The British Piano Sonata
1870–1945

This book considers the way in which British composers took an established Austro-German form as a starting-point. Influences from late romantic music, French impressionism, Russian nationalism, Scriabin, British folk music, African–American music and neo-classicism were all synthesized during this period, but the Austro-German tradition was ultimately to prove inescapable. The book also contains interesting and unique interviews, including one with Sir Michael Tippett, and includes a useful reference section, cataloguing the sonatas, as well as a full discography chronicling the recording history of each sonata, and numerous musical examples.

Dr LISA HARDY is a freelance music teacher and pianist.

The British Piano Sonata 1870–1945

Lisa Hardy

THE BOYDELL PRESS

© Lisa Hardy 2001

All Rights Reserved. Except as permitted under current legislation no part of this work may be photocopied, stored in a retrieval system, published, performed in public, adapted, broadcast, transmitted, recorded or reproduced in any form or by any means, without the prior permission of the copyright owner

The right of Lisa Hardy to be identified as the author of this work has been asserted in accordance with sections 77 and 78 of the Copyright, Designs and Patents Act 1988

First published 2001
The Boydell Press, Woodbridge
Reprinted in paperback 2012

ISBN 978-0-85115-822-8 hardback
ISBN 978-1-84383-798-5 paperback

Transferred to digital printing

The Boydell Press is an imprint of Boydell & Brewer Ltd
PO Box 9, Woodbridge, Suffolk IP12 3DF, UK
and of Boydell & Brewer Inc.
668 Mt. Hope Avenue, Rochester NY 14620, USA
website: www.boydellandbrewer.com

The publisher has no responsibility for the continued existence or accuracy of URLs for external or third-party internet websites referred to in this book, and does not guarantee that any content on such websites is, or will remain, accurate or appropriate

A CIP record for this title is available
from the British Library

This publication is printed on acid-free paper

Contents

List of musical examples and acknowledgements	vii
Acknowledgements	xv
Preface	xvii
Abbreviations	xix

	Introduction: the English Musical Renaissance	1
	Piano music in England in the early nineteenth century	1
	The role of the piano in British musical life	2
	The piano in the concert hall	2
	The piano in the home	5
	The dawn of a new era	6
1	**The Piano Sonatas 1870–1890**	9
	William Sterndale Bennett	9
	George Alexander Macfarren	11
	Charles Hubert Hastings Parry	14
	Charles Villiers Stanford	23
	Ethel Smyth	25
	Edward German	29
2	**The Piano Sonatas 1890–1910**	33
	Algernon Ashton	33
	A comparison between the Royal Academy of Music and the Royal College of Music	35
	John McEwen	36
	William Yeates Hurlstone	39
	Benjamin Dale	42
	York Bowen	48
	Dorothy Howell	52
	Leo Livens	52
	Cyril Scott	53
3	**Piano Sonatas by Bax, Ireland, Baines, Bush and Britten**	69
	Arnold Bax	69

Contents

	John Ireland	84
	William Baines	91
	Alan Bush	93
	Benjamin Britten	96
4	**Piano Sonatas by Sorabji and Bridge**	101
	Kaikhosru Shapurji Sorabji	101
	Frank Bridge	113
5	**The African–American Influence**	127
	African–American influences in Britain	127
	Constant Lambert	129
	Sir Michael Tippett	140
6	**Observations Drawn from Selected Sonatas 1930–1945**	159
	Howard Ferguson	160
	Malcolm Arnold	163
	Antony Hopkins	164
	Arnold Cooke	166
	Lennox Berkeley	168

Conclusions	171
Appendix 1: Interview transcriptions	175
Alan Bush	175
Geoffrey Bush	179
Howard Ferguson	186
Alan Frank	192
Antony Hopkins	198
Sir Michael Tippett	206
Appendix 2: Catalogue of Piano Sonatas 1870–1945	214
Appendix 3: Discography	223
Section 1: Recordings of Piano Sonatas	223
Section 2: Other recordings referred to in the text	230
Bibliography	233
Index	247

Musical Examples and Acknowledgements

The author and the publishers are grateful to all institutions for permission to reprint the materials for which they hold copyright. Every effort has been made to trace the copyright holders; we apologize for any omission in this regard, and will be pleased to add any necessary acknowledgements in subsequent editions.

Chapter 1

Fig. 1.1 Bennett, Sonata, Lamborn Cock, Fourth movement, Bars 1–8   11
Reproduced by kind permission of Stainer & Bell Ltd, London, England

Fig. 1.2 Macfarren, Third Sonata, Novello, First movement, Bars 1–8   13
Reproduced by kind permission of Novello & Co., Ltd (License No. PL 130999)

Fig. 1.3 Macfarren, Third Sonata, Second movement, Bars 1–10   13
Reproduced by kind permission of Novello & Co., Ltd (License No. PL 130999)

Fig. 1.4 Parry, Sonata No. 1, Lamborn Cock, First movement, Bars 1–9   17
Reproduced by kind permission of Stainer & Bell Ltd, London, England

Fig. 1.5 Parry, Sonata No. 1, First movement, Bars 16–21   18
Reproduced by kind permission of Stainer & Bell Ltd, London, England

Fig. 1.6 Parry, Sonata No. 1, First movement, Bars 51–4   19
Reproduced by kind permission of Stainer & Bell Ltd, London, England

Fig. 1.7 Parry, Sonata No. 2, Stanley Lucas, First movement, Bars 1–4   19
Reproduced by kind permission of Stainer & Bell Ltd, London, England

Fig. 1.8 Parry, Sonata No. 2, First movement, Bars 9–13   19
Reproduced by kind permission of Stainer & Bell Ltd, London, England

Fig. 1.9 Parry, Sonata No. 2, First movement, Bars 27–35   20

Musical Examples

Reproduced by kind permission of Stainer & Bell Ltd, London, England

Fig. 1.10 Parry, Sonata No. 1, Second movement, Bars 1–8   21
Reproduced by kind permission of Stainer & Bell Ltd, London, England

Fig. 1.11 Parry, Sonata No. 1, Second movement, Bars 48–56   21
Reproduced by kind permission of Stainer & Bell Ltd, London, England

Fig. 1.12 Parry, Sonata No. 2, Second movement, Bars 1–8   22
Reproduced by kind permission of Stainer & Bell Ltd, London, England

Fig. 1.13 Smyth, Sonata No. 1, Manuscript, First movement, Bars 1–11   26
Reproduced by kind permission of the Trustees of the Estate of Dame Ethel Smyth

Fig. 1.14 Smyth, Sonata No. 1, Fourth movement, Bars 1–8   27
Reproduced by kind permission of the Trustees of the Estate of Dame Ethel Smyth

Fig. 1.15 Smyth, Sonata No. 2, Manuscript, Third movement, Bars 1–4   28
Reproduced by kind permission of the Trustees of the Estate of Dame Ethel Smyth

Fig. 1.16 German, Sonata, Banks, Bars 1–4   30
Copyright 1987 Banks Music Publications. Reproduced by permission

Fig. 1.17 German, Sonata, Bars 48–51   30
Copyright 1987 Banks Music Publications. Reproduced by permission

Fig. 1.18 German, Sonata, Bars 63–6   31
Copyright 1987 Banks Music Publications. Reproduced by permission

Chapter 2

Fig. 2.1 Ashton, Sonata No. 3, Ries & Erler, First movement, Bars 1–5   34

Fig. 2.2 McEwen, Sonata, Novello, First movement, Bars 1–6   37

Fig. 2.3 McEwen, Sonata, First movement, Bars 84–91   38

Fig. 2.4 Hurlstone, Sonata, Manuscript, First movement, Bars 190–203   40
Reproduced by kind permission of the Royal College of Music

Fig. 2.5 Hurlstone, Sonata, Second movement, Bars 128–34   41
Reproduced by kind permission of the Royal College of Music

Musical Examples

Fig. 2.6 Dale, Sonata, Avison, First movement, Bars 1–8   43
Reproduced by permission of Novello & Co. Ltd (License No. PL 120900)

Fig. 2.7 Dale, Sonata, First movement, Bars 53–60   43
Reproduced by permission of Novello & Co. Ltd (License No. PL 120900)

Fig. 2.8 Dale, Sonata, First movement, Bars 85–94   44
Reproduced by permission of Novello & Co. Ltd (License No. PL 120900)

Fig. 2.9 Dale, Sonata, Second movement, Bars 1–17   45
Reproduced by permission of Novello & Co. Ltd (License No. PL 120900)

Fig. 2.10 Dale, Sonata, Finale, Bars 1–8   46
Reproduced by permission of Novello & Co. Ltd (License No. PL 120900)

Fig. 2.11 Bowen, Sonata No. 5, Swan, Second movement, Bars 57–70   51
© 1923 Josef Weinberger Ltd. Reprinted by permission of the copyright owner

Fig. 2.12 Scott, Sonata No. 1, Edwin Kalmus, Bars 1–19   55
Reproduced by permission of Novello & Co. Ltd (License No. PL 120900)

Fig. 2.13 Scott, Sonata No. 1, Bars 24–5   55
Reproduced by permission of Novello & Co. Ltd (License No. PL 120900)

Fig. 2.14 Scott, Sonata No. 1, Bars 56–7   56
Reproduced by permission of Novello & Co. Ltd (License No. PL 120900)

Fig. 2.15 Scott, Sonata No. 1, Bars 474–84   57
Reproduced by permission of Novello & Co. Ltd (License No. PL 120900)

Fig. 2.16 Scott, Sonata No. 1, Bars 420–4   60
Reproduced by permission of Novello & Co. Ltd (License No. PL 120900)

Fig. 2.17 Scott, Sonata No. 1, Revised version, Bars 1–19   62
Reproduced by permission of Novello & Co. Ltd (License No. PL 120900)

Fig. 2.18 Changes made to Sonata No. 1   63
Fig. 2.19 Scriabin, Mystic chord   66
Fig. 2.20 Scott, Sonata No. 2, Universal, Bars 10–13   66
Reproduced by permission of Novello & Co. Ltd (License No. PL 120900)

Musical Examples

Fig. 2.21 Scott, Sonata No. 2, Bars 205–12   67
Reproduced by permission of Novello & Co. Ltd (License No. PL 120900)

Chapter 3

Fig. 3.1 Bax, Sonata in D minor, Manuscript, Second movement,   70
Bars 1–8
Reproduced by kind permission of the Arnold Bax Trust and Lewis Foreman

Fig. 3.2 Bax, Sonata No. 1, Murdoch, First movement, Bars 1–4   72
© 1927 Murdoch, Murdoch & Company. Assigned to Warner/ Chappell Music Limited, London W6 8BS. Reproduced by permission of International Music Publications Ltd

Fig. 3.3 Bax, Sonata No. 1, First movement, Bars 24–7   72
© 1927 Murdoch, Murdoch & Company. Assigned to Warner/ Chappell Music Limited, London W6 8BS. Reproduced by permission of International Music Publications Ltd

Fig. 3.4 Bax, Sonata No. 1, First movement, Bars 76–7   73
© 1927 Murdoch, Murdoch & Company. Assigned to Warner/ Chappell Music Limited, London W6 8BS. Reproduced by permission of International Music Publications Ltd

Fig. 3.5 Bax, Sonata in F (No. 2 Scherzo), Manuscript, Bars 1–8   74
Reproduced by kind permission of the Arnold Bax Trust and Lewis Foreman

Fig. 3.6 Summary of main themes in Bax's Second Sonata   75

Fig. 3.7 Bax, Sonata No. 2, Murdoch, First movement, Bars 1–13   76
© 1927 Murdoch, Murdoch & Company. Assigned to Warner/ Chappell Music Limited, London W6 8BS. Reproduced by permission of International Music Publications Ltd

Fig. 3.8 Scriabin, Sonata No. 7, Dover, Bars 1–3   77
Reproduced by kind permission of Dover Publications Inc.

Fig. 3.9 Bax, Sonata No. 2, Manuscript, Extract from passage   78
inserted between Bars 185 and 186 of published version
Reproduced by kind permission of the Arnold Bax Trust and Lewis Foreman

Fig. 3.10 Bax, Sonata No. 3, Murdoch, First movement, Bars 1–5   80
© 1923 Murdoch, Murdoch & Company. Assigned to Warner/ Chappell Music Limited, London W6 8BS. Reproduced by permission of International Music Publications Ltd

Fig. 3.11 Bax, Sonata No. 3, First movement, Bars 175–82   80
© 1923 Murdoch, Murdoch & Company. Assigned to Warner/

Musical Examples

Chappell Music Limited, London W6 8BS. Reproduced by permission of International Music Publications Ltd

Fig. 3.12 Bax, Sonata No. 3, Second movement, Bars 67–72   81
© 1923 Murdoch, Murdoch & Company. Assigned to Warner/ Chappell Music Limited, London W6 8BS. Reproduced by permission of International Music Publications Ltd

Fig. 3.13 Bax, Sonata No. 4, Murdoch, First movement, Bars 15–19   82
© 1934 Murdoch, Murdoch & Company. Assigned to Warner/ Chappell Music Limited, London W6 8BS. Reproduced by permission of International Music Publications Ltd

Fig. 3.14 Ireland, Sonata, Stainer & Bell, First movement, Bars 1–4   86
Reproduced by kind permission of Stainer & Bell Ltd, London, England

Fig. 3.15 Ireland, *London Pieces*, Augener, *Ragamuffin*, Bars 41–4   87
Reproduced by kind permission of Stainer & Bell Ltd, London, England

Fig. 3.16 Debussy, Preludes, United Music Publishers, *General Lavine*, Bars 14–17   87
Reproduced by permission of United Music Publishers Ltd

Fig. 3.17 Baines, Sonata No. 2, Manuscript, First movement, Bars 1–4   92
Reproduced by kind permission of the Trustees of the Estate of William Baines

Fig. 3.18 Bush, Sonata No. 1, Murdoch, Bars 42–7   94
© 1923 Murdoch, Murdoch & Company. Assigned to Warner/ Chappell Music Limited, London W6 8BS. Reproduced by permission of International Music Publications Ltd

Fig. 3.19 Britten, Sonata in B flat (1925), Manuscript, Third movement, Bars 1–44   97
Unpublished excerpts from Benjamin Britten's Sonata in B flat (1925) are © copyright the Trustees of the Britten–Pears Foundation, and may not be further reproduced without the written permission of the Trustees

Fig. 3.20 Britten, Sonata in C sharp minor, Manuscript, Third movement, Bars 1–4   98
Unpublished excerpts from Benjamin Britten's Sonata in C sharp minor (1926) are © copyright the Trustees of the Britten–Pears Foundation, and may not be further reproduced without the written permission of the Trustees

Fig. 3.21 Britten, Sonata in B flat (1927), Manuscript, First movement, Bars 1–14   98
Unpublished excerpts from Benjamin Britten's Sonata in B flat (1927)

Musical Examples

are © copyright the Trustees of the Britten–Pears Foundation, and may not be further reproduced without the written permission of the Trustees

Fig. 3.22 Britten, Sonata in B flat (1927), Second movement, Bars 1–6   99

Unpublished excerpts from Benjamin Britten's Sonata in B flat (1927) are © copyright the Trustees of the Britten–Pears Foundation, and may not be further reproduced without the written permission of the Trustees

Chapter 4

Fig. 4.1 Sorabji, Sonata No. 1, London & Continental, Bars 1–4   103
Reproduced by kind permission of the Sorabji Archive and Alistair Hinton

Fig. 4.2 Recurrences of Sorabji's quasi-mystic motif   104

Fig. 4.3 Sorabji, Sonata No. 1, Bars 29–30   107
Reproduced by kind permission of the Sorabji Archive and Alistair Hinton

Fig. 4.4 Bridge, Piano Sonata, Stainer & Bell, First movement, Bars 11–15   115
Reproduced by kind permission of Stainer & Bell Ltd, London, England

Fig. 4.5 Bridge *Summer*, Stainer & Bell, Oboe 1, Bars 13–21   115
Reproduced by kind permission of Stainer & Bell Ltd, London, England

Fig. 4.6 Bridge, Four Songs, Augener, *Speak to Me, My Love*, Bars 10–20   116
Reproduced by kind permission of Stainer & Bell Ltd, London, England

Fig. 4.7 Bridge chord   117

Fig. 4.8 Scriabin, Sixth Piano Sonata, Dover, First movement, Bars 1–9   118
Reproduced by kind permission of Dover Publications Inc.

Fig. 4.9 Bridge Sonata, Second movement, Manuscript (RCM), Original version of Bars 1–6   122
Reproduced by kind permission of the Frank Bridge Trust

Chapter 5

Fig. 5.1 Dickinson, Types of Syncopation   131
Reproduced by kind permission of Peter Dickinson

Fig. 5.2 Lambert, *The Rio Grande*, OUP, Bars 39–40   134
© Oxford University Press, 1929. Reproduced by permission

Musical Examples

Fig. 5.3 Lambert, *Summer's Last Will and Testament*, OUP, Saraband, Bars 29–32   135
© Oxford University Press, 1929. Reproduced by permission

Fig. 5.4 Lambert, Sonata, Third movement, Bars 7–18   136
© Oxford University Press, 1930. Reproduced by permission

Fig. 5.5 Pentatonic fanfare   136
See Palmer, C: "Constant Lambert – A Postscript", *Music & Letters* lii, 1971, 173–6. Reproduced by permission of Oxford University Press

Fig. 5.6 Delius, *Appalachia*, Universal Edition, Bars 43–4   136
© Copyright 1906, 1951 by Hawkes & Son (London) Ltd. Reproduced by permission of Boosey & Hawkes Music Publishers Ltd

Fig. 5.7 Lambert, *The Rio Grande*, Bars 14–16   136
© Oxford University Press, 1929. Reproduced by permission

Fig. 5.8 Morris, *Canzoni Ricertati*, OUP, No. 1, Bars 98–105   144
© Oxford University Press, 1931. Reproduced by permission

Fig. 5.9 *Ca' the Yowes to the Knowes*, from G. F. Graham, *The Folksongs of Scotland*, Wood & Co.   146

Fig. 5.10 Tippett, Sonata No. 1, Second movement, Schott, Bars 1–16   147
Copyright 1954 by Schott & Co. Ltd, London. Reproduced by permission

Fig. 5.11 Tippett Sonata No. 1, Third movement   149

Fig. 5.12 Koninsky, *Eli Green's Cake Walk – Characteristic March*   151
[In *Ragtime Rarities: Complete Original Music for 63 Piano Rags*, ed. Trebor Jay Tichenor, Dover, 1975], Bars 1–16
Reproduced by kind permission of Dover Publications Inc.

Fig. 5.13 arr. Johnson, *Somebody's Knocking at your Door*, Viking, Bars 4–9   154
The Books of American Negro Spirituals by James Weldon Johnson and J. Rosamond Johnson, copyright 1925, 1926 by The Viking Press, Inc. renewed 1953 by Lawrence Brown, 1953, © 1954 by Grace Nail Johnson and J. Rosamond Johnson. Used by permission of Viking Penguin, a division of Penguin Puttnam Inc.

Fig. 5.14 arr. Johnson, *Peter, Go Ring Dem Bells*, Viking, Bars 1–10   154
The Books of American Negro Spirituals by James Weldon Johnson and J. Rosamond Johnson, copyright 1925, 1926 by The Viking Press, Inc. renewed 1953 by Lawrence Brown, 1953, © 1954 by Grace Nail Johnson and J. Rosamond Johnson. Used by permission of Viking Penguin, a division of Penguin Puttnam Inc.

Fig. 5.15 arr. Johnson, *Hallelujah!*, Viking, Bars 1–10   155
The Books of American Negro Spirituals by James Weldon Johnson

and J. Rosamond Johnson, copyright 1925, 1926 by The Viking Press, Inc. renewed 1953 by Lawrence Brown, 1953, © 1954 by Grace Nail Johnson and J. Rosamond Johnson. Used by permission of Viking Penguin, a division of Penguin Puttnam Inc.

Fig. 5.16 arr. Johnson, *John saw the Holy Number*, Viking, Bars 1–8   155
The Books of American Negro Spirituals by James Weldon Johnson and J. Rosamond Johnson, copyright 1925, 1926 by The Viking Press, Inc. renewed 1953 by Lawrence Brown, 1953, © 1954 by Grace Nail Johnson and J. Rosamond Johnson. Used by permission of Viking Penguin, a division of Penguin Puttnam Inc.

Fig. 5.17 arr. Johnson, *Do Don't Touch-a my Garment, Good Lord, I'm Gwine Home*, Chapman & Hall, Bars 5–12   156
The Books of American Negro Spirituals by James Weldon Johnson and J. Rosamond Johnson, copyright 1925, 1926 by The Viking Press, Inc. renewed 1953 by Lawrence Brown, 1953, © 1954 by Grace Nail Johnson and J. Rosamond Johnson. Used by permission of Viking Penguin, a division of Penguin Puttnam Inc.

Chapter 6

Fig. 6.1 Ferguson, Sonata, Boosey & Hawkes, First movement, Bars 1–6   162
© Copyright 1940 by Hawkes & Son (London) Ltd. Reprinted by permission of Boosey & Hawkes Music Publishers Ltd

Fig. 6.2 Arnold, Sonata, Roberton, Third movement, Bars 62–75   163
Reproduced by permission of Roberton Publications

Fig. 6.3 Hopkins, Sonata No. 1, Chester, First movement, Bars 12–24   164
Reproduced by permission of Chester Music Ltd (Licence No. PL 130999)

Fig. 6.4 Hopkins, Sonata No. 2, Manuscript, Third movement, Bars 1–5   165
Reproduced by kind permission of Antony Hopkins

Fig. 6.5 Tippett, Sonata No. 1, Schott, Third movement, Bars 93–9   165
Copyright 1954 by Schott & Co. Ltd, London. Reproduced by permission

Fig. 6.6 Berkeley, Sonata, Chester, First movement, Bars 99–106   169
Reproduced by permission of Chester Music Ltd (Licence No. PL 130999)

Fig. 6.7 Berkeley, Sonata, Fourth movement, Bars 1–4   170
Reproduced by permission of Chester Music Ltd (Licence No. PL 130999)

Acknowledgements

I am grateful to all those who have assisted me. Special thanks must go to Professor Peter Dickinson for his encouragement and advice.

I particularly appreciate the co-operation of the composers and performers whom I interviewed: the late Alan Bush, the late Geoffrey Bush, the late Howard Ferguson, the late Alan Frank, Antony Hopkins and the late Sir Michael Tippett.

I have had discussions or correspondence with the following: Professor Stephen Banfield, Michael Berkeley, Meirion Bowen, James Brown, Eric Fletcher, Christopher Foreman, Lewis Foreman, Paul Hindmarsh, Mike Hinson, Alistair Hinton, Colin Horsley, the late Dr Frederick Hudson, Dr David Russell Hulme, Michael Jones, Professor Ian Kemp, Dr Christian Kennett, Peter Lawson, John Lindsay, Celia Mike, Rachel O'Higgins, Eric Parkin, Professor Ian Parrott, Anthony Payne, Bruce Phillips, Laura Ponsonby, Guy Rickards, Kenneth Roberton, Eileen Roberts, Colin Scott-Sutherland, Marjorie Hartston Scott, Ronald Stevenson and Monica Watson.

Thanks are also due to the staff of the following libraries and institutions: Barbican Library; Birmingham Public Library; Bodleian Library, Oxford (Peter A. Ward Jones); British Film Institute; British Music Information Centre (Matthew Greenall, Tom Morgan); Britten–Pears Library (Dr Philip Reed, Helen Risdon, Jennifer Doctor); Goldsmiths' Library, University of London; Library of Congress, Washington DC; Henry Watson Music Library, Manchester; National Sound Archive; Royal Academy of Music; Royal College of Music; Sorabji Archive, Bath (Alistair Hinton); Trinity College of Music; University of London Library; Welsh Music Information Centre (Mr A. J. Heward Rees); Westminster Music Library.

Finally I should also like to thank my parents, Brian and Helen Farryan, for their constant support throughout my education. Above all, I thank my husband, Paul, who has patiently discussed aspects of my research and helped to solve many of my computer problems.

Preface

Any assessment of a single musical genre, such as the piano sonata, over a period of seventy-five years, must necessarily be selective. This study restricts itself to the solo piano sonata from the period of the English Musical Renaissance to World War II. Sonatas for piano duet are excluded, as are sonatinas. This book explores the composers' initial preoccupation with Germanic principles of sonata writing, and their subsequent exposure to influences outside this tradition. These include late romantic music, French impressionism, Russian nationalism, Scriabin, British folk music, African–American music and neo-classicism. Consideration is given to the education of each composer, in particular the climate at the Royal College and Royal Academy. World War I was to prove critical as a stimulus to creativity, and the immediate post-war years can be considered a golden age of piano sonatas. However, the Austro-German tradition was ultimately to prove inescapable.

One problem in detecting national trends is making a distinction between the British style and those of its component nations: England, Scotland, Wales and Ireland. The characteristics of individual nations are more easily discernible in folk music. Art music tended to be centralized, and in a city like London there was much foreign domination. Thus, following the example of many previous writers on this subject, the term English Musical Renaissance is used to include composers from the whole of the British Isles.

Detailed comments on certain key works show which influences and techniques affected the composers, and demonstrate their attitudes towards the sonata genre. Unpublished sonatas and works by lesser-known composers are included to illustrate the prevailing musical climate, and to substantiate trends observed in the key works. Consideration is given to the psychology of the British composer and the lack of contributions to the piano sonata repertoire from major figures.

Where a composer wrote more than one piano sonata before 1945, subsequent works are discussed in the same chapter as his first sonata, so that the stylistic development of that composer can be followed. Composers tended to make their impact with their first sonata but in certain cases a later work was more significant. In these cases the more important work is given greater attention.

Throughout the book, the reception history of the piano sonatas is also discussed, to build up a picture of public musical taste. The performance history of selected works within the chosen period is continued to the present day, and a discography is included in Appendix 3. Appendix 1 contains transcriptions of unique interviews which I conducted with composers whose works are discussed in the text, and Appendix 2 catalogues the sonatas.

Abbreviations

BBC	British Broadcasting Corporation
BMIC	British Music Information Centre
BMS Journal	*British Music Society Journal*
BMS News	*British Music Society News*
EPTA Journal	*European Piano Teachers' Association Journal*
Grove	*The Grove Dictionary of Music and Musicians,* ed. George Grove, 4 vols., first edition London, Macmillan, 1878
Lam	London – Royal Academy of Music
Lbm	London – British Library, Reference Division (formerly British Museum)
Lcm	London – Royal College of Music
LRAM	Licentiate of the Royal Academy of Music (Diploma Examination)
MGG	*Die Musik in Geschichte und Gegenwart,* ed. Friedrich Blume, 13 vols., Kassel, Bärenreiter-Verlag, 1949–86
ML	*Music and Letters*
MMR	*The Monthly Musical Record*
MO	*Musical Opinion*
MT	*Musical Times*
n.d.	no date
New Grove	*The New Grove Dictionary of Music and Musicians,* ed. Stanley Sadie, 20 vols., sixth edition, London, Macmillan, 1980
OUP	Oxford University Press
PRMA	*Proceedings of the Royal Musical Association*
RAM	Royal Academy of Music
RCM	Royal College of Music

Introduction: the English Musical Renaissance

Piano music in England in the early nineteenth century

Piano music had been particularly important in England from 1790 to 1830, as exemplified by the London Piano School. Muzio Clementi (1752–1832) and Jan Ladislav Dussek (1760–1812) were the most influential of the composers, Clementi's pupils having included John Baptist Cramer (1771–1858), John Field (1782–1837), George Frederick Pinto (1785–1806), Cipriani Potter (1792–1871) and Samuel Wesley (1766–1837). It was through these composers that serious concert piano music (as opposed to popular piano arrangements for domestic use) was kept alive during the first half of the nineteenth century. By 1830 composers attempted to preserve their artistic integrity and to resist commercial pressures. They achieved this by earning income from teaching in preference to writing popular music. Cipriani Potter led the Society of British Musicians at the Royal Academy of Music and taught them to respect German classical music. Although they believed that their mission was to preserve the high ideals of art, the exclusion of all foreign (non-British) music from their concert programmes meant that they were not taken seriously.[1]

Pianists of this period commonly performed their own compositions, as opposed to those of others, and performances were displays of technical brilliance. It was Chopin and Liszt who recognized the popular demand for virtuosity, sublimated it and cultivated a new style. England did not produce any composer-pianists of this stature, although foreign players did perform in this country. It is arguable that it was not until England itself produced good pianists that the music of her native composers could be effectively championed both at home and abroad. This did not happen until the twentieth century, when York Bowen, Harriet Cohen, Myra Hess and others regularly performed the piano works of British composers. Meanwhile, British composers turned to the Germans, especially Mendelssohn, for inspiration. By the beginning of the second half of the nineteenth century, Mendelssohn's style was outdated and did not appeal to the public. Despite the efforts of William Sterndale Bennett and George Macfarren, the two most prominent composers at this time,

---

[1] See Temperley, 1981, 400–34.

English piano music went into decline, and it took until the early years of the twentieth century before it could again be taken seriously.

Piano sonatas had been very important in Europe at the start of the nineteenth century, with Beethoven, Weber, Dussek, Schubert and others contributing to the repertoire. However, between 1840 and 1885 there was a slump in both the quality and quantity of piano sonatas, with the exception of those by Schumann, Chopin and Liszt, who produced a few excellent examples. The prevailing trend in piano music was to write many shorter and less formal works. A revival in interest in large-scale piano music was partly due to Brahms, although his three piano sonatas are early works. His major works for piano use variation techniques to provide structure and unity. It was not until the mid 1870s that people again became interested in all forms of chamber music. This revival of interest coincided with the birth of the English Musical Renaissance, and helped to foster a climate in which piano sonatas were written and performed.

The role of the piano in British musical life

The piano in the concert hall
In England in the early part of the nineteenth century there were few public solo piano recitals, although Clementi, Dussek, Cramer, Field and Moscheles were all active. In the 1830s, Moscheles took part in concerts that included trios and quartets in addition to piano solos. The principal music for the instrument could be heard at orchestral concerts, in concertos, and those performers who did give solos performed mainly their own works. It was Franz Liszt who pioneered the new concept of the solo piano recital to include other composers' works as well as his own. He began with a recital in Rome in 1839 and continued throughout the 1840s, including a recital in 1840 at the Hanover Square Rooms, London. These recitals included a selection of works, but no sonatas. Bennett was the chief British pioneer of this new trend, and he organized annual classical chamber music concerts, firstly in his own house and later at the Hanover Square Rooms, from 1842 to 1856. However, chamber music concerts usually consisted of a variety of ensembles, and it was unusual to hear piano sonatas, which at this stage may have been regarded as domestic rather than public music.

An important year was 1848: Chopin gave his first public recital in England, and Charles Hallé began a series of chamber concerts in Manchester. The latter were semi-public concerts, taking place in Hallé's own home, and Beethoven was the only composer to be featured. When Hallé performed Beethoven's Piano Sonata in E flat Op. 31/3 during this year, the director of the Musical Union told him that sonatas "were not works to be played in public" and that "no solo sonata had ever been included

Introduction: the English Musical Renaissance

in any [London] concert programme".[2] Beethoven's music was considered too serious to include in public recitals, as evidenced in E. M. Forster's *A Room With A View*. Lucy Honeychurch's performance of Beethoven's Piano Sonata Op. 111 at an amateur concert resulted in the vicar's disapproval. Yet within eight years, William Henry Holmes announced piano recitals that included sonatas each by J. W. Davison, G. Macfarren, Brahms, Rubinstein and two by Schumann.[3] Piano recitals were much longer than we are accustomed to today, although performers often played just one or two movements from a sonata.

Hallé subsequently performed a series of Beethoven's sonatas, playing all thirty-two works in eighteen concerts at St James' Hall, between 1861–3. He was the first pianist to attempt the complete cycle and within a short time, performers began to memorize the works.[4] Clara Schumann made annual visits to give recitals in England from 1867 to 1888. It was the Monday and Saturday 'Pops' concerts given at St James' Hall from 1865 to 1898 that established the vogue for chamber music. By the 1860s, pianists were more likely to be interpreters than composers, and proper concert venues began to replace salons.

Hans von Bülow made a dramatic impact on the British public in 1873. Audiences virtually idolized him, and his performances from memory set a new trend in England. Clara Schumann and some of her pupils had previously performed from memory, but von Bülow's cult status meant that his ideas were influential and in the following decades more pianists opted to perform without music. The first British pianist to play from memory may have been Franklin Taylor, when introducing Bennett's Sonata, *The Maid of Orleans*, to the Crystal Palace audience in December 1873.

> Solo instrumental music in the concert context had only a limited role at the [Crystal] Palace. Instrumental solos appeared as items to complement the main concerto or concert piece in the programme: this is where the many performances of solo pieces by Chopin and Liszt found a place, alongside the small vocal items which the soloist often accompanied.[5]

Despite the growing trend for piano recitals, mixed recitals were still popular. This is a sample programme from a concert at the Philharmonic Hall, Liverpool, given on 17 December 1873:[6]

---

[2] C. E. and M. Hallé, 1896, 10. See Schonberg, 1964, 221, who doubts the validity of this claim.
[3] Holmes, *MT*, 1856, 177.
[4] Newman, 1969, 13.
[5] Musgrave, 1995, 144.
[6] Anon., *MT*, 1874, 367.

Schumann	Quartet in A Op. 41/3
Hummel	Song, *L'ombrosa notte vien*
Sir W. S. Bennett	*The Maid of Orleans* Piano Sonata
	INTERVAL
Rubinstein	Sonata Duet for Piano and Cello
Schumann	Two Songs
Beethoven	Grand Trio in D Op. 70/1

In 1885–6 Anton Rubinstein gave seven consecutive recitals covering the history of pianoforte music throughout Europe. They contained music ranging from the mid sixteenth century to the mid nineteenth century, including many sonatas, and each programme was extremely long.[7]

Gradually the sonata gained an important place in piano recitals. New sonatas were introduced to the European public by travelling recitalists and publishers. Many did not gain a permanent place in the repertoire as performers and publishers became inundated with compositions, all competing for an airing. Sonatas were not the most profitable music to publish and publishers were reluctant to invest in serious music written by unknown composers. If a composer could get his sonatas printed, they would have been likely to have to compete in a catalogue full of salon music. Often a composer considered launching his career with a published sonata, which would demonstrate not only his command of compositional technique, but would also show off a performer's skill.

Wagner's Op. 1 was a Piano Sonata, Brahms' only Piano Sonatas are Opp. 1, 2 and 5 and Berg's Piano Sonata is his Op. 2. A similar trend is observed in British piano sonatas. Parry's and Stanford's Sonatas are relatively early works; those of Smyth, German and Hurlstone, although unpublished, are student compositions. So was the Piano Sonata by Dale, which was published and did effectively launch his career. The sonata was seen as an ideal of technical and musical achievement to which a composer might aspire. In this sense it ranked with the symphony and string quartet. Music critics were likely to praise sonatas, merely because their name showed a serious intention.

By the 1890s, piano recitals were becoming extremely popular. Paderewski, Pachmann, Busoni, Moszkowski and Rachmaninov performed in England.

> The disease of the day is evidently "pianism". During the present season there have appeared at the three principal West End concert halls very nearly seventy solo pianists.[8]

---

[7] Newman, 1969, 14.
[8] Anon., *MT*, 1890, 402.

Introduction: the English Musical Renaissance

The pianists mainly performed familiar pieces, and works by Liszt were the most frequently played. The content of the programmes was fairly inflexible, as described by John E. Borland in a paper of 1897.

> It was customary to commence with a Bach prelude and fugue (usually perverted from one intended for the organ), a Beethoven sonata (choice limited to about four or five), some Chopin pieces (there were about twelve orthodox ones to select from), and a Liszt rhapsody.[9]

Most pianists kept to this framework, which was remarkably similar to the LRAM syllabus for most of the twentieth century. The more adventurous did risk playing some Schumann or Brahms!

The piano in the home
The main reason that British piano sonatas were not widely heard was that by the late nineteenth century they were intended for professional virtuosi and were beyond the capabilities of the average amateur. Some foreign composers, such as Kuhlau and Reinecke, wrote two types of sonata, using one style for art works and another for pedagogical sonatas. Amateurs needed music that required the minimum of technique, and preferred playing popular arrangements or easy original works. Many of these pieces had French titles, as the Victorian ladies sought to be like Parisian ones. The classical music that was attempted by them included Mendelssohn's *Songs without Words*, Chopin's Nocturnes, the easy sonatas by Beethoven, Schubert's Impromptus and pieces by Grieg. On the whole, piano sonatas were too serious, although sometimes one movement of a work was played. Publishers took advantage of this fact and printed extracts from sonatas. The British public had a lighter taste; they preferred Gilbert and Sullivan operettas and music hall to classical highbrow music. The editor of the *Musical Times* recognized this problem.

> The publisher who can induce our Baxes, Irelands and Dales to write pianoforte sonatas that can be played by five thousand amateur pianists instead of by a mere score or so of professionals will do everybody a good turn – himself above all.[10]

This illustrates that publishing piano sonatas was not financially viable, and undoubtedly accounts for the fact that many remained in manuscript.

Professional pianists of the Victorian era were generally male, although during the second half of the nineteenth century, women began to perform in public. Initially, the absence of professional training for pianists in this country hampered progress and resulted in amateur mediocrity. Following the establishment of the Royal Academy of Music in 1822, Trinity College

---

[9] See Scholes, 1947, 309.
[10] Anon., *MT*, 1923, 613.

in 1875, the Guildhall School of Music in 1880 and the Royal College of Music in 1883, the situation began to change.

Paradoxically, despite the poor standards of native composition and performance, London had been the centre of piano manufacture in the early Victorian period. At the Great Exhibition of 1851, thirty-eight English manufacturers exhibited sixty-six pianos, which was far more than France, Germany and the United States. There were about two hundred piano manufacturing firms in England, mainly in London.[11]

During the 1870s, hire purchase schemes were available for piano purchasers.[12] By the early 1900s, one Englishman in six bought a new piano every year (with the older model moving to the humbler classes). Moderately priced pianos were imported, and by 1910, there were between two and four million pianos in Britain – approximately one piano for every ten to twenty people. This was far more than the number in France or Germany.[13] Sheet music was bought regularly, and the piano was the centre of domestic entertainment. *Harrison's Weekly Pianoforte Magazine* published pieces for home enjoyment. As living standards had improved, people had money to spend on leisure activities such as pianos, music and lessons, and there was a wider appreciation of music. The middle classes saw playing the piano as a symbol of aspiration to higher ideals. It advanced a person's education, both musical and social, and provided an emotional outlet.

The dawn of a new era

It is difficult to identify precisely when the English Musical Renaissance occurred. J. A. Fuller-Maitland considered that it began with the first performance of Parry's *Prometheus Unbound* on 7 September 1880. Many other writers, including Ernest Walker, Stanford and Frank Howes, adopted this view. However, Robert Stradling and Meirion Hughes present a different view of the situation.[14] They claim that the importance attached to *Prometheus Unbound* came retrospectively. Its supposed genius was not noted in reviews following its first performance, and the first broadcast of Parry's crucially important work came as late as 1980 – one hundred years after its composition.[15]

Another composer who was regarded by some as the founder of the renaissance was Arthur Sullivan (1842–1900). H. C. Colles cited *Trial By Jury* (1875) as the turning point in British music history. Previously *The Tempest* (1862) had been a huge success, and two theatres were constructed

---

[11] Ehrlich, 1990, 28.
[12] Ibid., 98.
[13] Ibid., 91.
[14] Stradling and Hughes, 1993.
[15] Anon., *MT*, 1880, 498–9.

Introduction: the English Musical Renaissance

in London for Sullivan's work. The Palace Theatre in Cambridge Circus was intended to be the English equivalent of Bayreuth. However, Sullivan could not lead the renaissance, as his music was not serious enough, despite being more widely known to the general public than Parry's. Thus some people considered that Parry usurped Sullivan as the true founder of the renaissance.

A lecture entitled "The Musical Renaissance in England", given by Morton Latham at Cambridge in June 1888, provided a name for this new musical movement. This was followed in 1890 by the publication of Latham's book, *The Renaissance of Music*.

To try to attribute the English Musical Renaissance to one composer would be a vast over-simplification. The seeds for change were sown by composers of the previous generation (Macfarren and Bennett, amongst others) and were nurtured by Parry and Stanford, but the fruits of their labours did not emerge until the beginning of the twentieth century. These composers made an important contribution to musical life in Britain.

One of the main problems for the nineteenth-century British composer was that there was little genuine native tradition on which he could build. In the words of T. S. Eliot, a composer needs "a perception, not only of the pastness of the past, but of its presence".[16] Although there was a strong performing tradition in the field of choral music, the prevailing style was derived from Handel. The last great British composer had been Purcell, who died in 1695.

There was an absence of revolution in England – one source of inspiration to many other European nationalist movements. Thus the English lacked a sense of national musical identity, despite the importance of its trade and empire. English musicians were not respected in society and many found more sympathy abroad, particularly in Germany. During the classical and early romantic periods, Germany had developed and refined sonata form, which the English composers took over. However, by the mid 1860s, attitudes were beginning to change and the English started to realize that musical success could be a source of national pride, at least in the case of popular music.

The acceptance of the status of musicians did not come until universities offered taught music degrees. These had been awarded at Cambridge since 1464, and at Oxford since 1511, but formal courses did not exist elsewhere. A music faculty and chair were established at Trinity College, Dublin, in 1861. Music degrees were awarded at the universities of London (from 1879), Edinburgh (1893), Wales and Manchester (both 1894) and Durham (1897). The syllabuses included the study of harmony, counterpoint, imitative composition and history of music. However, universities were inadequately supplied with textbooks and courses often covered the subjects

---

[16] Eliot, "Tradition and the Individual Talent" (1919), in 1951, 14.

only superficially. Students would have studied sonata form as exemplified by the music of Mozart, Haydn and Beethoven, and traditional attitudes to this form would have affected their own interpretation of the sonata genre. The ways in which composers brought their own personalities to bear on this form is the basis of my subsequent discussion.

1

The Piano Sonatas 1870–1890

During the mid nineteenth century, the most influential figures in British music were William Sterndale Bennett and George Macfarren. These two composers helped to raise the status of music, in preparation for the English Musical Renaissance.

William Sterndale Bennett (1816–1875)

Bennett knew both Mendelssohn and Schumann, having visited Germany three times between 1836 and 1842. He had made an impressive debut as pianist and composer, but to earn a living he was forced to divide his time between composing, performing, teaching, conducting, and organizing concerts. In 1856 he was appointed Professor of Music at Cambridge and in 1866 he became the Principal of the Royal Academy of Music. He also founded the Bach Society. Thus he composed very little music after 1844.

As with other British composers of the period, Bennett was brought up to believe that he should follow in the footsteps of Mozart and Haydn, so much of his music is derived from the classical style. Other composers whose music he admired included Bach, Spohr, Clementi, Hummel and Moscheles. His keyboard writing was heavily influenced by Mendelssohn. It was Bennett, through the Philharmonic Society, who was responsible for bringing the music of Schumann to the English public. Schumann praised Bennett's keyboard works in 1837, although by 1843 he thought that his musical style had failed to develop.[1]

Bennett's Sonata No. 1 Op. 13 dates from 1837 and is dedicated to Mendelssohn, and the *Suite de Pièces*, possibly his best piano work, was written in 1841. Bennett performed only occasionally from the 1840s onwards, and possibly as a consequence, he wrote very little piano music after this time. He began writing the second movement of the Sonata Op. 46, *The Maid of Orleans*, in 1869. The introductory movement and third

[1] Spink, *MT*, 1964, 419.

movement were completed in August and September 1872, during Bennett's holiday, whilst the final movement was completed in 1873.

This Sonata was written for and dedicated to Arabella Goddard, who had regularly performed Bennett's piano works during the previous twenty-one years. Each movement is titled and preceded by a description of the programme, taken from Schiller's *Joan of Arc*. Bennett attempts to translate programmatic elements to music, but the programmatic allusions are very simplistic.

> It is easy to suggest pastoral scenes: a few pedal notes, a certain simplicity of melody, and a few realistic touches expressive of the waving of branches of trees, or the meandering of a brook, and the thing is accomplished.[2]

Detailed representation of the story is not suited to a sonata, and its melodramatic style would have been more appropriate as an accompaniment to a silent movie.[3] The themes are not substantial enough to convey Bennett's intentions. Melodies are fresh and lyrical, but accompaniments are rudimentary and soon become monotonous. Overall, the movements are heard as separate entities, almost like tone poems, and there is a lack of clear structural coherence.

Despite its dedication, the Sonata was first performed in 1873 by a Miss Channell, at a concert given by Rebecca Jewell, as Goddard was on tour at this time.[4] Lamborn Cock first published the Sonata in London not later than July 1873 and by December of that year, Bennett wrote to his son, "they have printed 1150 copies of the Sonata".[5] This was a rare achievement for a piano sonata, and Kistner reissued the work early in 1876. A favourable review of the publication appeared in the *Musical Times*.[6]

The Sonata Op. 46 may have appealed to amateur pianists. It is technically not too demanding, although the final movement is not very pianistic in style. Contemporary critics, who had not expected Bennett to write any further piano works, are said to have been surprised and delighted with the outcome, one writing that "there can be no doubt that it will stand as an enduring work of genius on account of its intensity of expression".[7]

However, twentieth-century critics have a very different perspective. Michael Hurd, in his review of the Sonata, considers that "the last movement ('The End. Moto di passione') is more suggestive of the toasting of muffins than the roasting of human flesh"![8] This movement is illustrated

---

[2] Shedlock, 1964, 232.
[3] Programmaticism can be suited to a sonata, as in Beethoven's *Les Adieux*.
[4] J. R. S. Bennett, 1907, 442.
[5] Ibid., 442.
[6] Anon., *MT*, 1874, 391.
[7] Statham, *MT*, 1878, 130–4.
[8] Hurd, *BMS News*, 1992, 159–60.

in Fig. 1.1. Even Geoffrey Bush, who has championed the music of Bennett, admitted that this work is a failure.[9]

Fig. 1.1 Bennett, Sonata, Lamborn Cock, Fourth movement, Bars 1–8

Bennett's Sonata was clearly a great success during the late nineteenth century, owing to its pictorial approach. It received more performances than any other British piano sonata of the period.[10] Audiences who found the typical classical piano sonatas too highbrow would have appreciated the immediacy of impact that this sonata made, owing to its depiction of the life of Joan of Arc. Although short character pieces were popular with romantic composers, and orchestral tone poems commonly used extra-musical influences, Bennett's was the only British piano sonata to include a programme. Performers and critics of the present time tend to see this as a hindrance to the work's appreciation rather than a virtue. Nevertheless, it is interesting to note that three pianists have recorded it.

George Alexander Macfarren (1813–1887)

Chronologically, the discussion of Macfarren's Third Piano Sonata should follow that of Parry's sonatas, as it was published in 1880. However, Macfarren was part of the generation preceding Parry. With Bennett he helped to prepare the way for the English Musical Renaissance, and so it seems more appropriate to consider his work at this point.

Macfarren wrote three piano sonatas, which span his career. Sonata No. 1 in E flat was published in 1842 and revised in 1887. No. 2 in A, *Ma*

---

[9] Bush, 1983, 74.
[10] For reviews of performances of this work, see the following volumes of *MT*:
1874, 359 (Franklin Taylor, Crystal Palace, Dec. 1873, from memory)
1874, 367 (Hans von Bülow, Liverpool Philharmonic Hall, 17 Dec. 1873)

Cousine, was published in 1845 and No. 3 in G minor appeared in May 1880. There is the possible indication of a further two piano sonatas, one of which was written for Agnes Zimmermann and performed by her in 1866.[11]

Macfarren had studied at the Royal Academy of Music under Cipriani Potter from 1829. He returned there as a Professor in 1837 and was one of the most prolific English composers of the nineteenth century. He had ambitions to become a successful opera composer, and wrote music in practically every genre. He was one of the few Englishmen of his generation to continue writing symphonies. His views were old-fashioned and he used Mozart and Beethoven as his models, rather than contemporary romantic composers. He deplored musical innovation and despised the early music revival, though his ideal was the "unweariedly staunch advocacy of English music".[12] Much of his importance was due to his scholarship. He lectured and wrote on many subjects and in 1875 he succeeded Bennett as Professor of Music at Cambridge and Principal of the Royal Academy. Despite becoming totally blind from 1860, he was able to write, lecture and compose with the aid of amanuenses.

His Third Sonata, in four movements, was written for and dedicated to Agnes Zimmermann. In the first movement there are no clear boundaries between themes or sections and the themes are constantly being varied. This continuity disguises the underlying outline of sonata form, and the exposition is presented without a repeat. The exposition contains three themes: an opening one in the tonic [Fig. 1.2], a second in D flat (tritone relationship) and a third in E flat.

The second movement, in ternary form, contrasts even and dotted quavers [Fig. 1.3]. The harmonies remain unadventurously diatonic throughout. It is surprising that Macfarren, an academic composer, uses consecutive fifths in bar 9 of this example. The second section (*Cantabile*) is unusual; it contains no key signature, but expands the minor third interval characteristic of the opening section to a major third and develops it. The

    1874, 427 (Frank Spinney, Royal Musical Hall, Leamington, 29 Jan. 1873)
    1874, 544 (R. Blagrove, Beethoven Rooms, 4 June 1874)
    1874, 723 (E. M. Lawrence, Rugby, 19 Nov. 1874)
    1875–6, 58 (F. Taylor performed 2 movements in memory of Bennett, 4 March 1875)
    1877, 20 (W. S. Hoyte, Assembly Rooms, St John's Wood, 5 Dec. 1876)
    1878, 40 (Arabella Goddard, Victoria Rooms, Clifton, 4 Dec. 1877)
    1878, 685 (F. E. L. Barnes, Synod Hall, Montreal, 4 Nov. 1878)
    1880, 91 (Frank Barnard, Putney, 19 Jan. 1880)
    1881, 378 (Clara Lilwall, RAM pupil, Royal Hotel, Birmingham, 1 June 1881)
    1881, 430 (Miss Emilie Scott, Association Hall, Mount Pleasant, Liverpool, 25 June 1881)
    1884, 338 (von Bülow, London?, 15 May 1884); reviewer notes "the work was not improved by the player's exaggerated expression and an over-indulgence in the rubato style"
    See also *MMR*, iii, 1873, 104–5 (first review?).
[11] Newman, 1969, 580. *MT*, 1866, 339.
[12] Banister, 1891, 407.

The Piano Sonatas 1870–1890

Fig. 1.2 Macfarren, Third Sonata, Novello, First movement, Bars 1–8

Fig. 1.3 Macfarren, Third Sonata, Second movement, Bars 1–10

third section returns to the opening theme, now with a new accompaniment, and the movement ends with a coda.

The third movement, Scherzo, is in C minor, with a Trio in C major. It is unusual to find such a movement in 2/4, although the thematic material itself is relatively undistinguished and reminiscent of Haydn.

The final movement, Allegro Agitato, returns to G minor. It is long and rambling, filling fifteen of the score's forty pages. An introductory passage in octaves precedes the main theme. The thematic material here has little potential, yet it is spun out with almost incessant quaver accompaniment. However, one unusual feature is that the D flat theme from the first movement returns.

There is confusing evidence relating to the premiere. The *Musical Times* carries an advertisement for the first performance of Macfarren's Piano Sonata at a Concert for New Compositions at the Royal Academy of Music on 26 April 1879.[13] Another advertisement announces the performance of New Compositions by the Musical Artists' Society on 5 March 1881, including Macfarren's Third Sonata.[14]

This Sonata shows the complete dominance of Germanic ideas of form, style and harmony and it is not surprising that the work has not been recorded. Macfarren proved himself capable of writing a pastiche sonata, but was unable to express his individuality through this genre. As we shall see, Macfarren's traditional Mendelssohnian-derived style was his legacy to his pupils. Parry took lessons from him in 1875 and dedicated *Variations on a theme by Bach* (1873–5) to him.

Charles Hubert Hastings Parry (1848–1918)

It is with Parry that we see important attempts to advance the style of the piano sonata. Like Bennett and Macfarren, Parry begins with elements of Beethoven's, Mendelssohn's and Schumann's styles, but it is the way in which he is able to assimilate elements of Brahms' and Wagner's harmonic language that are of particular interest.

Parry's education included a period of study at Exeter College, Oxford, where he read Law and History, matriculating in 1867. As might be expected in an upper-class family, he was subjected to a certain amount of career pressure and as a result held a position in insurance at Lloyd's Register of Shipping from 1870 to 1876.

Nevertheless, Parry's interest in music took him to Stuttgart in 1867, to study instrumentation and composition with the English composer Henry Hugo Pierson (1815–73), whose works include songs, choral music, the patriotic *Hurrah for Merry England* (1880) and an oratorio *Jerusalem* (1852). Pierson had left England because he had found the ecclesiastical bias to university degrees intolerable. Having been elected Reid Professor of Music in Edinburgh, he resigned from this post and took voluntary exile in Germany instead. It was extremely unusual for a British composer to take such a step, as it meant effectively competing with the great German composers in their own land. Like Bennett, Pierson had met both Mendelssohn and Schumann.

In addition to his musical studies, Parry learnt to speak German and he absorbed the culture, later learning French in Belgium in 1869. Parry did not learn much from his subsequent teacher Bennett, with whom he studied in 1870, because Bennett was insufficiently critical. Through Clara Schumann, Joseph Joachim and Julius Stockhausen, Parry learnt of Brahms, who was then relatively unknown in England. Parry wanted to take lessons with Brahms, and Walter Broadwood contacted Joachim to enquire about

---

[13] *MT*, 1879, 185. The number of the Sonata is not given.
[14] *MT*, 1881, 105. The instrument is not mentioned.

The Piano Sonatas 1870–1890

this possibility, but Brahms declined. Parry's circle of close musical friends consisted largely of Germans, and thus he would have felt a closer affinity with the German tradition than the English music of the period.

From November 1873 Parry studied Brahms' Piano Sonata Op. 5 and his Piano Quintet Op. 34 with Edward Dannreuther. Dannreuther's influence on Parry was far-reaching. At his house in London Parry's early chamber music was performed, and it was he who introduced Parry to the music of Wagner, which was to prove crucial in his musical development.

Dannreuther was the main champion of Wagner in England. In 1867, the pianists Dannreuther, Fritz Hartvigson, Walter Bache and Karl Klindworth had formed The Working Men's Society, with the aim of performing contemporary orchestral music in arrangements for two pianos. This included Liszt's arrangement of Beethoven's Ninth Symphony, works by Berlioz, Rubinstein and Wagner. Klindworth played *Das Rheingold* and *Die Walküre* in 1868, and Dannreuther introduced the society to *Tristan und Isolde*. By 1872, Dannreuther had inaugurated the Wagner Society.

Parry heard concert performances of *The Ring* in London, given by the Wagner Society, and attended *The Ring* cycle at Bayreuth from 20 to 23 August 1876. The following year, Wagner came to England for a festival of six concerts that ultimately proved a financial disaster. Parry had carefully studied the scores of Wagner's operas before the performances, and was extremely moved by them. At Bayreuth Parry met Liszt, Tchaikovsky, Cui, N. Rubinstein, d'Indy, Saint-Saëns, Grieg and Bruckner.

The dates of composition of Parry's piano sonatas are somewhat confusing. Dibble states that they were both written in 1876, although No. 2 in A preceded No. 1 in F by a matter of months.[15] However, the style of Sonata No. 1 in F seems to suggest a much earlier period of composition, as will be demonstrated in the following discussion. There is an entry from Parry's diary on 4 October 1873 referring to a Sonatina in F, although no trace of this work exists today. There is also another entry from 28 October 1876, "... finished my [?Sonata ?Suite] for Pianof. in F ma." [16] Possibly Parry began the work in 1873, intending it to be a Sonatina, and then later decided to expand its scope and to re-name it Sonata. This may explain why it was published as No. 1, despite being completed after No. 2.

It is likely that Parry completed the Sonata in F before the diary entry of October 1876. In a letter to Edward W. Hamilton dated 7 May 1876, Parry thanks him for looking over his movement, and goes on to say that he has already sent it to Lamborn Cock, who hopes to bring it out in the autumn.[17] The implication is that the Sonata is already finished.

These were not the first attempts that Parry had made to write a piano sonata. In 1865 he had written a Sonata in F minor for piano duet that

---

[15] Dibble, 1992, 136–8.
[16] Private correspondence with Laura Ponsonby. Diaries held at Shulbrede Priory.
[17] Lbm Add MS 48621.

remains unpublished, influenced by Mendelssohn.[18] In 1872 he wrote *Charakterbilder – Seven Ages of Mind – Studies for the Pianoforte*, which are Schumannesque. His *Großes Duo* in E minor, written in January 1876, demonstrates the influence of Bach. Thus the piano works that Parry wrote immediately before his two sonatas demonstrate influences ranging from the baroque to the early romantic periods.

The manuscripts of both solo piano sonatas are held at the Bodleian Library, Oxford. Sonata No. 1 in F consists of the first three movements, and an incomplete fourth movement, but of Sonata No. 2 in A there are only the last seven bars of the first movement followed by the second movement. Both sonatas were published, No. 1 in F by Lamborn Cock in 1877, and No. 2 in A by Stanley Lucas in 1878. In the letter to Edward W. Hamilton, already mentioned, Parry says that he turned his attention to things rustic when he wrote the F major Sonata, and intended to call it *Arcadia*. He had intended to dedicate it to Lady Pembroke, but as relations with her were strained he dedicated it to George Grove instead. The Second Sonata bears a dedication on its title page, the decorative typeface leading to some confusion over whether the dedicatee's name was Tora or Cora. Augener erroneously printed Cora on the title page of their reissue. Dibble tells us that Parry's friend was Tora Gordon, and that he wrote the sonata in honour of her engagement to Victor Marshall.[19]

> ... as I began the sonata I began to idealize the object of it and to make a Romance out of it; and love grew till in my heart she was only second to Maudie [his wife]. The result was a rapidly produced work. I wrote my four movements and an introduction in less than 3 weeks and with the doctoring it afterwards received partly from my own criticisms and partly from Macfarren's valuable suggestions I think it is the best work I have written yet.[20]

Parry's attitude to sonata form is revealed in the article *Sonata* that he wrote in 1877 for the first edition of Grove's dictionary and his *Art of Music*.

> In the early sonatas both halves of the movement were played twice. As artistic feeling developed, the repetition of the second half was frequently dispensed with, but the repetition of the first half was maintained, mainly to help the mind to grasp firmly the principle of contrast between the two keys. In modern times the repetition of the first half is also commonly dispensed with, because the musical instinct has become so quick to grasp any indication of design that it no longer requires to have such things insisted on; and also the progress of music towards a more passionately

---

[18] Dibble, 1992, 34.
[19] Dibble, 1992, 136.
[20] Diary [?Jan. – Mar.] 1876, Shulbrede Priory. This implies that the Sonata was completed early in 1876.

Fig. 1.4 Parry, Sonata No. 1, Lamborn Cock, First movement, Bars 1–9

emotional phase makes it noticeably anomalous to go through the same exciting crises twice over.[21]

Here Parry illustrates the notion of progress in music during the nineteenth century. His own Piano Sonatas demonstrate the conflict between looking backwards, taking Beethoven as a model, and looking forwards to the new Wagnerian style. The first movement of Sonata No. 1 in F follows a sonata form plan in which the exposition is repeated – a feature that Parry considered to be classical. However, the first movement of the Second Sonata in A, also in sonata form, dispenses with the repeat, and is more overtly emotional. The presence of the expositional repeat in Sonata No. 1 supports the view that it was composed considerably earlier than Sonata No. 2. Comparison of the opening movements of both Sonatas will illustrate their stylistic differences.

The opening theme of the first movement of Sonata No. 1 consists of a descending arpeggio followed by chords, all of which firmly fix the tonic key, F major [Fig. 1.4]. Parry discusses in *Art of Music* how Beethoven uses the opening arpeggio in Sonata Op. 2/1 in F minor, raising it with sequences until it reaches a peak of intensity, and only then relaxing the tension.[22] This

[21] Parry, 1893, 259.
[22] Ibid., 288–90.

seems to be what Parry is trying to achieve with his F major arpeggio. Although it is a descending pattern, he raises the highest note and transposes it to reach a climax at the sforzando in bar 7. This leads immediately into a new theme, a more melodious figure (poco marcato), which is heard first in the bass register in bar 7 and then in the treble. The second subject emerges through an abrupt modulation to the expected dominant key, C major [Fig. 1.5], and builds up to a well-timed climax before dying away.

Fig. 1.5 Parry, Sonata No. 1, First movement, Bars 16–21

The development opens with the first subject transposed into C major. The musical material is clearly divided into sections marked by double bar lines. The sections explore remote keys including B and D majors. The B major section [Fig. 1.6] is reminiscent of bars 17–20 from *Reconnaissance* in Schumann's *Carnaval*, also in the same key. Both composers alternate the tune between melody and bass, and accompany it with semiquavers.

Parry's first movement ends with a recapitulation of themes in the tonic as expected, and sequences are used to build to a loud climax. The final ten bars use a descending arpeggio and they decrease in volume, which is the reverse of the procedure used at the start of the movement.

To contrast with the classical form of the first movement of Sonata No. 1, the first movement of Sonata No. 2 is more imaginative. It begins with an introduction in A minor that uses a variant on Wagner's Tristan chord in the first bar [Fig. 1.7]. Parry's chord superimposes fourths, replicating the structure of Wagner's chord. Although Parry's chord could be heard as a diminished seventh, the melodic line rises in a similar manner to the opening melody of Wagner's *Tristan* Prelude. Additionally, Parry's chord resolves onto E7 and uses pitches that are identical to the opening of the *Tristan* Prelude. These similarities are unlikely to be coincidental. This opening of

Fig. 1.6 Parry, Sonata No. 1, First movement, Bars 51–54

Parry's Sonata No. 2 uses a curious stylistic mixture. Besides the chromaticism, there is a diatonic linking phrase almost akin to a Baroque French Overture.

Fig. 1.7 Parry, Sonata No. 2, Stanley Lucas, First movement, Bars 1–4

The introduction consists of two parts; the second of which is very similar to the arioso dolente in Beethoven's Piano Sonata Op. 110 in A flat (Adagio ma non troppo, Bars 3–6), and Parry even uses the same key (enharmonically) as Beethoven [Fig. 1.8]. This theme is used in imitation with tenths, which are difficult for most pianists.

Fig. 1.8 Parry, Sonata No. 2, First movement, Bars 9–13

Parry uses this lyrical theme later in the movement, immediately before the recapitulation. This is similar to the way in which Beethoven uses the Grave theme from his Sonata Pathétique Op. 13 at important structural points.

The first subject of the main section of Sonata No. 2 has a Brahmsian character, with the melody doubled in thirds and octaves [Fig. 1.9]. Parry uses far-ranging modulations from the tonic A minor, including a passage in E flat (a tritone away) in the development. The whole movement uses a successfully integrated design.

Fig. 1.9 Parry, Sonata No. 2, First movement, Bars 27–35

Parry's attitude to form is much more flexible in the Second Sonata than the First, leading Fuller-Maitland to describe the first movement as a rhapsody on contrasting themes that do not conform to a classical plan.[23] In the First Sonata, the classical standpoint dominates, whereas in the Second the romantic view is more important. As demonstrated above, the main influences seen in the type of figurations used in the First Sonata are those of the early romantic composers, Beethoven and Schumann, whereas the Second also demonstrates those of the later romantic composers, Brahms and Wagner. These observations are also borne out by consideration of the remaining movements of the two sonatas.

Returning to the First Sonata, the second movement is of lower density [Fig. 1.10]. Rather surprisingly, it must have worked as a salon piece, as it was the only movement from either of Parry's Sonatas to be published separately. The style of the first section is similar to *Arlequin* from Schumann's *Carnaval*. *Arlequin* is a lively movement, also rhythmically monotonous and containing much repetition.

---

[23] Fuller-Maitland, 1934, 25.

Fig. 1.10 Parry, Sonata No. 1, Second movement, Bars 1–8

The three sections of this movement contain completely different material, with no obvious thematic connections. Unlike the first section, the second and third sections are both in 4/4. The second section uses thick chords, and it is not clear whether it should be played at a slower tempo than the first [Fig. 1.11]. The style of this example now seems very Elgarian, almost like a *Pomp and Circumstance* march, although it predates the Elgar by about twenty-five years. It is in quadruple metre, with a firm plodding bass on every beat. Sequences and repetition are used to build the melody to a climax, whilst there is a logical harmonic structure and directness of approach. Leaps of a sixth and an octave are found throughout, and all of these features can be found in Elgar's marches. These similarities may indicate the existence of a truly British musical tradition that has its origins in our popular music, especially the ceremonial march.

Fig. 1.11 Parry, Sonata No. 1, Second movement, Bars 48–56

The third movement of the First Sonata, Andante, has the character of a barcarolle in its undulating quaver accompaniment, which suggests the influence of Mendelssohn. It is in modified ternary form, beginning and ending in B flat major, with a middle section in the expected dominant key, F major.

The final movement of the First Sonata consists of an Andante introduction to the main Allegretto in F major. It is a fast, virtuosic movement that is possibly an attempt to emulate the style of Chopin's finales. The main section is like a rondo, with four main themes that are developed by sequences (heavily relied upon!), modulations, transposition from major to minor and dialogue between the hands. The coda combines elements of two themes to build to a climax.

Like his First Sonata, Parry's Second Sonata follows a four-movement plan, but its second movement is the slow movement, and its third a scherzo.

The second movement has a binary structure with two themes in each section. The first theme is based in C sharp minor [Fig. 1.12] and the second in E major. The influence of Schubert can be seen in its lyricism, whilst the harmonies show an awareness of Wagner and illustrate a romantic aesthetic rather than a classical one.

Fig. 1.12 Parry, Sonata No. 2, Second movement, Bars 1–8

The third movement is a Scherzo in A major with a trio section (Meno mosso) in C major. The scherzo section is based on semiquaver scale patterns, whilst the trio contrasts with quaver movement. The movement ends by way of an enharmonic change with a coda that recalls both themes.

The fourth movement is a rondo, with its main theme in A major. As would be expected in a rondo, there is more repetition than development, and Parry transposes his themes by octaves.

The character of this Sonata is much more overtly romantic and emotional than the First. Themes are subjected to development rather than merely repeated and sequences are less obvious. In this Sonata Parry seems to have more fully assimilated his style, supporting my view that it was composed considerably later than Sonata No. 1.

It is difficult to assess accurately the influence that Parry's piano sonatas had on subsequent composers. Despite being published, there is no evidence to suggest that they were ever publicly performed. This contrasts with the frequent reporting of Bennett's Sonata in the *Musical Times*. However, both of Parry's sonatas lie easily under the fingers (with one or two exceptions) and could have been played by amateurs.

Parry did not have an international reputation to match that of Stanford or Elgar; and after World War I, his reputation in England declined. Although for much of the twentieth century writers on music have had almost an obsession with the major figures and originality, now we are more able to appreciate composers' works on their own terms. Thus Parry's own music is now enjoying a revival, with recordings of all of his Symphonies available. Some of his piano music, including the two Sonatas, has been performed on Parry's own piano at Shulbrede Priory and recorded on compact disc. Jeremy Dibble has made a major study of Parry's life and works, which has generated renewed interest in his music. No longer is Parry remembered solely for his achievements in music education, helping to improve standards of performance, composition and criticism, but also for his own compositions. As Parry's Second Sonata is the most important example of the British piano sonata to have been written in the nineteenth century, it deserves to be more widely known.

To conclude, Parry was obliged to attach himself to the dominant Austro-German tradition and it was within this that he had to learn to express his own individuality. His piano sonatas illustrate the early stages of this process. Whereas the piano sonatas by Bennett and Macfarren followed almost exclusively in the tradition of Mendelssohn, Parry's sonatas embrace the influence of Brahms and, most importantly, if tentatively, Wagner. The Wagnerian influence was not seen again in the British piano sonata until two decades later, when Dale's Piano Sonata was published. Parry finally achieved his goal more creditably than most of his contemporaries and set intellectual standards that influenced future generations of British composers.

Charles Villiers Stanford (1852–1924)

Stanford was subjected to a similar type of education and family career-pressure as Parry. He attended Queens' College, Cambridge as a choral scholar, reading Classics, and his father planned for him to enter the legal profession. Stanford also spent a period in Germany. In 1874 he studied composition with Carl Heinrich Reinecke and pianoforte with Papperitz in Leipzig and in 1876 he studied with Friedrich Kiel in Berlin.

From the *New Grove* we learn that Stanford wrote a Piano Sonata in D flat, Op. 20, which is unpublished. I corresponded with the author of the article, the late Dr Frederick Hudson, but unfortunately, even after thirty years of investigation, he was unable to trace the location of the manuscript.

Stanford included a performance of this Sonata in a Cambridge University Music Society Pop concert on 25 February 1885. It had also been previously performed at a concert in St James' Hall, London, on 4 February 1884. From this one assumes that the work was written *c*. 1884. The *Musical Times* of 1 March 1884 contains a review of the Sonata.

> Some listeners have professed to perceive in the work a deliberate intention to violate the established laws of form, but we confess that to us no such design is apparent. In matters of detail, Mr. Stanford shows himself an independent thinker, but in all essentials his newest work is as classical in outline as could possibly be desired. The opening *adagio* is exceedingly impressive, and the succeeding *allegro moderato* is worked out with splendid mastery of the subject matter, the general effect being that of a lofty design carried into execution by a thoroughly experienced hand. The succeeding *allegro grazioso,* a modified kind of scherzo, is vigorous, and the final *allegro commodo* with its excellent first subject, seems scarcely less important than the first movement, though for some mysterious reason no analysis was vouchsafed of this portion of the work. We have no hesitation in characterising it as one of the most important compositions for piano solo produced within the present generation. It was very finely played by Miss Zimmermann, and composer and executant were called to the platform and loudly cheered. The Sonata was repeated by Miss Zimmermann on the following Saturday, and again favourably received, its merits more conspicuous on second hearing.[24]

Agnes Zimmermann was a noted interpreter of British piano sonatas. She was the dedicatee of Macfarren's Third Sonata.

Stanford rarely deserted classical forms and said, "The road [of orthodoxy] may be sometimes dusty and heavy, but it was made by the experience of our forefathers, who found out the best direction for ensuring our progress." [25] He felt that only when a composer had absorbed the rules could he know when it was appropriate to break them. Stanford insisted that his pupils at the Royal College of Music studied strict counterpoint, and later chapters demonstrate the effects this had on his pupils.

Stanford wrote twelve sonatas in total. The five organ sonatas date from 1917 to 1921, and hence detailed study of them is unlikely to provide information about procedures he may have used in the Piano Sonata. The only other sonatas that he wrote during a similar period to the Piano Sonata are the First Cello Sonata in A, Op. 9 (*c*. 1878) and the First Violin Sonata in D, Op. 11 (*c*.1880).

In contrast to Parry, Stanford had an international reputation, especially

---

[24] Anon., *MT*, 1884, 147. See also Shedlock, 1964, 233–4.
[25] Greene, 1935, 224.

in Germany, although one can only speculate whether the Piano Sonata was ever performed there.

Ethel Smyth (1858–1944)

As the three Piano Sonatas by Ethel Smyth were written between September and December 1877, they are clearly student works. Towards the end of her life, Smyth prepared a catalogue of her works, but omitted these three sonatas from it, possibly indicating that she placed little value on them. Like Stanford's Sonata, they were never published, but the manuscripts can be seen in the British Library. Smyth never published any piano works, yet it was the only instrument that she played. As no record of the Sonatas being performed exists, they are unlikely to have influenced other composers, but it is interesting to see how this British composer responded to the dominant Germanic influences.

Smyth's natural musical gifts manifested themselves early in her childhood. She transposed and played by ear from an early age, encouraged by her mother, who was herself a talented musician. Smyth sang duets with her sister, and her first attempts at composition were chants and hymns. Her first real contact with the world of classical music came at the age of twelve, with the arrival of a governess who had studied music at Leipzig Conservatoire. Smyth obtained a copy of Beethoven's Piano Sonatas and began to study them. It was then that she conceived her plan of going to study music in Leipzig, a plan that her father opposed as he believed that artists were of low moral standards. This attitude prevailed at the time, and as already seen, both Parry and Stanford had to overcome parental pressure to become musicians.

Through Mr Ewing, the music master at her school in Putney, Smyth learned of Wagner and she read Berlioz's *Treatise on Orchestration*. She often travelled alone to London, to attend concerts. She was very moved by her first hearing of Brahms – the *Liebeslieder* waltzes – and queued to see Joachim. Eventually her father agreed to let her go to Leipzig, as she was to stay with friends.

Smyth entered the Leipzig Conservatoire in the autumn of 1877, where she studied composition with Reinecke, as had Stanford, three years earlier. She was the first woman to be admitted to his class. She also studied counterpoint and theory with Salomon Jadassohn and piano with Maas. Smyth did not find her teachers to be particularly sympathetic, so she left the conservatoire and took private lessons with Heinrich von Herzogenberg.

Smyth spoke fluent French and German, and in later years wrote her own libretti in these languages. Some of her operas were first performed in Germany, as was the case with Stanford also. Her musical language in the Piano Sonatas is derivative of the classical–romantic German tradition, although some of her early choral works show the influence of English Church music, with which she would have been familiar.

As in the case of Parry's two sonatas, Smyth's Sonata No. 1 is essentially a classical piece, whereas her Sonata No. 2 is a more romantic work. Sonata No. 1 in C, dedicated to *la Madre*, was completed by September 1877. It was written as an exercise for her teacher, and Smyth wrote on 22 August 1877, "I have done three movements and very ugly two of them are".[26]

The first movement is in a small-scale sonata form, carefully worked out [Fig. 1.13]. The first subject is almost Mozartian, the textures are clear, and there is frequent use of ornaments throughout. The second subject is in the expected dominant key. More remote modulations seem to present problems for Smyth, and there are a number of occasions on which a diminished seventh chord is used to wrench the phrase into a new key. Her phrases are consistently short, and this interrupts the flow of the music.

Fig. 1.13 Smyth, Sonata No. 1, Manuscript, First movement, Bars 1–11

The second movement consists of a Minuet in A major and Trio in A minor, but the musical ideas are undistinguished. The third movement is a funeral march that opens with low thick chords, doubled in octaves and filled-in with thirds in the manner of Brahms. Its second theme is lyrical, marked dolore, but the quaver accompaniment to it is uninteresting and it almost grinds to a halt at this tempo. Even Smyth admitted that this movement was not successful, pencilling in the comment, "Ein langweiliger Satz – keine Bewegung" [A boring movement – no movement]!

The mood of the final movement is similar to that of the first, but it is in rondo form. Fig. 1.14 begins with a pedal C, above which the themes unfold. There is an unbroken succession of two and four bar phrases. Röntgen, the leader of the Gewandhaus Orchestra, commented, "that Rondo theme is so pure and fresh that I could almost swear it was by

[26] In Dale, *ML*, 1949, 329–36.

Mozart" – hardly a compliment for a work written almost a hundred years later![27] A heavy Alla Burla section is used towards the end, and the Sonata ends fortissimo.

Fig. 1.14 Smyth, Sonata No. 1, Fourth movement, Bars 1–8

The Second Sonata in C sharp minor, *Geistinger*, written in November–December 1877, demands a more advanced piano technique as its scales are virtuosic and it is dramatic and emotional in mood. Whereas the First Sonata contained four movements, the Second has only three.

The German actress Marie Geistinger inspired the Second Sonata, and the first movement is descriptive of Smyth's first visit to her. It begins stormily; the introduction contrasts high and low registers and the descending lines are meant to suggest her ascent of the staircase! Rapid scales follow, and Smyth's knock at the door is depicted. The movement uses a sonata form structure from the main section (Allegro Moderato) onwards. Many self-contained phrases conjure up "the most banal of all banal conversations I have ever taken part in".[28] The rhythm of the main theme (a crotchet, followed by four quavers) is used as an ostinato.

The second movement has a lilting feel, and its use of 9/8 metre makes it similar to a barcarolle.[29] It is in the key of D flat major, the enharmonic equivalent of the tonic major. Smyth is harmonically quite adventurous and the movement contains frequent modulations and chromatic notes, although it lapses into sentimentality in parts. The movement is in ternary form, with a middle section in the contrasting key of F major.

The finale begins boldly in octaves, using the rhythm of a Bourrée [Fig. 1.15]. The lower auxiliary motif is used throughout the movement and beats are divided into two or three. It uses chromatic harmonies and frequent modulations.

[27] Ibid.
[28] Ibid.
[29] Serbescu, *EPTA Journal*, 1995, 12.

Fig. 1.15 Smyth, Sonata No. 2, Manuscript, Third movement, Bars 1–4

Considering that this Sonata was written immediately after the First, there has been a dramatic change in Smyth's approach to composition, and it is unlikely that anyone would attribute her Second Sonata to Mozart!

Smyth began her Third Sonata in D major, which consists of only two movements, in December 1877. The manuscript is in very poor condition and it is hard to see even the staves. Smyth's handwriting is almost illegible, possibly indicating that the Sonata was hurriedly written. Key signatures only appear on the first line of each section, and there are virtually no dynamic or phrase markings. Even the quality of the ideas and their working out is much weaker than in the other sonatas, leading me to question the accuracy of the date of it. Serbescu notices its pastoral character, resulting from fifths in the bass part of the first movement (Allegro).[30] Smyth alternates the time signature between 3/4 and 6/8 so that the quavers flow freely and she makes little distinction between the two subjects. The second movement is a Scherzo and Trio in D minor. This type of structure was uncommon as a final movement, and the use of the minor mode suggests that Smyth may have originally intended to write a third movement.

Despite Smyth's love for the music of Brahms and her admiration of Wagner, these two composers do not significantly influence her musical language in the sonatas. Mozart and Beethoven remain the chief stylistic influences, possibly because Smyth played their piano works herself. Her use of programmatic elements as inspiration for the musical ideas can be compared to Bennett's, although Smyth does not annotate her scores with any clues to the source of her ideas. Extra-musical influences make the Second Sonata considerably more successful than the First and it is a pity that Smyth did not return to the piano sonata genre when her style had fully developed.

Smyth's music has been the focus of a recent reappraisal, owing to the current fashion for gender studies in music. Her opera, *The Wreckers*, was performed at the Promenade concerts in London in 1995 and Serbescu has recorded the complete piano music. Now her oeuvre is accessible to scholars, but the piano sonatas are unlikely ever to be included in recitals as their style is too immature.

---

[30] Ibid.

Edward German (1862–1936)

German's work was written as an entry for the 1884 Lucas Medal Competition at the Royal Academy of Music, which required entrants to submit the first movement of a sonata for piano. In the event the competition, between over thirty works, was won by Stewart Macpherson, whilst German came second.[31] Septimus Webbe performed German's Sonata at the Royal Academy of Music.[32]

The manuscript survives apart from about a page at the end. In the version published by Banks Music, James Brown has supplied a conclusion amounting to five bars. Unfortunately, the published score does not distinguish between German's original music and Brown's later annotations or additions. A comparison between the published score and German's manuscript reveals that, apart from Brown's conclusion, his editing mainly concerns details of phrasing and articulation. He helpfully clarifies ambiguities in the score, such as using explicit triplet markings over groups of three quavers. Other differences between the manuscript and score seem rather odd, such as Brown's substitution of 4/4 for German's C. Brown alters the phrasing of the second subject into long-breathed phrases, rather than using the one-bar phrases seen on the manuscript, which presumably are German's. The printed version does seem to make more musical sense, but full details should have been provided. Other changes concern the irresponsible addition of accents and expression markings such as espress. and animato, that are not in the manuscript. The first twenty-three bars are clearly intended to serve as an introduction. Despite German's underlining of this word on the manuscript, the title is omitted from the published score.

This work was only intended to serve as a first movement, rather than a complete sonata, hence its published title is inaccurate. It is not surprising to find that sonata form is used. The introduction in G minor provides a confident start. It consists of two ideas, a chordal theme [Fig. 1.16] and a meno mosso section. The former recurs at the end of the exposition and at the end of the sonata, and the latter recurs during the development. Thus German uses principles of cyclic form, as seen in music by Schubert and Liszt.

The introduction shares some material with the first movement of German's unpublished Piano Trio in D, written in 1883. Both works are in major keys but with minor introductions. The Piano Trio uses a first phrase of five bars as opposed to the Piano Sonata's four. It omits the triplets and presents the second half of the phrase in octaves rather than with harmonization.

---

[31] Scott, 1932, 22.
[32] Ibid., 28.

Fig. 1.16 German, Sonata, Banks, Bars 1–4

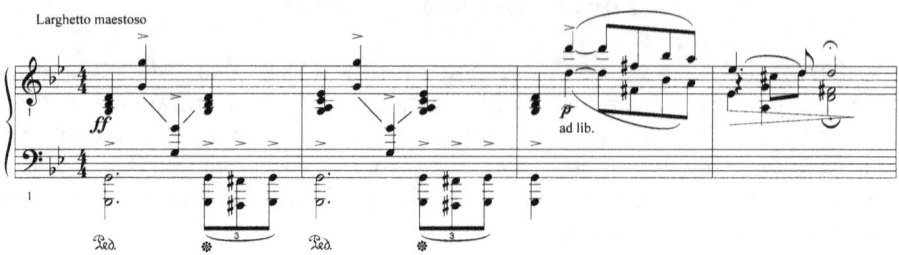

The main Allegro spiritoso of the Piano Sonata is in G major and uses a syncopated theme. A new theme, using triplets, reaches an Elgarian climax [Fig. 1.17]. As in Parry's First Sonata, this prompts the question whether there is a British tradition emerging from our popular music.

Fig. 1.17 German, Sonata, Bars 48–51

German mainly wrote comic operas, incidental and light music, although piano transcriptions of these works were published. He became particularly popular after the death of Sullivan in 1900. The *Musical Times* summarized his contribution to musical life in 1927.

> Mr. German is second to no composer today as a writer of light music, and he has done incalculable service to the art by showing over and over again that music so tuneful and attractive as to please the lay ear immediately, may yet be unexceptional on artistic grounds. We doubt if any other English composer has so consistently captured both general and musical public.[33]

The second subject in D major [Fig. 1.18] is almost identical to one of the main themes from Liszt's Piano Sonata in B minor (1854, bars 153–6). This could be coincidental, but the same theme is used in German's First Impromptu, written *c.* 1883 and published as part of his Suite by Edwin Ashdown in 1889. This is followed by a hymn-like theme marked sostenuto, also in D major, and the exposition ends with a variant on the introduction.

---

[33] Anon., *MT*, 1927, 135.

The Piano Sonatas 1870–1890

The texture of this seems orchestrally conceived as it uses tremolos. The exposition is repeated.

Fig. 1.18 German, Sonata, Bars 63–66

The development further explores the main themes in the keys of E major, E minor and B minor. The Lisztian theme is cleverly accompanied by the left hand, in the rhythm of the introduction. The recapitulation brings us back to G major with the expected return to the main section. The themes are slightly modified and the Elgarian climax omitted, but it follows essentially the same order of presentation as the exposition. This Sonata uses a diatonic vocabulary. German avoided the chromatic sentimentality typical of much Victorian music, although some of his salon music is akin to Fauré.

The Piano Sonata was not published until 1987, a wait of over a hundred years! Thus its interest is that of a curiosity. It is unlikely that German would have expected his student Piano Sonata to reach the public, especially as it consisted of only one movement. Interestingly, his was the first British piano sonata to illustrate the influence of Liszt. The connection between Liszt and the Royal Academy of Music will be discussed further in Chapter 2 (pp. 35–6).

This chapter has surveyed the most important developments in the British piano sonata from 1870 to 1890. Some other, minor composers, wrote sonatas during this period, but there is insufficient space to discuss their work here, although details are provided in the catalogue.[34]

Elgar did not write a piano sonata, although his Sonatina was originally written in 1889, revised in 1931 and published in 1932. He was another composer who played the piano as a child, and his father was a piano tuner. However, he claimed to "know nothing about piano music" and to "hate the piano".[35] Piano music spans his musical career, but he preferred the organ, possibly because it is capable of sustaining a musical line whereas the piano is not. His Organ Sonata No. 1 in G was written in 1895, and it is a fine example of the form. It pre-dates his symphonies but it uses a similar large-scale four-movement plan.

The piano sonatas discussed in detail above have demonstrated the

---

[34] See also Newman, 1969, 584–601.
[35] Anderson, 1993, 393–5.

prevailing attitude towards composition among British composers in the late nineteenth century. Every composer, not just in Britain, conformed to the Austro-German tradition, which was an international language. All of the composers, to some extent, owed a debt to Haydn, Mozart and Beethoven. Bennett and Macfarren also looked to the early nineteenth-century composers, mainly Mendelssohn. Even the minor German composers, such as Rheinberger, Raff and Reger, used this approach. It was not musical pastiche, but a method of using other composers' ideas to develop one's own. The works that were the most successful managed to blend a variety of influences, as exemplified by Parry's Sonatas. He synthesized influences from Mendelssohn, Schumann, Brahms and Wagner, and his piano sonatas also contain individual fingerprints – they are not merely derivative in style. The following chapters attempt to trace the development of the British piano sonata as composers begin to move outside the dominating Austro-German orbit.

2

The Piano Sonatas 1890–1910

During this period, we see the emergence of several different styles in British piano sonatas. None of the composers discussed in this chapter established a reputation to match that of Parry or Stanford, but the Piano Sonatas by Benjamin Dale and Cyril Scott are significant contributions.

Algernon (Bennet Langton) Ashton (1859–1937)

Music by Ashton is virtually unknown. Despite more than 160 of his works being published, the British Library holds fewer than half of his scores. Ashton was an English composer, but he spent the formative years of his life in Germany, living in Leipzig from 1863, hence his music is based on the Teutonic tradition. His teachers included Iwan Knorr, the teacher of Cyril Scott and the Frankfurt Group, Reinecke and Raff.

Ashton returned to London at the age of twenty-two and from 1885 he taught the piano at the Royal College of Music. He wrote music in all the major genres, except opera. Much of his music was published in Germany, and it achieved a better reputation on the continent than at home. The British composers Pierson, Smyth, Stanford, Delius and to some extent Elgar, also found a more enthusiastic audience abroad. The English treated Ashton as an eccentric, and did not take him seriously. His two hobbies, writing incessantly to newspapers and tidying graves, did nothing to improve matters.

It is very difficult to clarify details of Ashton's piano sonatas, as there is so much conflicting evidence. Lewis Foreman's article for *The New Grove* states that Ashton wrote twenty-four piano sonatas, one in every major and minor key.[1] Patrick Webb claims that there are eight piano sonatas, the first being published in 1882, but Newman says there are only seven, which were

---

[1] See Sadie, S. (ed.), *New Grove*, 2, 654–5. Supported by Abraham in Blume (ed.), *MGG*, i, 750.

published between 1899 and 1925.² Harold Truscott observed that the first of the eight sonatas, in E flat minor, was published in 1888.³ I can confirm that at least eight were published between 1899 and 1926, six of these in Germany.⁴ The Hofbauer catalogue of 1898 lists Ashton's Opp. 1–100, which does not include any piano sonatas. When the sonatas were published they did not appear chronologically, so the opus numbers do not give any indication of their order of composition.

Ashton is blandly content with traditional forms and harmony, although the keyboard writing is idiomatic and sonorous. His Piano Sonatas do not form a major contribution to the genre and are rather derivative. His style is summarized in the following contemporary review:

> The whole work is full of sound thought and clever workmanship, but to those who know Mr. Ashton's music these qualities will not come as a surprise. The composer's subjection to the school of Schumann and Brahms is very evident, and it probably proves a bar to the full manifestation of his individuality.⁵

The opening of Sonata No. 3 [Fig. 2.1] is typical of his piano music.

Fig. 2.1 Ashton, Sonata No. 3, Ries & Erler, First movement, Bars 1–5

Ashton is unusual in having written such a large number of Piano Sonatas – the composers discussed in Chapter 1 did not write more than three. It is unlikely that he would have written so many if there had been no prospect of having them performed, and he probably played them himself.

[2] Webb, *BMS Journal*, 1992, 26. Newman, 1969, 592. There are scores of seven piano sonatas at the Library of Congress, Washington.
[3] Truscott, *MMR*, 1959, 142. His article may not be reliable – Truscott also refers to four piano sonatas by Parry, which were allegedly written towards the end of his life. Parry wrote only two sonatas, which are early works.
[4] See Appendix 2, p. 214.
[5] Anon., *MT*, 1893, 613. A review of Sonata No. 2 for Cello and Piano Op. 75.

The Piano Sonatas 1890–1910

Yet even today, when there is a revival of music from this period, including recordings of Parry's piano sonatas and Smyth's complete piano music, none of Ashton's works has been performed or recorded. His position in British music history is that of an outsider.

A comparison between the Royal Academy of Music and the Royal College of Music

Some of the most significant developments in the period 1890–1910 occurred at the Royal Academy of Music. It is worth briefly considering the history of the London music institutions before discussing the music that resulted.

The Royal Academy of Music had been founded in 1822 with William Crotch as Principal. He was succeeded by Cipriani Potter (1832–59), Charles Lucas (1859–66), William Sterndale Bennett (1866–75), George Macfarren (1875–87) and Alexander Mackenzie (1888–1924). The Academy was originally modelled on Mendelssohnian Leipzig, and by the 1870s it was criticized for the quality of its teaching. The public view was that the Academy was inadequate to compete with continental conservatoires, and it was proposed that a new conservatoire should be established in London.

The National Training School for Music was founded in 1876, with Arthur Sullivan as its Principal. He remained in this position until 1881, when John Stainer succeeded him. A proposal to merge the Academy and National Training School was considered, but rejected. In 1883 the National Training School was superseded by the Royal College of Music with George Grove as Director. Parry took over as Director in 1895, remaining in this post until his death in 1918. Grove's original staff included Parry as Professor of Composition, Stanford as Professor of Composition and Orchestral Conducting and Walter Parratt as Professor of Organ.

Both Parry and Stanford had received German training and thus the Teutonic tradition was continued in South Kensington. Despite Parry's early enthusiasm for Wagner, in later years he became very conservative in his musical tastes and Grove was not keen on Wagner either. Stanford, too, disliked modernity and followed in the Brahmsian tradition, although he did support opera, which Parry hated. Stanford was often criticized for the ease with which he composed and was reproached for being too academic in his choice of musical forms. Parry and Stanford had university connections – Parry was Professor at Oxford from 1900 to 1908, and Stanford was at Cambridge from 1887. Both undeniably helped to raise the standard of musical education and scholarship through their own writings.

Mackenzie, the Principal of the Royal Academy, had received a much broader musical education. Whilst a student in Germany, he had played second violin in the Sondershausen orchestra, performing the contemporary music of Liszt, Berlioz and Wagner. Mackenzie used Wagnerian leitmotifs in his own compositions, which included operas and oratorios. He conducted a range of musical organizations including the Novello Oratorio Concerts, the Royal Choral Society and the Philharmonic Society. It was through the latter organization that he gave the first English performance of Tchaikovsky's Sixth Symphony and Borodin's Second Symphony. On his tour of Canada in 1903, he promoted music by British composers. Consequently, the ideals of the Academy embraced these wider influences.

Also on the staff at the Royal Academy was Frederick Corder, Professor of Composition from 1888. Having studied with Hiller in Cologne, he hoped to start an English opera tradition, but was forced to abandon his plan. Together with his wife he made translations of Wagner's libretti, and he wrote books on Beethoven, Liszt and Wagner. He was also fond of the music of Dvorák, according to Bax, who recalled Corder's eagerness to "point out the Czech composer's piquant rhythmical ingenuities ... and the picturesqueness of his harmonic devices".[6] Although Corder's musical sympathies were very broad, they did not extend to the modernist composers, and he confessed to failing to understand the music of Debussy.

It was through the teaching of Mackenzie and Corder that pupils at the Royal Academy became aware of late romantic music, styles with which the Royal College teachers were not in sympathy. By the turn of the century, the Brahmsian style that typified the Royal College was seen as conservative and outmoded, whereas the Wagnerian style of the Royal Academy was progressive. The following examples illustrate the differences between the music that resulted.

John McEwen (1868–1948)

McEwen was educated at the Royal Academy of Music from 1893 to 1895, where his teachers included Prout, Corder and Matthay. He was a pianist, and taught at the Athenaeum School (now the Royal Scottish Academy of Music and Drama). In 1898 he joined the staff of the Royal Academy as Professor of Harmony and Composition. He was responsible for influencing both the institution and its pupils towards a liberal outlook. McEwen was a keen promoter of British music, although not of his own compositions. He never wrote for festivals, and was never commissioned, but wrote exactly what he wanted to. This included much chamber music, especially string quartets, choral and orchestral music. He helped to establish the Anglo-French Music publishing company and was music adviser to the Aeolian company, but on becoming the Principal of the Royal Academy in 1924 he was forced to relinquish many of these activities. He wrote many books, including *The Foundation of Musical Aesthetics* and *An Introduction to the Unpublished Edition of the Piano Sonatas of Beethoven*. He was an

---

[6] Bax, *The Times*, 27 August 1932, 12.

academic composer and his studies of classical sonatas undoubtedly affected his attitude to the genre.

McEwen's Sonata in E minor was written in 1903 and published in 1904 by Novello. Today it is virtually unknown and out of print. It is a four-movement work, "... an individual, dignified, and forceful work of ample dimensions, broad ideas, and spacious technique".[7] The first movement is in sonata form, beginning loudly, with dense chords accompanied by semiquavers over a pedal E [Fig. 2.2]. The opening of Grieg's Piano Sonata, also in E minor and marked *Allegro moderato*, uses a similar left hand accompaniment pattern and its first phrase, like McEwen's, ends with an upward flourish.

Fig. 2.2 McEwen, Sonata, Novello, First movement, Bars 1–6

McEwen pays careful attention to the sonorities. The hands begin widely spaced and then move in contrary motion. Whereas the right hand descends diatonically, the inner voice of the left hand rises chromatically. The second subject contrasts in mood and is in the expected dominant key. McEwen's rhythm is very flexible. Different irregular subdivisions of the beat appear in each hand [Fig. 2.3], giving the work a virtuosic character. McEwen uses chromatic, Wagnerian harmonies and he makes much use of augmented chords, as seen in bars 86 and 89 in Fig. 2.3. These features mark a significant advance on the style of previous piano sonatas, making this work unsuitable for amateurs.

The second movement is an Adagio in B flat minor, a tritone above E. The tonality and solemn mood of the music invite comparison with the funeral march in Chopin's Second Piano Sonata Op. 35. The improvisatory

[7] Anon., *MT*, 1905, 31–2.

Fig. 2.3 McEwen, Sonata, First movement, Bars 84–91

introduction is followed by a solemn melody that is varied, building to a series of climaxes.

The third movement is a Scherzo and Trio. The Scherzo is in G major, Vivace, in 6/16 metre, whereas the Trio is slower, in E major and in 2/4. It is light-hearted, providing welcome relief from the gloom of the previous movement. Varied groupings of semiquavers provide hemiola effects, again illustrating McEwen's rhythmic vitality. The Trio section begins with a light three-part texture and becomes progressively denser by doubling the parts in octaves.

The final movement provides a return to the serious mood and the E minor tonality of the first movement. It has a short Largo introduction in which low and high registers are contrasted. The main Allegro con fuoco is in rondo form and its main theme is presented in octaves. This is alternated with a more lyrical episode, although both themes consist of unrelenting semiquavers. The movement ends with a Presto coda based on the movement's main theme.

The work does not introduce any structural innovations, using traditional classical forms, but its content is original and it works well as a virtuoso piece. Every movement except the second relies on continuous semiquaver figuration, which is a weakness as it becomes monotonous, despite helping to unify the work. The outer movements rely heavily on bare and filled in octaves. The Sonata shows great promise, yet it is McEwen's only piano sonata.[8] He wrote a Sonatina in G minor, published in 1919, but this is regressive in style and could easily be played by an amateur. In later years McEwen was very busy with administration and teaching duties and he had little time to compose. The Sonata deserves to be performed and recorded and it is surprising that no-one has championed this neglected work.

William Yeates Hurlstone (1876–1906)

There are parallels between the Piano Sonatas of William Yeates Hurlstone and Benjamin Dale. Both composers were child prodigies; Hurlstone wrote his Sonata at the age of eighteen, whilst Dale began his Sonata at the age of seventeen.[9] Neither composer wrote a second piano sonata. The most significant difference between the two composers was that Hurlstone studied at the Royal College of Music from 1894 to 1898 whilst Dale studied at the Royal Academy of Music from 1900 to 1906. Although it is an over-simplification, Hurlstone's Sonata follows in the Brahmsian tradition, whereas Dale's can be seen to follow on from Liszt, R. Strauss and Wagner.

Hurlstone wrote *Five Easy Waltzes* for piano at the age of nine, and a Piano Trio Op. 2 at the age of fifteen, both of which were published by his father, an amateur musician. As a young boy, Hurlstone read textbooks to discover the rules of composition, he was a chorister for a short time before succumbing to asthma, and he had piano lessons from 1886 to 1894 with Mr Arthur Wilmot in Croydon. At the age of eighteen, Hurlstone won a scholarship to the Royal College, where he studied composition with Stanford and piano with Algernon Ashton and Edward Dannreuther. His fellow students included Thomas Dunhill, John Ireland, Frank Bridge and Samuel Coleridge-Taylor.

Hurlstone's Sonata in F minor was written in 1894. It is in three movements (fast-slow-fast) and the first follows the expected sonata form using traditional key relationships. Hurlstone uses cyclic themes, showing an awareness of procedures used by Beethoven, Schubert and

---

[8] Newman, 1969, 598 indicates a Second Sonata in A minor, published in 1918. The British Library Catalogue of Printed Music does not contain details of it.
[9] Articles by Corder, 1918, and Evans, E., 1919, give 1902, but Evans gives 1905 in Colles, H. C. (ed.), *Grove* iii (1927). The end of the first movement is dated 24 October 1904 (Lbm MS) and the printed version gives the completion date July 1905.

Liszt. The main themes of the first and second movements recur in the final movement and the same motif opens the first and third movements. Fig. 2.4 is taken from the middle of the recapitulation, but further development of the material results from the use of an interrupted cadence in bars 190–91. Modulations, of which there are many, result from the use of diminished seventh chords (as in the left hand of bars 193 and 195) or enharmonic relationships (as in bars 196–7, where C flat becomes B), and the harmonic language is chromatic.

Fig. 2.4 Hurlstone, Sonata, Manuscript, First movement, Bars 190–203

The slow movement, which is melodious, demonstrates the influence of Chopin in its use of rapid decorative chromatic scales [Fig. 2.5]. In the outer movements, textures are often thick, using octave doublings and melodies in low registers, and Brahms' influence can be discerned. Hurlstone's Capriccio in B minor, published in 1907 by Avison, was clearly modelled on Brahms' Rhapsody in B minor Op. 79/1.

Hurlstone's Piano Sonata is a showy piece, containing frequent changes of metre, cross-rhythms, extended fast sections in octaves and frequent

Fig. 2.5 Hurlstone, Sonata, Second movement, Bars 128–34

modulations. There is no evidence to suggest that the Sonata was ever performed, and it was never published. Stanford showed it to the pianist Ernst Pauer, who felt that it remained for too long in one key.[10] Stanford did not agree with this view, indeed it is hard to believe that anyone could reach this conclusion, given the proliferation of accidentals and numerous key signature changes in the Sonata! Hurlstone was an accomplished pianist, having played the solo part in his Concerto in D at St James' Hall in 1896, and so he may have given private performances of his Sonata. An audience in Walsall hailed him as a second Paderewski! However, Hurlstone was of retiring disposition and he was often forced to cancel concerts owing to the ill health that plagued him throughout his life.

Hurlstone was self-critical, hence his output remained small. Some works were well received, such as the Phantasy String Quartet, which won the first Cobbett prize in 1906. In 1904, W. H. Thomas identified Hurlstone as a

---

[10] Hurlstone (ed.), 1947, 15–16. See also Newell, 1936.

young composer who placed England on the eve of a golden age of music.[11] Unfortunately the dawn he predicted failed to materialize. Of the five composers mentioned by Thomas, the only one whose music is performed today (albeit rarely) is York Bowen. Hurlstone died less than two years later, yet "he was regarded by those in whose company he studied as unquestionably the most significant figure of his generation".[12] Today his name is barely known, although the Associated Board of the Royal Schools of Music have selected Hurlstone's *Four Characteristic Pieces* for clarinet as examination pieces.

Benjamin Dale (1885–1943)

The fourteen-year-old Dale made his début as a composer with the performance of his orchestral overture *Horatius*. At the Royal Academy of Music, where he enrolled in 1900 on the same day as Arnold Bax, Dale's teachers included Corder for composition, Howard-Jones and Lake for pianoforte and Richards for organ.

Dale's ambitious Piano Sonata consists of four substantial movements, lasting in total about forty-five minutes and covering sixty-two pages of printed music. An opening Allegro in D minor follows the outlines of an enlarged sonata form. The main subject is affirmative [Fig. 2.6], and the second subject provides a lyrical contrast in F major [Fig. 2.7]. The principal themes are subjected to variation, as in the thematic transformations of Liszt's Sonata in B minor.[13] This helps to sustain the listener's interest throughout the length of the work. In Fig. 2.8, the second subject is varied from bar 91, which should be compared with Fig. 2.7. It begins in the same key of F major, but after two bars the melody is altered. The hands are widely spaced and triplet scales provide decoration. The dynamic change (from pianissimo to fortissimo) could not be more extreme! Dale, like Bax, pays careful attention to details. Nearly every note has articulation and dynamic markings attached. The textures are intricate, with much polyphony.

Fig. 2.8 illustrates one of the most harmonically complex passages of the Sonata, and builds up to a huge climax. The continuous bold, upward thrusts, appoggiaturas, anticipations and passing notes demonstrate the influence of R. Strauss.[14] Bars 86 and 91 use second inversion chords in the manner of Strauss and augmented eleventh chords are used, as seen in bar 60 [Fig. 2.7]. Dale's cadenza-like sections and his propensity for variation

---

[11] W. H. Thomas, "Are we on the eve of a great musical triumph?" *Daily Mail*, 5 August 1904, 7. The other four composers were Henry E. Geehl, York Bowen, Paul Corder and Adam Carse.
[12] Quotation by Dunhill in Trend, 1985, 48.
[13] Demuth, 1952, 121–2 rates it as the best European piano sonata since Liszt's.
[14] Newman, 1969, 594.

Fig. 2.6 Dale, Sonata, Avison, First movement, Bars 1–8

Fig. 2.7 Dale, Sonata, First movement, Bars 53–60

form are similar to the methods of Reger.[15] Enharmonic modulation, a keyboard technique, is used and the modulations are very wide-ranging. One German reviewer found the fast sections of the outer movements formally confusing and tiring to listen to, preferring the clear structure of the variations.[16] The influences of Liszt, Wagner and Strauss are hardly surprising, given that Corder was Dale's composition teacher. The first movement also demonstrates the influence of Glazunov's First Piano Sonata of 1901, which Corder had probably introduced his pupils to.

---

[15] Redlich in Blume (ed.), *MGG*, ii, 1871. He notes that Dale's Sonata aroused unusual attention and cites it as being the best piano sonata since Brahms.
[16] Leitzmann, *Die Musik*, 1906–7, 306.

Fig. 2.8 Dale, Sonata, First movement, Bars 85–94

The remaining part of Dale's Sonata consists of a theme and variations in the remote key of G sharp minor (a tritone relationship with D minor). They are grouped into sections: a slow movement (Variations I–IV), scherzo (Variations V–VII) and lead by way of a bridge passage to the finale in D major. This is unusual and there is no precedent in the piano sonata repertoire, although Dale may have known Tchaikovsky's Piano Trio in A minor Op. 50. After conventional first movements, both Tchaikovsky and Dale use a theme and variations for the remaining part of the work.

The Piano Sonatas 1890–1910

Corder recalled that Dale's original intention was to group the slow variations together and follow this with a group of faster ones to create the impression of a slow movement followed by a scherzo.[17] However, to relieve the monotony of a succession of slow variations, Dale opted for an Allegretto third variation.

Fig. 2.9 Dale, Sonata, Second movement, Bars 1–17

The theme [Fig. 2.9] has a two-part structure; the first part is low and in octaves, whereas the second is high and lyrical. The first two variations preserve the distinction between the two halves of the theme. Variation 1 accompanies the first half of the theme with a descant and the second half is transferred to the bass register in octaves. Variation 2, in the relative major (B major), expands the first half of the theme and contracts the second, as well as altering the metre to 4/8. The third variation maintains the 4/8 metre but reverts to G sharp minor. The tempo is slightly increased, to Allegretto con grazia. The whole variation uses similar figuration and it departs substantially from the original theme. Variation 4 returns to a slow tempo, B major and is in 3/4 metre. It maintains the outlines of the melody of the first half of the theme, although the rhythm is modified. It demonstrates the influence of Schumann.

The fifth variation, in G sharp minor and 6/8 metre, marks the beginning

---

[17] Corder, *MT*, 1918, 166.

of the scherzo section. Its main idea is derived from the descending fifth motif seen in the second part of the theme and it has a ternary structure. Variation 6 is a Mazurka in E major. This dance movement acts as a trio, owing to its central placement in the scherzo. The seventh variation is a moto perpetuo, almost a self-contained piece, which is highly chromatic and extremely difficult for the pianist to play at this speed, let alone pianissimo. Dale takes the theme as a starting point, using fragments of it to form the basis of the variations. In some variations, as in the last, the theme is virtually unrecognizable. The variations work successfully in that they contrast a variety of keys, metres, speeds and motifs.

The transition to the finale recalls the opening theme of the first movement. The finale is in rondo form, with a virtuosic main theme [Fig. 2.10]. Fragments of previous themes are hinted at throughout the movement and it builds to a loud and virtuosic climax. A Lento coda in D minor follows, in which the first part of the theme is recalled and harmonized. The second part of the theme reappears and the movement ends *pppp*. It is surprising that after the exuberance of the earlier part of the Sonata, the work ends slowly and sadly in D minor, although this was the precedent set by Liszt's Sonata.

Fig. 2.10 Dale, Sonata, Finale, Bars 1–8

Dale's Sonata was the first outstanding British piano sonata. Its harmonic language avoided the clichés of the Beethoven–Brahms style and utilized the resources of Straussian and Wagnerian chromaticism to an unprecedented level. In a sense, however, it marked the end of an era, as this was as far as late romantic harmonies could be taken. Dale's Sonata may have been the best British piano sonata to date, but, compared to the music of our European contemporaries, we were still lagging behind. Dale had successfully fused various elements of a late romantic style, but he was not the founder of a new musical style.

Dale's output remained small, and he was interned in Germany during World War I. For the last thirty-five years of his life Dale taught composition at the Royal Academy, and he was one of three musicians to be appointed to the BBC's Advisory Panel in 1936. Edwin Evans noted, "a certain fastidiousness prevents his output from becoming considerable, but also ensures the maintenance of a high standard".[18] Corder once claimed that Dale had [in 1918] written "fewer and better works than any English composer of his generation".[19] Dale had a precocious talent and it is remarkable that a young student composer could assimilate this style so quickly. However, it burnt him out.

No commercial publisher would have risked publishing such a long and difficult work by an unknown student. However, Corder, McEwen and Matthay had established the Society of British Composers at the Royal Academy in June 1905, to promote this type of work.[20] Its resources were limited, but Dale's Sonata was first published in 1906 as the Avison Edition, being printed through Breitkopf and Härtel. Subsequently it was published by Cary & Co., which was taken over by Novello c. 1908.

Dale was a pianist and organist and hence he shows a clear understanding of the potential of the instrument. Nevertheless, the epic scale and fiendish technical demands of the Piano Sonata deter all but the most committed pianist. Dale's use of the total range of the piano poses one of the biggest problems for the performer, coupled with the fact that the hands have to move around the keyboard so quickly. The hands often combine different cross-rhythms; melodies to be projected are placed in the middle of the texture, or in canon. Whole sections are built upon rapid octaves or thick chords, and the twisting, chromatic semiquavers demand a prodigious technique.

Dale dedicated his Piano Sonata to York Bowen, who played the first movement at the Queen's Hall on 22 February 1905 and the whole Sonata at the Bechstein Hall on 14 November 1905.

At the beginning of the twentieth century, the Russian pianist Mark Hambourg established an annual competition for a new piano work at the Royal Academy. At the last minute, Dale decided to submit his Piano Sonata, which was chosen as the winner from sixty entries.[21] Hambourg played only the variations in the concert at the Queen's Hall on 16 June 1906, and his interpretation was not faithful to Dale's score. Dale refused to

---

[18] Evans in Colles (ed.), *Grove* ii, 2. See also Evans, *MT*, 1919, 201.
[19] Corder, *MT*, 1918, 166.
[20] The Society held musical evenings consisting of all-British programmes. *The Society of British Composers Yearbook 1907–8* records that there were 254 members, and that they had published 44 works.
[21] The judges included Coleridge-Taylor, Arthur Hervey and Landon Ronald.

join him on stage, despite the rapturous reception, and he subsequently returned the prize.

The Sonata had been well received by the press, with both Cyril Scott and Joseph Holbrooke writing articles praising it. Dale's Academy friends, Myra Hess and Irene Scharrer, both performed it in 1906, and by 1907 it was a popular recital piece. Hess and Scharrer were both pupils of Tobias Matthay, Professor at the Royal Academy from 1880 to 1925, who founded his own school of piano playing in 1900. His other famous pupils included Harold Craxton and Harriet Cohen. The rise in standard of British pianists inspired their fellow composers, including Dale, Bax and Bowen, to write increasingly demanding works.

The technical demands of Dale's Sonata and its colossal length prevented it from establishing itself firmly in the repertoire. The movements were sometimes performed separately, but the issue of the Sonata on pianola roll in 1910 and its subsequent reissue in 1924, helped to bring the work to a wider public. It is arguable that listening to a performance on pianola roll is the best way to hear Dale's Sonata. However, a technically perfect performance is not a substitute for an impassioned interpretation, and the tempo would be left to the discretion of the pianola operator.

Other pianists who performed Dale's Sonata include Leo Livens, Benno Moiseiwitsch, Vivian Langrish, Effie Kalisz, John Tobin, Moura Lympany and Frank Merrick. York Bowen and Myra Hess continued to keep it in their repertoire. However, by 1923, *The Times* reported that the work was beginning to date. By 1925, its reputation was declining and Gerald Abraham included it in an article, *The Great Unplayed*.[22]

Dale's Sonata was never released on gramophone and it was neglected until the 1970s, when Peter Jacobs began to include it in recitals, and he recorded it on compact disc in 1992. Even today, it is rarely included in piano recitals and only the devoted enthusiasts of British music know of its significance.

(Edwin) York Bowen (1884–1961)

Although the main focus for my discussion of Bowen is his Fifth Sonata, published in 1923, I have included him in the chapter spanning the period 1890–1910 because he was a contemporary of Dale at the Royal Academy of Music. When he was fourteen he won the Erard scholarship, studying composition with Corder and piano with Matthay as well as viola and horn. He was also a proficient organist, enabling him to write idiomatically for a variety of instruments. Bowen toured Britain, performing his own compositions, including his First Piano Concerto in December 1903, as well as solos

---

[22] See Foreman's notes to Continuum CCD 1044. Also see *RAM Magazine* no. 15 (1905), p. 14; no. 17 (1907), p. 8; no. 20 (1907), p. 13 for further details.

by Chopin, Liszt, Scriabin and Tchaikovsky. Saint-Saëns praised, "the most remarkable of the young British composers"[23] and considered Bowen's potential to be greater than that of his fellow student Bax, who had made his impact as a prodigious pianist but not yet as a composer.

Bowen was one of Dale's closest friends and they frequently attended performances of Wagner's operas at Covent Garden together. Whereas Dale's Piano Sonata received immediate acclaim, Bowen's Sonata No. 1 in B minor (1900) did not make a significant impact, despite being published and performed. A review of its performance on 21 February 1901 cited the influence of Grieg.[24] Bowen took longer than Dale to develop his style and he wrote several unpublished piano sonatas during his student days. Bowen continued writing piano sonatas throughout his career, and his Sixth Piano Sonata Op. 160 dates from 1961. Liszt's Piano Sonata in B minor had been a significant landmark in the form, and many British composers, including McEwen, Hurlstone, Dale and Bowen, also wrote minor key sonatas. Bowen's Sonata No. 3 (1912) uses the key of D minor, like Dale's.

As would be expected from a pupil of Corder, Bowen's early musical style was influenced by the music of Liszt, Wagner, Strauss, and the Russian nationalists. He was fascinated by the music of Debussy and Ravel, and temporarily resigned his professorship at the Royal Academy in 1909 as a protest against the views of the Principal, Mackenzie, who considered their music to be "immoral"![25] Bowen began his compositional career when abstract romantic music was popular and he continued writing in this lyrical style long after the end of World War I, when it was considered old-fashioned. He considered the most important quality that music should possess was that of beauty.

> Some of the things we are expected to digest today are audacious insults. They may be clever, but these effusions which have no sense of key, melodic line or shape of any kind, cannot be regarded as music ... If modern life is ugly, then there is all the more reason why music should bring beauty into it.[26]

World War I had signalled a turning point for many European composers, including his contemporaries Bax, Ireland and Bridge, as will be shown in Chapters 3 and 4, but Bowen disapproved of all modernist trends, vehemently objecting to music that lacked tonality and melody. His rejection of prevailing fashions won him the admiration of Kaikhosru Sorabji, who hired the Bechstein Hall in about 1946 to hear Bowen play his Twenty-Four Preludes and Fugues Op. 102 under ideal conditions.[27]

---

[23] F. Potts, *York Bowen: piano music*, Hyperion 66838 (notes to CD).
[24] In Watson, 1984, 12.
[25] Ibid., 15.
[26] Brook, 1946. See Watson, 1984, 67.
[27] Sorabji, 1947, 235–9.

Bowen followed the tradition of the composer-pianist. He possessed a formidable technique that many envied, performing the most demanding pieces by Liapunov, Liszt, Rachmaninov and Medtner. Few pianists other than Bowen performed his piano sonatas and with the exceptions of the First, Fifth and Sixth sonatas, they remain in manuscript. Like Dale's Sonata, they are virtuosic works, and their technical demands placed them beyond the grasp of many. Bowen wrote a vast amount of piano music, including short pieces for amateurs, and this may have affected his reputation as a serious composer. Bowen was a polymath; in addition to playing the piano, viola, horn and organ, he conducted, composed and taught at the Royal Academy. The public became sceptical of his many talents, and like Constant Lambert (see pp. 129–40), Bowen failed to gain recognition and appreciation.

The first movement of Bowen's Sonata No. 5 in F minor (published in 1923) uses a modified sonata form. Cyclic procedures are used, and the introduction to the first movement is recalled in the coda to the last movement. Bowen frequently reharmonizes melodies when they are repeated, in order to cast new colours on the original theme. Bowen uses a subtle palette of shifting harmonies as the themes journey over the range of the keyboard. Virtuosic demisemiquaver scales in the outer movements place the highest demands on the performer and are marked *brilliante* or *glissando*.

The second movement is in ternary form, a form that was commonly used by Bowen in his slow movements. It uses modal diatonicism, as in bars 67–70 of Fig. 2.11, which mark the return of the opening theme, and the quavers flow freely. Its middle section uses higher diatonic triads and chords built from piled-up fourths. Bars 61–4 of Fig. 2.11 seem to anticipate Lennox Berkeley's musical language (see pp. 168–70).

The writing is always pianistic, but extrovert, especially in the finale. Like the composer-pianist Rachmaninov, Bowen wrote virtuosic music within a tonal idiom. Bowen premiered this Sonata in January 1924 and it met with critical acclaim from the public. The critic of *The Observer* praised its "clear, easily remembered themes".[28] This work must have been one of the few British piano sonatas written in the 1920s that did receive a favourable reception. Clinton Gray-Fisk's review of the work noted

> Mr. Bowen's Sonata in F minor (Op. 72) is a massive three-movement work, superbly written for the keyboard, teeming with inventive interest and memorable at least, for its eloquently expressive Andante. Delivered with Mr. Bowen's verve and sensitivity it made overwhelming effect, but the work's demands in the matter of virtuosity are formidable and this may to some extent account for its comparative neglect.[29]

---

[28] In Watson, 1984, 30.
[29] Gray-Fisk, *MO*, 1956, 71.

Fig. 2.11 Bowen, Sonata No. 5, Swan, Second movement, Bars 57–70

© 1923 Josef Weinberger Ltd. Reprinted by permission of the copyright owner.

However, this review dates from 1956, by which time the late romantic style was considered very old-fashioned. Bowen's and Dale's music had been neglected since the 1940s for this reason. Bowen recorded a few of his own short pieces around 1924 for Vocalion, for whom he also made the first recording of Beethoven's Fourth Piano Concerto with his own cadenzas. In the 1960s, Lyrita produced a record of Bowen playing his own music, but it did not include any sonatas.[30] It is encouraging to note that there has recently been a revival of interest in Bowen's piano music and a couple of recordings have resulted. Josef Weinberger has reprinted the Fifth Sonata, the Twenty-four Preludes and Sonata in B flat minor Op. 160 and so it is to be hoped that more pianists will include Bowen's pieces in their recitals.

---

[30] Watson, 1984, 83.

Other composers who studied at the Royal Academy of Music during this period include Dorothy Howell, Leo and Evangeline Livens, Alan Bush and Arnold Bax.

Dorothy Howell (1898–1982) studied under Matthay and McEwen for piano and composition respectively. She wrote a Piano Sonata in 1916, during her second year at the Royal Academy. This work remains in manuscript, and is held by her family. She made her Proms debut in 1919 with *Lamia*. A review of this work by the *Daily Sketch* referred to her as "the English Strauss".[31] Subsequently, her musical style became more economical and in 1955 she wrote another Piano Sonata which is influenced by the neo-classical style.

Leo Livens (?1896–c.1961) attended the Royal Academy from 1912 to 1920, and was a contemporary of Howell. He performed the first movement of Dale's Sonata in 1915, and wrote a Piano Sonata in 1914, which was published. It is a virtuosic work, in the late romantic vein, and Livens uses florid pianistic figurations in the manner of Chopin. Like Dale, he failed to fulfil his early promise and although he was appointed Professor in 1922, by 1928 he had been admitted to a mental institution, where he remained at least until 1959. His sister, Evangeline, also studied at the Royal Academy and wrote a Piano Sonata, which she performed there in 1915.

Alan Bush studied at the Royal Academy from 1918 to 1922, and may have known Livens. Like Bax, he was another composer-pianist who studied with Corder and Matthay. Their piano sonatas are discussed in Chapter 3 (pp. 69–84 and 93–5).

In the period from 1900 to 1920, the main piano sonatas to have been written were composed by students of the Royal Academy, with the exception of Cyril Scott's First Sonata. Thus the climate at this institution was worth investigation since it played a crucial role in the development of the British piano sonata. It may have been that writing a piano sonata was a requirement of the composition syllabus, owing to the proliferation of this genre. German's Piano Sonata was written for a competition and in 1907 the Royal Academy club prize was awarded to the composer of the best single movement for piano in sonata form. In lessons, composers would have been required to demonstrate their understanding of sonata form, and most chose to write for the piano, as they were mainly pianists. Using the title sonata indicated that the composition was to be considered an important and abstract work. It would commonly be a technically challenging composition that demonstrated the ability of the performer.

It is interesting that only the Royal Academy students wrote piano sonatas in an attempt to launch their composing careers. The situation

---

[31] In Mike, *BMS Journal*, 1992, 51.

was not paralleled at the Royal College, despite the fact that the Royal College teachers held a strong Austro-German bias. The explanation has to be that the Royal Academy had a piano-orientated culture. During this period the growth of Matthay's school of piano playing encouraged pianists to attend this institution rather than the College.

One further point that requires explanation is why the piano sonatas written by the Academy pupils have generally failed to hold a place in the repertoire. The student works by Dale, Bowen, Livens and Bush were published, but their immaturity may have prejudiced audiences and critics.

The ability of a composer to mature and develop is essential. The most successful of the Academy composers was Bax. He was able to build upon his training at the Royal Academy to cultivate a personal style, whereas Dale and Bowen changed very little over the course of their careers. Thus Bax's Piano Sonatas, written some years after his training, synthesize his range of musical experiences, whereas Bowen's later Piano Sonatas fail to do this.

Cyril Scott (1879–1970)

Like Smyth and Ashton, Scott's education included periods spent in Germany. However, unlike them, he was able to distance himself from the Teutonic tradition and develop his own individual style. Scott's Piano Sonata No. 1 (1908) was the next important British piano sonata after Dale's.

In 1891 Scott went to Frankfurt for eighteen months to study the piano with Lazzaro Uzielli, a pupil of Clara Schumann, and theory with Engelbert Humperdinck. He was back in Frankfurt from 1895 to 1898 to study composition with Iwan Knorr. Knorr (1853–1916) had spent a large part of his life in Russia and loved Russian music, especially Glazunov and Tchaikovsky. Scott's fellow students included Norman O'Neill, Roger Quilter, Balfour Gardiner and Percy Grainger, who collectively became known as the Frankfurt Gang. Although they did not attempt to write in the same style, they were united in their hatred of Beethoven! Grainger provided the most important influence on Scott's style, and he regularly performed Scott's piano music.

Scott had a cosmopolitan outlook, owing to his training abroad. He was essentially a romantic artist, approving of originality, but not at the expense of beauty.[32] Like the other members of the Frankfurt Gang, Scott was interested in Pre-Raphaelite art and the work of William Morris. Scott introduced the others to the plays of the Belgian Symbolist and philosopher Maurice Maeterlinck (1862–1949) and the poems of Stefan George (1868–1933), whom he had known from his student days in Frankfurt. Grainger tried to assess this influence in his memoirs:

[32] Scott, 1917, 3–4.

Perhaps it might be true to say that we were all of us PRERAPHAELITE composers ... under 'preraphaelite' I understand art which takes a conscious charm from what is archaic ... And what musical medium could provide the agonized emotionality needed? ... I think the answer is the CHORD. The chord has the heartrending power we preraphaelites needed. Based on Bach, Scriabine, Wagner, Grieg and César Franck Cyril, Balfour and I became chord-masters indeed.[33]

Scott composed a one-movement Piano Sonata *c.* 1901, which he abandoned after the first performance by Evelyn Suart in 1903. Grainger suggested that it could be reworked under his editorship, and the result was Scott's *Handelian Rhapsody* of 1909. Its textures are clearly influenced by Grainger's piano writing, with reliance on octaves and filled in chords, often stretching a tenth.

Scott's Piano Sonata No. 1 was composed in Shere in the summer of 1908, premièred at the Bechstein Hall by the composer on 17 May 1909, and subsequently revised in 1910.[34] Scott had two publishers: Schott of Mainz published the large-scale works and Elkin published the salon music. He was financially independent, enabling him to devote his time to composition without worrying about obtaining employment or teaching to earn a living. Thus he could write for any medium that inspired him, regardless of its marketability. However, Elkin required him to write a certain number of small piano pieces and songs each year as part of his contract. These pieces were widely circulated, accessible to amateurs and became quite popular, although Banfield notes that some of the songs were less easy to promote.[35] Elkin were reluctant to take the financial risk of publishing Scott's First Piano Sonata and one of his friends contributed towards the engraving.[36] Scott destroyed all of his early works, written up to *c.* 1912, unless they had already been published, and so Piano Sonata No. 1 had a lucky escape.

Scott's Sonata No. 1 is to be played continuously, but it is divided into sections. The first movement is an Allegro con spirito that follows a modified sonata form. The two main themes are heard in alternation and are developed throughout. Thematic transformation is an important part of Scott's style – themes are rarely repeated exactly. Transformations of the first subject (bars 6–7 in Fig. 2.12) can be seen in Figs. 2.13 and 2.14. Bar 7 of Fig. 2.12 retains its rhythmic identity in each case, and its melodic shape remains similar, although the melody of bar 6 is simplified. However, the metre is varied, as demonstrated by comparing Fig. 2.13 with 2.14. The latter shortens the bar length by one semiquaver.

---

[33] In Palmer, *MT*, 1979, 738.
[34] It is not clear what revisions were made. Marjorie Hartston Scott, in a letter dated 21 March 1995, stated that the revised version was published by Elkin in 1909, and that Schott published it in 1910.
[35] Banfield, 1985, 93.
[36] Scott, 1969, 99.

Fig. 2.12 Scott, Sonata No. 1, Kalmus, Bars 1–19

Fig. 2.13 Scott, Sonata no. 1, Bars 24–25

Fig. 2.14 Scott, Sonata No. 1, Bars 56–7

A transition leads straight into the Adagio second movement without a break. It is in modified ternary form and has the emotional intensity of Scott's shorter piano pieces and songs. One of the hallmarks of Scott's style is the way that he uses chords and harmonies. Harmonies are used non-functionally and impressionistically, as in the music of Debussy. Scott juxtaposes unrelated chords, creating interesting harmonic colour and adding to the sense of tonal ambiguity. Often the chords involve the use of added notes, especially at points of repose, and chords are presented in unusual spacings. Scott tends to avoid passing notes and prefers to harmonize every note of the melody. However, he still uses chords in second inversion in the manner of Richard Strauss [See Fig. 2.12, bar 12], which relate back to functional harmony. Enharmonic modulation enables Scott to slip effortlessly through different tonal centres.

At the end of the second movement, Scott recalls previous themes, and there is another seamless join to the third movement. This exuberant, scherzo-like movement also recalls earlier thematic motives.

The final section (it is not labelled fourth movement, although it functions as such) is a three-part fugue, influenced by Scott's fondness for Bach [Fig. 2.15]. The fugue subject is treated freely and is rhythmically modified to fit the irregular metres. Even the second entry of the fugue subject (bar 478) uses different rhythms as well as a different metre to the first. Nevertheless, each entry of the fugue subject is clearly recognizable. The ensuing development recalls themes of the first movement in alternation with the fugue subject. The work ends with a majestic coda that recalls the opening of the Sonata. After approximately twenty-five minutes of continuous music with virtually no rests and no breaks between movements, silence proves a welcome relief to both listener and performer!

It seems somewhat paradoxical that someone who rejected the Austro-German tradition should use traditional genres for his works, but in addition to three piano sonatas, Scott wrote two symphonies and five concertos. It is arguable whether Scott's sonatas should be linked with sonata form, as they have more in common with a tone poem. However, Scott considered that all great composers attempted to introduce new formal strategies and he wrote about his ideas for a new sonata form in 1917.[37] Scott

---

[37] Scott, 1917, 53–9 and Scott, *MMR*, 1917, 104.

Fig. 2.15 Scott, Sonata No. 1, Bars 474–8

was concerned that the separate movements of sonatas rarely had any connection with one another and that only the first movement had structural importance. To achieve unity, logic and a sense of flow, Scott suggested that the final movement should contain a recapitulation of the principal themes from previous movements. In a symphonic poem, the unfolding of drama was due to the re-introduction of themes, frequently transformed. Scott felt that themes could similarly be used in a sonata, changing it from a purely abstract form to an epic or dramatic one.

Scott presents a theory that other composers were already using instinctively. Cyclic principles had been used by Schubert in his *Wanderer Fantasia*, developed further in Liszt's Piano Sonata and Tchaikovsky's Fourth Symphony as well as in Dale's Piano Sonata. All three of Scott's piano sonatas illustrate his theories. When the themes recur they are subject to melodic and harmonic transformation, although Scott's varying metres permit complicated rhythmic alterations that his predecessors had not explored.

Scott was an accomplished improviser, capable of creating lengthy pastiches in the style of Bach or Handel, so that he was able to convince friends that he had memorized actual pieces by these composers. Scott originally trained as a concert pianist, and he performed almost exclusively his own compositions. He recalled cursing himself for making Sonata No. 1 so difficult.[38] He composed at the piano, and his facility as an improviser is a vital clue in helping to account for the style of his compositions.[39] Despite the work's adherence to a type of sonata structure, the musical content sounds spontaneous, like a written-out improvisation. In this respect it can be compared with the Piano Sonatas by Sorabji (see pp. 101–12) and Lambert (see pp. 129–40).

The most striking aspects of Sonata No. 1 are its continuity, the frequent changes of time signatures and the surprising degree of dissonance for its time. The use of multimetricism was not original; Scott had borrowed the technique from Grainger, who had used it in *Train Music* (1900–1), *Bush Music* (1900), and *Hill Songs 1* and *2* (1901–2 and 1907). Grainger cannot claim to have invented the technique, as Antoine Reicha (1770–1836) had used combined metres and polymetres in his Thirty-six Fugues (1803).[40] Nineteenth-century Russian composers had used this device; Debussy uses it in *Prelude à l'après midi d'un faune* (1892–4) and later piano works, Ravel uses it in *Oiseaux tristes* and *La Vallée des cloches* (both 1905), and Delius had used it. However, their use of changing metres was occasional whereas Grainger and Scott tend to change the metre almost every bar [Fig. 2.12].

Scott's Piano Sonata consolidated various stylistic traits seen in the shorter piano pieces that he had written before 1908. His *Scherzo* Op. 25 (1904) was the first piece in which he abandoned key signatures and its varying subdivisions of beats anticipated multimetricism. In *Vesperale* (1904), Scott inserted a bar of 3/4 in a piece predominantly in 2/4, but he did not really exploit the potential of multimetricism. It is a technique that may have been derived from the desire to set words naturally, but there is little evidence of this in Scott's early songs. Multimetricism was not used in songs until *Nocturne* and *Spring Song* (published 1913). Scott's consistent development of multimetricism within a sonata structure represents a great innovation. However, he fails to provide sections in regular metres to provide a contrast.

There is much of Delius' influence in the way that Scott's music flows freely, and like Scott, Delius was also an improviser. There is an abundance of rhapsodic textures in Sonata No. 1, similar to those of Delius. Little of Delius' music had been performed in England; apart from a concert he promoted in 1899, nothing was heard until *Appalachia* and the Piano Concerto in 1907. Grainger met Delius in April 1907, and in the following year Delius dedicated *Brigg Fair* to him. Grainger helped to secure performances of Delius' music and so he may have introduced Delius' music to Scott.

Delius' music is freely evolving and uses transformation of motifs. He

---

[38] Scott, 1969, 138.
[39] Fisher, *Recorded Sound*, 1976, 503.
[40] Stevenson, 1971, 188.

The Piano Sonatas 1890–1910

avoids cadences and the form of his music emerges as a result of changing harmonic tensions. Like Scott, Delius wrote many works in extended one-movement forms, rather like tone poems. Delius' chords are mainly triads, secondary sevenths and dominant discords, but he uses chromatic alterations also. Thus his harmonic language is similar to Scott's, although his music is less dissonant and more melodic. It was not until 1911 onwards that Delius attempted a more radical juxtaposition of unrelated chords. The first five bars of Fig. 2.12 use typical Delian harmonies, although Scott's rate of harmonic change is much faster than Delius'.

Scott considered melody to be a very important part of modern music. His melodies are plastic lines, shaped and unimpeded by traditional cadences, providing a continual sense of flow. The lack of textural, dynamic and rhythmic contrasts threatens monotony, which only a sensitive interpreter can avoid. Scott does not base many of his melodies on the pentatonic or whole-tone scales, but prefers to use modal and exotic scales. He avoids key-signatures and gives equal importance to the twelve semitones, describing his music as non-tonal.

Scott met Fauré, Debussy and Ravel in 1902. Of these, Scott was most in sympathy with Ravel, and they often played their music to each other. Scott was unfairly nick-named "the English Debussy", owing to his impressionistic textures. The non-functional use of harmony, fluid phrases and parallel chords were seen as early as 1904, in Scott's *Pierrot Piece No. 1*. *Lotus Land* used chords with added notes, sevenths, pentatonic and whole-tone scales in the style of Debussy. Fig. 2.16, taken from Scott's Sonata, seems reminiscent of *Reflets dans l'eau* (1905). Impressionism did play a part in Scott's music. He was concerned with the expressive power of chords and colour in music, but his music was more dissonant than Debussy's. Debussy was not very tolerant towards other contemporary composers, but Scott visited him sporadically between 1902 and 1913.[41] They discussed Scott's Piano Sonata and Debussy's comment, "Cyril Scott is one of the rarest artists of the present generation" appears at the top of the score of Scott's *A Little Russian Suite*, published by Elkin in 1909.[42]

Scott frequently uses arabesques to decorate the melody, another texture used by Debussy. These weaving patterns occur in the inner parts and provide another method of varying themes. The writing is suited to a pianist with large hands, and lies under the fingers, as would be expected from an accomplished pianist like Scott. He requires a glissando in the third movement, which he did not find a problem to play but Grainger clearly disliked it. Ronald Stevenson recalls how Grainger marked the copy of his score with an instruction to place a handkerchief attached to an elastic band into his breast pocket, which he could whip out at the required moment to place over his fingers to play the glissando. He would

---

[41] Scott, 1969, 125.
[42] Scott, 1924, 104.

Fig. 2.16 Scott, Sonata No. 1, Bars 420–4

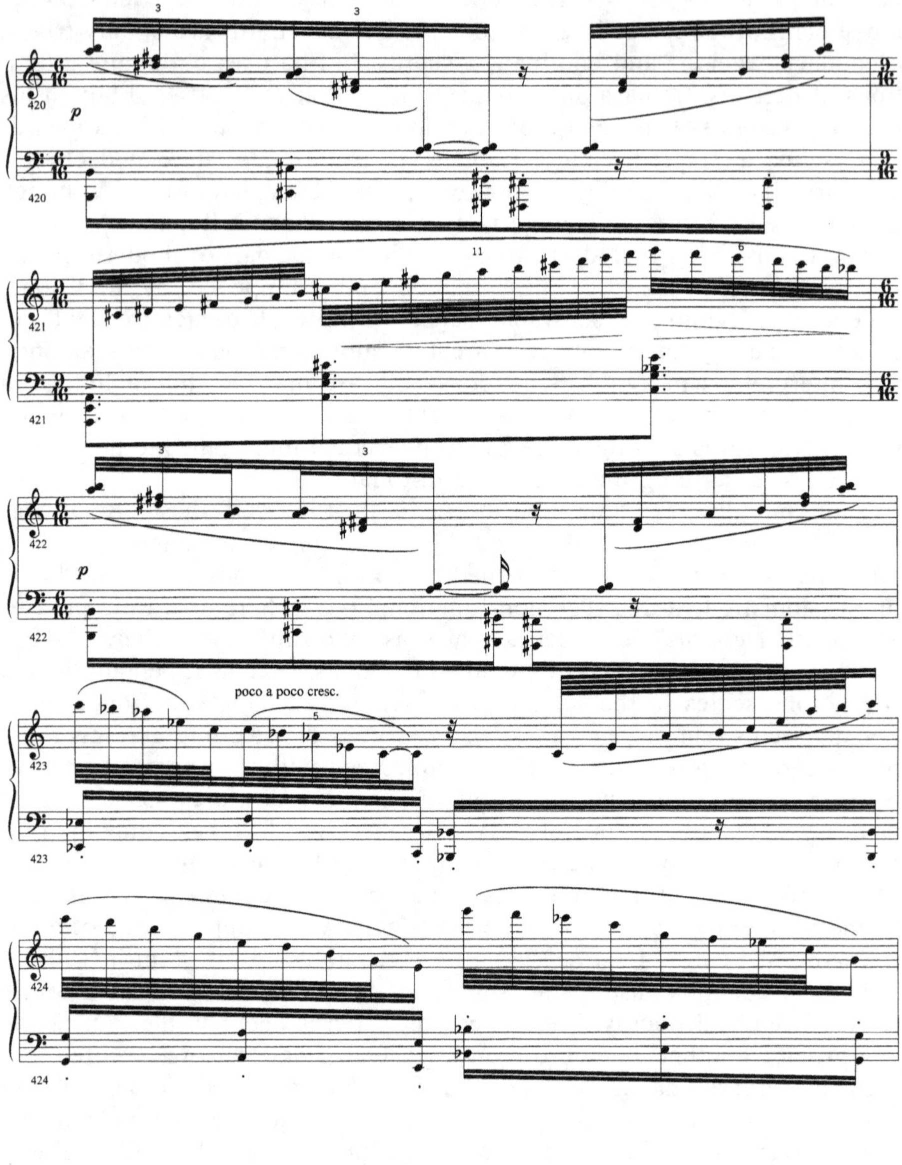

then release the handkerchief and the elastic would ensure that it returned to his pocket![43]

Scott must have known some Scriabin, since he had written his first five piano sonatas by 1907. However, Scott's rhythms are much more flexible than Scriabin's owing to his improvisatory approach. Scriabin only

[43] In Foreman (ed.), 1981, 121.

The Piano Sonatas 1890–1910

abandoned key signatures from his Sixth Sonata (1911) and it is only from his Fifth Sonata onwards that he adopted a one-movement form. Both composers share certain harmonic characteristics, using rich diatonic harmony with chromaticism. In Scriabin's Fourth and Fifth Sonatas he avoids cadences and uses ambiguous tonality, as does Scott. Both composers had an interest in the occult, although it is difficult to asses how this extra-musical influence affected their piano works. Some of Scott's shorter pieces (*Lotus Land* of 1905 and *Chinese Songs* published in 1906) show the influence of Eastern music. Scott had never been to the East and claimed to have heard little of its music, but he had a keen interest in Eastern philosophy, leading him to the conclusion that music can influence the mind and emotions.[44]

Scott's circumstances are paralleled by those of the American composer, Edward MacDowell (1860–1908), who had studied in Frankfurt from 1879 to 1880, some years before him. MacDowell responded to the commercial demand for piano music and songs by writing miniatures, yet he wrote four piano sonatas between 1891 and 1900. He had a romantic temperament, and like Scott, sometimes used literary mottoes at the head of his works. MacDowell was influenced by Schumann, Liszt, Wagner, Raff, Rubinstein and Grieg. As he was no real innovator, it is difficult to assess his impact on others, although at the turn of the century he occupied a leading place in American music.

The first movements of Charles Ives' Piano Sonata No. 1 (1902–10) and his *Concord* Sonata (1912–15) contain examples of free flowing phrases, flexible rhythms and multimetricism. Both Scott's and Ives' works are expansive and improvisatory in character, but they must have come to similar conclusions independently.

Scott issued a rhythmically and harmonically revised version of Sonata No. 1 c.1935.[45] Fig. 2.17 shows the first nineteen bars of the revised version, which should be compared with Fig. 2.12. Fig. 2.18 documents the changes made by Scott.

The principle used by Scott in his revision seems to be an avoidance of triadic formations. He does this by adding notes (mainly seconds) to chords, and substituting notes for those of the expected triad. Thirds are omitted, exposing open fifths. Dominant seventh chords are avoided, and replaced by the 1–4–7 chord (e.g. C–F–B flat) typical of his Second Sonata, discussed later (p. 66). Passages that formerly used parallel sixths are modified to use fifths and less consonant intervals.

Some of the changes made by Scott seem fussy and are inexplicable. In bar 6, he changes the F of the melody to F sharp, ruining the modal tune.

---

[44] Scott, 1950, 25.
[45] Exact year unknown. Darson, 1979, suggests 1935. Changes that Scott made to the original version would seem to be consistent with his musical style dating from the 1930s.

Fig. 2.17 Scott, Sonata No. 1, Revised version, Bars 1–19

Bars 7 and 8 use a mixture of F and F sharp, indicating that Scott is undecided exactly what to do. Some alterations are made to single notes in dense chords, such as in the left hand of bar 2, and the added second interval in bar 11 lasts only a semiquaver. These changes are barely noticeable during a performance. The instability of the details confirms weaknesses in Scott's whole approach.

The Piano Sonatas 1890–1910

Fig. 2.18 Changes made to Sonata No. 1

Bar	Quaver	Voice	Changes	Effect
1	2	RH	Adds A	Destroys melody, creates 5th
	4	LH	Omits F sharp	Destroys bass line, no root in chord
	6	LH	Omits E flat	Dom 7th becomes maj triad
2	1	RH	Adds A	Open 5th
	1	LH	Adds A	Chord contains only root and 5th
	3	RH	Adds C	Chord contains only root and 5th
	5–6	LH	D sharp to C sharp	Creates F sharp triad in LH
	7–8	RH	G sharp to A	Creates A min triad in RH
	7–8	LH	G sharp to G, adds B flat	Like 1–4–7 chord, plus B flat
3	None			
4	1	LH	G to A	Triad with added 2nd
5	1	RH	F to F sharp, adds G	Triad and added 2nd, avoids original aug 6th chord
	6	RH	Adds F	Added 2nd
6	6	RH	F to F sharp	
7	1	LH	G to A	Added 6th
	3–4	LH	G to G sharp	Avoids G7
8	1	RH	Omits tie	
	1	LH	C to D, G omitted	Added 2nd, avoids doubling 5th
	2	RH	Adds F sharp	
	3	LH	Adds A	
	4	RH	Adds D, B flat	Creates maj triad
	5	RH	Adds C, A	Creates min triad
9	4–5	RH	Adds D	Added aug 4th
10	1	RH	Adds D	Added 2nd
	5	RH	C to D	Adds aug 4th, avoids triad
	7	RH	Adds A flat	
	7	LH	E flat omitted	
11	1	RH	Adds grace note, D	
	1–2	LH	G sharp to F sharp	Omits 3rd, adds 2nd
	3	RH	Adds A	Semiquaver, not noticeable
	3–4	LH	A to G	Omits 3rd, adds 2nd

Fig. 2.18 (*cont.*)

Bar	Quaver	Voice	Changes	Effect
11	5	RH	Adds grace note, D sharp, and omits C	Triad without 3rd
	5		Run includes B	Added 2nd
	5–6	LH	Omits A	Omits 3rd
12	1	LH	Adds D	Added 2nd
	3–4	RH	Adds D	Added 2nd
	6	RH	C to C sharp, adds G, alters rhythm	C sharp opposes C tonality
13	1	RH	F to F sharp, rhythm altered	
	1	LH	Single G reiterated	
14	1	RH	Adds D	Adds aug 4th
	2	RH LH	Chord renotated	Explicitly see 1–4–7 in bass
15	1–3	RH	Renotated	
16	1–3	LH	G to F	Omits 3rd, adds 2nd
	4	LH	Adds A flat, bass not held through	Open 5ths in bass
17	1	LH	Adds A	Added 2nd
	5	LH	F to G	Avoids triads
	6	LH	G to A	Avoids triads
18	1–2	LH	G flat to B flat	Added 2nd
	3	LH	G to B	Added 2nd
19			None	

Scott also made changes to the rhythms. One example of this was to alter a 13/16 time signature into 3/4 by contracting five semiquavers into a quintuplet. Bar 24 in Fig. 2.13 is altered in this way. Scott did this so that a single beat value (here, a crotchet) could be maintained for longer. To compensate for the loss of flexibility, Scott indicates metronome marks in each section and asks that phrases should be played with greater rubato. The changes are most extensive in the first and third movements, and Scott generally retains the same structural outline throughout. It is only in the second movement that he cuts bars. The part writing in the fugue remains virtually the same although the rhythms are simplified. The changes do not significantly alter the demands made on the player's technique, and the second version is not necessarily the best. Edwin Kalmus have recently reissued Scott's Sonata as part of a compilation of his piano music, but they

The Piano Sonatas 1890–1910

have inexplicably reproduced the original 1909 version, complete with mistakes, and have provided no editorial notes.[46]

To understand the reasons behind the development of Scott's style, it is useful to consider his reception both in England and abroad. He had first come to the attention of the London public in 1901 with a performance of his Pianoforte Quartet, in which Kreisler played the violin. Scott's Violin Sonata preceded his First Piano Sonata, although it was not published until 1910. The two works were very similar and the multimetricism of the Violin Sonata was considered revolutionary by the academics.[47] At this time, the work of Parry and Stanford was influential and Scott was regarded as an "enfant terrible" in English music, rather than a pioneer.

The public preferred Scott's small piano pieces that were accessible to amateurs, to a large-scale Piano Sonata that seemed dissonant, long and rambling. As in the case of Smyth, Ashton, Delius and Elgar, Scott had a better reputation in Germany than in England. Cyril Scott Evenings took place in Frankfurt, Vienna and Cologne, where Scott played his Sonata No. 1, and it was also played in Berlin and Hamburg.[48] Mahler's widow contacted Scott to tell him that she had played his First Violin Sonata and admired his work. Scott played his Sonata and other piano works in Florence and Milan, where he received the medal of the Leonardo da Vinci Society.

The Musical League was inaugurated in 1908. The original idea behind it came from Delius. Elgar, Bantock, Henry Wood and the critic W. G. McNaught supported its aims, which were to create an annual festival for new or unfamiliar compositions by composers from home or abroad. A continuing tradition was not established, but the first festival took place in Liverpool from 24–25 September 1909. There were concerts of chamber, orchestral and choral music. Grainger performed piano works by Scott (*Handelian Rhapsody*) and Stanford (*Irish Dances*), and Bax played the piano in a concert given in the Yamen Rooms. Another festival occurred in 1913 but the League lacked momentum and it was never really effective in promoting British music. Grainger continued to perform Scott's First Piano Sonata until the 1950s, although there is no evidence to indicate which version of the Sonata he played.

One of the main factors affecting the reception of Scott's works was World War I. Scott was declared medically unfit and he played in benefit concerts during this time. After the war, the public no longer wanted music of a late romantic style and Scott's music suffered a fate similar to that of Bowen and Dale. Pre-Raphaelite influences had reached the continent before they reached England and were outdated by the time that the Frankfurt Gang reached maturity.

---

[46] Edwin Kalmus Classic Edition, K 09966, Florida, no date. Also contains *Chimes* Op. 40/3, *Impromptu* Op. 41 and *Summerland* Op. 54.
[47] Scott, 1969, 121.
[48] Ibid., 137–8.

Unfortunately, the innovations of Scott's First Sonata were not matched in his subsequent sonatas. The Second Sonata (1935) is in one movement. It is dedicated to Walter Gieseking, who had been a keen interpreter of Scott's First Sonata, and he sight-read the Second Sonata from the manuscript.[49] It consists of three subject groups, the third of which is marked Andante and later functions in place of a slow movement. Like the First Sonata, the second is played continuously and Scott re-introduces variants on the three subject groups as a recapitulation. The work ends with a coda that is derived from the first subject material. This work uses much simpler textures than the First Sonata.

It was not until the period between these two sonatas that Scott really systematized his use of chords built upon the interval of the fourth. This chord dominates the Second Sonata and is used also in the Third Sonata (1956). Scott explained the use of the 1–4–7 chord (for example C–F–B flat) in *Bone of Contention.*[50] He preferred this chord to the dominant seventh chord and noted that it is identical to the upper part of Scriabin's mystic chord [Fig. 2.19]. It has similarities with the harmonies of Sorabji, whose five piano sonatas were all written in the period between Scott's First and Second Sonatas [see pp. 101–12]. Scott's chord can also be related to the quartal harmonies of Hindemith and Bartók. It is used harmonically and as an ostinato, as seen in Fig. 2.20, and it generates the thematic material for the Sonata.

Fig. 2.19 Scriabin, Mystic chord

Fig. 2.20 Scott, Sonata No. 2, Universal, Bars 10–13

In the development section, pairs of notes ascend in the rhythm of six against seven [Bars 209–11 in Fig. 2.21]. This was the first time that Scott's metres had been superimposed rather than juxtaposed.

[49] Scott, 1969, 137–8.

Fig. 2.21 Scott, Sonata No. 2, Bars 205–12

Parallel chords are used to harmonize the third subject in a chorale-like style, recalling Scott's earlier ideas of Pre-Raphaelite music. Triadic harmony appears briefly in the development of the second subject, but this gives way to very dissonant mixed interval chords which use the 1–4–7 chord in the bass. Triads also occur in the recapitulation of the third subject, where trill-tremolos recall Scriabin. Even the conclusion of the Sonata is tonally ambiguous, although the pedal C major chord provides an anchor. The final C major chord contains an added second and is preceded by a decoration on C sharp minor.

When Scott wrote his Second Sonata, he was no longer considered an avant-gardist and this work did not provoke a hostile reaction. Between the 1930s and 1950s, Scott's compositional output declined. He read widely and wrote much, including books on the occult, alternative medicine and an autobiography. This may have been a contributory factor in the problem of his recognition, even though he had established himself as a composer long before this time. The public is sceptical of a person with many wide-ranging interests. Demuth noted, "a prophet is often unhonoured in his own country, but the complete neglect of Scott is something inexplicable".[51] Little has been written about him. A biography by A. Eaglefield Hull was published in 1926, which he outlived by another forty-four years. In 1962, an attempt was made to form a Cyril Scott Society, but it did not survive owing to the lack of a secretary. Although both the First and Third Piano Sonatas have been recorded, the Second has not.

Scott did not teach others, with the exception of Rubbra, and he had few connections in musical circles. He had always distanced himself from the establishment and he seemed to have little awareness of other contemporary British composers. Sir Thomas Armstrong noted that Scott and the rest of the Frankfurt Gang were free from the "Three Choirs Festival outlook".[52]

---

[50] Ibid., 237.
[51] Demuth, 1952, 119.
[52] Armstrong, *PRMA*, 1958, 1.

Scott wrote little about the music of Vaughan Williams, Holst or Bridge, and his only real contact with another composer in Britain was with Grainger, who was of Australian origin. Scott was not interested in writing music based on folksong or Tudor music and therefore stood apart from the prevailing nationalist trends. However, he was a pioneer of British piano music, producing more piano works in the period 1903–14 than any other British composer and any other international one with the exception of Scriabin.[53]

Bacharach detected in Scott's music a showy and commonplace element that clashed with its mystical inspiration.[54] The *Musical Opinion* of 1949 noted that Scott's pianism was dated, garish and crude.[55] Even though Sorabji's free flowing and improvisatory style had some similarities with Scott's, he wrote that Scott's idiom was one "which underneath its trumpery finery of ninths, elevenths, added sixths, joss-sticks, papier-Asie Orientalism and pinchbeck Brummagem-Benares nick-nackery, oozes with glutinous commonplace".[56]

Cyril Scott was a key figure before World War I in helping Britain to break away from musical conservatism and the prevailing Germanic influences. His style was eclectic yet personal, a result of "selection, combination and limitation".[57] It developed from a language influenced by the harmonies of Wagner and Strauss, through one influenced by Russian music and French impressionism, into his own personal style. This evolved into a dissonant idiom early on, possibly influenced by the decadence of the 1890s, as shown by his choice of poets. Scott's attempt to use multimetricism consistently on a large scale was innovative. Although it may not always work successfully, it demonstrates a rhythmic freedom never seen before in any piano sonata.

During the period 1890–1910, composers began to embrace wider influences in their piano sonatas. These included late romantic and impressionistic harmonies, Russian nationalism, orientalism, Scriabin and Delius. The role of French and Russian music is the next significant contribution.

---

[53] Darson, 1979.
[54] Bacharach (ed.), 1946, 189.
[55] Ottaway, *MO*, 1949, 143.
[56] Sorabji, 1932, 63.
[57] Scott, 1969, 192.

3

Piano Sonatas by Bax, Ireland, Baines, Bush and Britten

During this period there is a consolidation of several important strands first noted in the previous chapter.

Firstly, the Royal Academy's progressive teaching, with a particular emphasis on the music of Liszt, Wagner, Strauss and the Russian nationalists, affected the style of Arnold Bax's and Alan Bush's Piano Sonatas.

Secondly, the influence of Scriabin becomes particularly apparent. This has already been noted in Scott's Sonatas and it continues in the Sonatas written by Bax, William Baines, Kaikhosru Sorabji and Frank Bridge. The last two composers are considered in Chapter 4 (pp. 101–26). Scriabin visited London in 1914, performing his Piano Concerto and *Prometheus*. His Sixth Piano Sonata was published by Koussevitzky in Russia in 1912 and his Seventh the following year. Hence, by the period under discussion his music was becoming increasingly well known. Scriabin was an important influence upon British composers at this time, as he had developed the piano sonata to the limits of avant-garde techniques.

Thirdly, French impressionism, another stylistic trait observed in Scott's Sonata, contributed towards the development of Bax, Ireland and Baines.

Arnold Bax (1883–1953)

Bax's family encouraged his musical talents, and he was unable to recall a time when he could not play the piano. From 1896, Bax accompanied the choral society that his father sponsored and its director suggested that Bax should receive a formal musical education. By his mid teens Bax had attempted to play most of Beethoven's piano sonatas, and he began to compose.

There is a notebook containing some of his earliest compositions, dated 1897–8, in the British Library. These *Clavierstücke* are neatly written in ink, and the note stems all appear on the right hand side of the note-heads, regardless of their direction. One of the works is a Sonata in D minor, labelled No. 5. It consists of three movements, the last of which has been abandoned. The influence of the classical masters, especially Haydn and Beethoven, is clear in the thematic ideas and their treatment. The chords are generally triadic, although the second movement, in the style of a berceuse, uses more subtle inner voices [Fig. 3.1]. It is written in the key of D flat major, tonally very distant from D minor. These harmonies and the rhythmic flexibility of the first movement are affected by Chopin. Chopin remained an important influence upon Bax's pianistic writing, especially in his use of lyrical melodies.

Fig. 3.1 Bax, Sonata in D minor, Manuscript, Second movement, Bars 1–8

It was September 1900 when Bax entered the Royal Academy of Music, commencing his studies on the same day as Dale. He trained as a pianist, winning the Gold Medal in 1905, but decided to turn his attention to composition, and subsequently rarely played in public. In 1906–7 he went to Dresden to see operas by Wagner and Strauss, and he also heard music by Mahler and Bruckner. He admitted, "for a dozen years of my youth I wallowed in Wagner's music to the almost total exclusion – until I became aware of Richard Strauss – of any other".[1] Like most of the composers being considered, Bax was fortunate to have a private income and he was able to devote his life to composing and travelling.

Unlike his contemporaries Dale and Bowen, it was not until Bax left the Royal Academy in 1905 that he developed his own personal style. His mature style owes very little to the Teutonic tradition. During World War I, he even wrote to *The Sunday Times*, suggesting banning all German music, although his view was not widely supported.

Irish legend and folk music were to be the forces that liberated Bax from the constraints of Austro-German music. He became interested in the poetry of W. B. Yeats and wrote short stories and poems under the pseudonym Dermot O'Byrne between 1905 and 1919. The Irish literary renaissance coincided with the English musical renaissance. It provided another world of inspiration, one which was not too exotic and not too far away. Bax grew to love the landscape of Ireland and visited the country

---

[1] Bax, *National and English Review*, March 1952, 172–4.

frequently throughout his life. Aspects of nature, especially the sea, stimulated his imagination.

The other country that inspired his music was Russia. In 1910 he fell in love with a girl from the Ukraine and accompanied her on her return to Russia. The *Romantic Tone Poem*, which Myra Hess premièred at the Bechstein Hall on 25 April 1911, was written as a result.

> As a technical exercise, one could wish for nothing more exacting than the *Romantic Tone Poem* by Mr. Arnold Bax ... The composer presumably had some "programme" in his mind when he wrote it, but since no clue was afforded of its meaning, the audience was left to imagine the romance that had inspired music so rhetorical as this proved to be.[2]

It was revised between 1917 and 1920. Hess performed the second version, called *Symphonic Phantasy*, at the Wigmore Hall on 9 October 1919[3] and Harriet Cohen performed it with the title Sonata at the Wigmore Hall on 15 June 1920. Bax's revisions were finally completed and Cohen performed the First Piano Sonata in F sharp minor on 12 April 1921.

Cohen described how the illimitable distances of the Russian plain inspired the early part of the development section.[4] She recalled that Bax's revisions included the addition of a coda that interlaced phrases of the main theme, for the first time heard in a major key, with bell sounds.[5] These bell-like textures may have been influenced by Liapunov's *Etudes d'exécution Transcendante* Op. 11 Nos. 3 and 8 (1900–05), which Bax knew.[6] He notated the coda on four staves, in order that the separate parts could be clearly distinguished.

Bax followed Liszt by writing his First Sonata in a minor key in one movement, although Liszt's Sonata closes quietly, whereas Bax's ends triumphantly. Development occurs through organic growth, a technique typical of a symphonic poem, which is essentially how Bax conceived his Sonata. From Liszt, Bax adopts the device of thematic transformation, seen also in the sonatas by Dale and Scott.

---

[2] Anon., *The Queen*, 6 May 1911, 781. In *The Society of British Composers Yearbook 1912*, 28.

[3] Evans, *Pall Mall Gazette*, 10 October 1919. He recalls, incorrectly, that this work was originally called Sonata. At the Aeolian Hall on 2 June 1911, Hess played the first movement of a Sonata in D minor, which was never mentioned in any lists of Bax's music published in his lifetime. Evans may have confused the *Symphonic Phantasy* with this work. The *Symphonic Phantasy* rarely uses D minor, and so it is unlikely to be a later version of the Sonata. See also Anon., *The Times*, 10 October 1919, which confirms that the *Symphonic Phantasy* is an earlier version of the First Piano Sonata, citing the bells.

[4] In Bacharach (ed.), 1946, 127.

[5] Ibid. Her comments suggest that the *Romantic Tone Poem* lacked this ending. The Easter bells that Bax heard on his arrival in St Petersburg may have inspired this. See sleeve notes of Frank Merrick Society 7.

[6] Letter to Arthur Alexander, n.d., in Foreman, 1988, 170.

The opening of Bax's First Sonata is shown in Fig. 3.2. At the third presentation of the first subject, Bax treats each of his three parts independently and the result is the subdivision of a beat into five and six semiquavers simultaneously [Fig. 3.3]. Especially in the earlier piano sonatas, Bax's harmony results from the combination of a number of polyphonic parts. In some cases, this leads to chords that consist of sharps, flats and naturals, making it difficult for the pianist to read, but demonstrating Bax's talent for hearing music orchestrally and playing from scores.

Fig. 3.2 Bax, Sonata No. 1, Murdoch, First movement, Bars 1–4

Fig. 3.3 Bax, Sonata No. 1, First movement, Bars 24–7

For altering the second subject, Bax includes florid decorations in a high register that recall the techniques of Field and Chopin, whilst the main theme sounds in the tenor register [Fig. 3.4]. Similar influences are seen from the early sonatas of Scriabin, who varies a simple melody by presenting it in various registers and decorating it with counter-melodies. The decoration of melodies using arabesques is an impressionistic feature seen in the music of Debussy, Scott and in the first movement of Scriabin's Second Sonata. In the second movement of Scriabin's First Sonata, he presents a simple song-like melody and later complicates it with semiquavers, as Bax is fond of doing. Bax changes the character of the theme by altering its dynamics and accentuation. At one point, the lyrical theme is distorted into an ironic march.

Fig. 3.4 Bax, Sonata No. 1, First movement, Bars 76–7

The opulence, pagan exoticism and artistic innovations of Diaghilev's ballet company made a tremendous impression upon Bax when it toured Britain in 1911. Influences from Russian composers such as Balakirev, Mussorgsky, Medtner, Scriabin and Rachmaninov contribute to the style of the First Sonata. Bax, like Dale, knew works by Glazunov. From 1908, he and Arthur Alexander, a pianist from New Zealand, used to play the symphonies of Glazunov, and works by Borodin, Rimsky-Korsakov and Balakirev, in piano duet arrangements.[7] Glazunov's two Piano Sonatas date from 1901 and there are certain textural similarities with Bax's style. Both composers use long-breathed tunes with semiquaver accompaniments and their rhythmic groupings are flexible. Additionally, they both use frequent modulation to colour their music. Bax always uses tonalities in his piano sonatas, but his essentially diatonic vocabulary is constantly embellished by chromatic and modal elements.

The following example is briefly mentioned in order to illustrate Bax's developing musical style. There exists a manuscript of a Scherzo (second movement) from an aborted Piano Sonata dated 17 October 1913. Down the left hand side of the page, Bax lists the scoring for the piece, which was performed in an orchestral version at the Proms in September 1917. It is surprisingly long, considering that a scherzo is usually the most light-weight movement in a sonata, and it was cut for a pianola roll version in 1920.[8] There is heavy reliance on quaver and dotted quaver rhythms, often on a monotone [Fig. 3.5].

Bax was reticent and shy, and did little to actively promote his music. The Society of British Composers published a Trio in 1907, which he was later embarrassed by. His student years at the Royal Academy of Music had led him into contact with Hess, who performed many of Bax's early works. It was through her playing that Bax was introduced to Dr L. Strecker of Augener's publishing company, who agreed to publish Bax's short piano

---

[7] Ibid., 54–5. They were amongst the first in England to play *Petrushka* and *The Rite of Spring*, although Bax preferred the romantic and nationalist Russian repertoire.

[8] Piano Rolls – Aeolian 1951; Universal Music Co. 513620; Broadwood Piano Co. 513620; Artistyle 93519. In 1981 it was recorded by Pearl.

Fig. 3.5 Bax, Sonata in F (No. 2 Scherzo), Manuscript, Bars 1–8

pieces. In the early years of World War I, Bax heard Cohen perform his piano pieces with great sympathy. She made her début at a solo recital in June 1918 and at the Proms in 1920, where she performed Bax's *Symphonic Variations*. Thus Bax had two champions of his music, and had to try to define their territory. For Harriet (whom Bax called Tania), he composed several short pieces, such as *Mountain Mood, Winter Waters* and *Ideala*. In 1922, Bax's principal publishers, Murdoch, Murdoch & Co., sponsored a concert of his piano works, songs and orchestral music. It included a performance of the Second Sonata given by Cohen. Although she was reported to have struggled with the demands placed on her, as a result of the concert Bax was launched as the leading composer of the day.[9]

Bax's Second Sonata was written in 1919, whilst he was in the process of revising the First. Arthur Alexander performed it on 24 November 1919. Bax withdrew the work until 15 June 1920, when Cohen played it at the Queen's Hall. According to Bax, the Second Sonata is epic and dramatic in construction, and deals with the conflict of good and evil.[10] It marks a significant advance on his First Sonata.

The one-movement form and methods of thematic transformation are inherited from Liszt, although by now, one-movement phantasy forms were widely used, owing to Cobbett's chamber music competitions. Bax's single movement is ambitious in its scope and it demands an assured technique. The modified ternary form of the piece is summarized in Fig. 3.6.

The Sonata's lengthy introduction, of which the beginning is illustrated in Fig. 3.7, is very similar in harmony and mood to the opening of Scriabin's Seventh Sonata [Fig. 3.8]. The work is described as being in G, but as in bar 5, the introduction avoids any reference to this key by the use of a bitonal aggregation consisting of C minor and B major triads, which share a mediant (E flat/D sharp). This chord is built upwards from the low C.

[9] Evans, *MT*, 1922, 874. The first major article about Bax was Evans, *MT*, 1919, 103–5 and 154–6.
[10] Bax told Frank Merrick this. See sleeve notes of FMS 6. See also Cohen in Bacharach (ed.), 1946, 127.

Fig. 3.6 Summary of main themes in Bax's Second Sonata

Bars	Main key	Theme
1–46	C minor	**"A" Section** *Introduction.* Lento, Tenebroso. Subsections: 1–9, 10–17, 18–26. Bars 10–17 contain important motto. Repeated, modified, on F minor, 27–46. Motto 35–8.
47–51		Transition.
52–107	G major	*First Subject.* Moderato Eroico. 52–69, 70–91, 92–107.
108–113		Motto modified. Lento. Focal note E flat.
114–75	E minor	*Second Subject.* (Lento) – Allegro Moderato. Subsections: 114–33, 134–47, 148–72, 173–5.
176–81		Transition. Presto.
182–5		Motto. Lento. Focal note A.
186–223	E flat major	**"B" Section** *Third Subject.* Lento. 186–211, 212–23.
224–49		*Fourth Subject.* Vivace.
250–65		*Third Subject.* Lento, Trionfale.
266–303	E flat/B min	**"A" Section** Introduction developed. Lento. 266–75, Motto 276–8, 279–90 introduces new tuba motif, motto 291–3, 294–303.
304–45	B minor and others	*Fourth Subject.* At 334–5 and 340–1, motto is superimposed.
346–81	G major	*First Subject.* Molto Largamente.
382–404	(G minor)	*Second Subject*, accompanied by *First Subject*.
405–16	F sharp	*Third Subject.* Lento.
417–24	E minor	Transition. Poco più mosso.
425–47	G min/maj	Motto. Ends in G major, Più lento.

Tritones (F sharps) are used to negate tonality, appearing in the bitonal chord and as appoggiaturas, as in bar 2.

Bax's introduction creates a sinister mood, owing to its use of bitonality, tritones and augmented triads, features that are typical of Scriabin. Beginning in bar 10, the main theme is doubled in octaves in the middle of the texture and accompanied by thick chords in the outer parts. This theme is the most important one in the Sonata and acts as a recurring motto, reminding the listener of the evil that is constantly present. Augmented triads are exposed above the motto, blurring the sense of tonality. When the motto is repeated, the chordal accompaniment rises to a higher register. This is typical of Bax – he rarely repeats a theme exactly.

Other typical Russian features can be observed in the introduction, including fragments of an octatonic scale (consisting of alternating tones

Fig. 3.7 Bax, Sonata No. 2, Murdoch, First movement, Bars 1–13

and semitones) and ostinati. An ostinato based on the root, dominant and ritone (C, G, F sharp) is sounded, above which a melody rises from the depths, using tritones both melodically and harmonically.

The sinister mood of the introduction leads into the first subject in G major. The frequent repetition of the tonic in its melody gives it a Russian character. Initially it is presented in octaves in the right hand, accompanied

Fig. 3.8 Scriabin, Sonata No. 7, Dover, Bars 1–3

by open fifths in the left. This theme is freely developed. Repetitions are modified by chromatic alterations to the harmonies and phrases are irregularly extended, including one bar of 1/4 metre. When it returns at bar 92, it is marked fortissimo and slower. The chords are filled in, and the accompanying parts move chromatically. Bax adds seconds to the chords, in the manner of John Ireland.

The second subject illustrates the influence of Irish folk music. A syncopated left hand ostinato is established before parallel sixths are added. This is followed by a simple folk-like melody in the transposed Dorian mode at bar 122.

The development section provides the central focus for the ternary form. Here Bax introduces another two themes, having already developed the first two subjects in the exposition. The third subject is in the contrasting key of E flat and the harmonies are based upon decorations and alterations of dominant sevenths, ninths and elevenths, a characteristic feature of Bax's style. This is a technique used by Scriabin and also adopted by Bridge in the slow movement of his Piano Sonata.

The recapitulation recalls the gloomy introduction and extends it. Each of the four subjects returns, and between bars 382–5, the first and second subjects sound together. When the motto returns from bar 429 it is transformed into the major mode and is marked tranquillo. The key of G major is firmly established, demonstrating that good will triumph, and the Sonata ends slowly and diatonically.

Bax's piano writing seems orchestrally conceived. This is confirmed by his instruction *quasi Trombe* (bar 70), and elsewhere (as in bar 425) by tremolandos. His piano writing is always idiomatic and themes are always voiced appropriately to express his ideas in orchestral colours. The music is crammed with ornamental detail, but the lack of tone colours available on the piano exposes the quality of Bax's thematic writing. In comparison with his lavish orchestral scores, the result seems monochromatic.

The manuscript of the Second Sonata can be seen at the British Library. This copy was used by Harriet Cohen, and contains her fingering. Annotations in blue pencil such as "keep going" and accidental signs were performing indications. The Sonata was mostly written without alterations and where changes occur, they concern fairly large sections rather than single notes. These must be the amendments that Bax made following the first performance.

The most significant alteration was at the start of the development section (bar 186). Bax originally began with an eighteen bar Andante con moto that led directly into the present Lento without a break. Fig. 3.9 illustrates its first four bars. Like the Scherzo [Fig. 3.5], this theme made much use of quaver and dotted quaver patterns.

Fig. 3.9 Bax, Sonata No. 2, Manuscript, Extract from passage inserted between Bars 185 and 186 of published version

Following bar 265, one whole page of manuscript and the following eight bars, containing material derived from the discarded Andante, were removed. Two pages of the manuscript were discarded after bar 416. The deletion of these sections helped to tighten up the structure of the Sonata and improved its overall effect.

Bax's Second Sonata has rightly been considered the best of his Piano Sonatas. He developed the idea of conflict between tonal and less tonal areas and between the characters of the main themes. The motto is brooding and dissonant, whereas the first subject is jubilant and clearly diatonic. Thus the ideas are well contrasted for identity and juxtaposition. Bax's single-movement Sonata No. 2 is more successful than Scott's single-movement Sonata No. 1 because of the contrasts between themes. Each theme retains its own identity, even when transformed, so that the listener can distinguish between them. Bax uses textural contrasts more effectively than Scott, and the overall ternary form of Sonata No. 2 works successfully.

In 1922, Bax wrote a third piano sonata. Cohen claimed to have suggested that he should orchestrate it.[11] This he did, re-writing the slow movement, and it became his First Symphony. Bax composed at the piano, and occasionally did not decide until later whether a work should remain as such or be orchestrated. *Paean* and *Mediterranean* (both 1920) began life as piano works and were later arranged for orchestra.

Cohen was an extravagant personality and championed the music of British composers. Ireland, Vaughan Williams, Bliss and Bartók all wrote pieces for her and Kodály, Janácek and Sibelius admired her. Unfortunately, she was domineering and possessive. She told Bax which instruments he should not write for, and she wanted the exclusive rights to perform works that Bax wrote for her, in particular the *Symphonic Variations*.[12] This meant that the work was infrequently heard and not published. When Patrick Piggott recorded the work for the BBC as late as 1963, Cohen threatened legal action. In 1935, Bax wrote *Legend* for the pianist John Simons, who had impressed him with his interpretation of the Third Sonata. Somehow Cohen obtained the manuscript and never passed it on to him until many years later, when he had finished concert work.[13]

Cohen did perform Bax's Piano Sonatas fairly frequently. She was the dedicatee of the Second and Third and gave the first performance of the Fourth. She played expressively, although her technique was not brilliant and she was hampered by the fact that she could not stretch a ninth. Surprisingly, Bax's writing in his Piano Sonatas does not make any concessions for her limited span. By the 1940s her technique was deteriorating and the BBC began to neglect her.

Bax wrote his Third Sonata in 1926. For the first time in his piano sonatas, Bax uses three distinct movements, the first of which follows a modified sonata form. He recalls the opening section in a coda at the end of the last movement, in much the same way that Dale recalled his slow movement theme at the end of his finale.

The Third Sonata is described as being in G sharp minor, although the opening page sounds in C sharp minor because Bax uses an ostinato outlining a C sharp minor ninth chord [Fig. 3.10]. Paradoxically, at the end of the whole sonata he uses a C sharp minor key signature, with an ostinato based on G sharp minor. Further contrast arises from the fact that one of the main themes is based in G major.

The development transforms the opening theme into an Irish dance. As in the development section of his Second Sonata, the harmonies here make use of extended dominant ninths, elevenths and thirteenths. There is also some evidence of Bax experimenting with quartal harmonies, as seen at the

---

[11] Foreman, 1988, 190. Noemy Belinkaya performed it as a piano piece at the Purcell Room, 16 October 1983.
[12] Ibid., 207.
[13] He played it on Radio 3 in 1969, and at the British Music Information Centre in October 1983.

Fig. 3.10 Bax, Sonata No. 3, Murdoch, First movement, Bars 1–5

Fig. 3.11 Bax, Sonata No. 3, First movement, Bars 175–82

beginning of Fig. 3.11. These chords lead into arpeggio figuration, suggesting the influence of impressionism.

The second movement is based on an original folk-like melody, in ternary form. Colin Scott-Sutherland suggests that the opening of this movement recalls the third movement of MacDowell's *Eroica* Sonata, although the links are tenuous.[14] Like Bax, MacDowell wrote four piano sonatas that contain orchestral-like trills and large chords. Their epic titles could easily refer to works by Bax. MacDowell uses heroic and folk themes in a similar way to Bax, although with less harmonic distinctiveness. It may have been their common heritage that provides the link, rather than direct influence.

By this time, Bax was increasingly using vertical harmony rather than linear harmony resulting from polyphony. One example is at the end of the second section of the second movement [Fig. 3.12]. In the closing bars of this movement, Bax juxtaposes the two main themes. The inclusion of both first and second themes in the final section of ternary form is a feature that Bax commonly used as a way of creating unity.

Fig. 3.12 Bax, Sonata No. 3, Second movement, Bars 67–72

---

[14] Scott-Sutherland, 1973, 107 footnotes.

The last movement is a toccata, again in ternary form, whose semiquaver figures relate it to the first movement.

In the manuscript, Bax made no alterations to the two outer movements. The middle movement has a couple of pages deleted at the end of the first section, which contained a variant on the Andante con moto theme from the first movement. Now, the only remaining cross-referencing of themes between movements is in the coda to the last movement, which recalls the opening.

Cohen gave the first performance of the Third Sonata on 18 November 1927 at the Liverpool Centre of the British Music Society. It was reviewed favourably, although the reviewer was puzzled by the first movement and suggested it needed a further hearing to appreciate it.[15] In this Sonata, a change in the way that Bax develops his themes is observable. He uses the motivic development of small cells, instead of the variation or transformation of a longer phrase. This may reflect Bax's increasing admiration for Sibelius, whom he visited in 1931–2. Just as Sibelius' later style, as demonstrated by his Seventh Symphony (1924), tended towards consolidation rather than expansion, Bax's style in his Fourth Sonata (1932) is more economical. Another possible explanation for this is the growth of the neoclassical movement from the early 1920s, as illustrated by works of Ravel, Stravinsky, Hindemith and the pupils of Boulanger.

Like the Third Sonata, the Fourth has three movements. The first movement contains a tune in an inner part, which has been compared to the woodwind melody in Sibelius' *Finlandia* [Fig. 3.13].

The work is modal, using sharpened fourths and flattened sevenths, and is influenced by folk music. The second movement contains a beautiful long flowing melody, accompanied by a syncopated pedal note, which Bax understandably considered one of his favourite movements. This theme is later accompanied by modal parallel thirds. Cohen performed the Fourth Sonata in New York on 1 February 1934, although it was dedicated to the Irish pianist, Charles Lynch.[16]

Fig. 3.13 Bax, Sonata No. 4, Murdoch, First movement, Bars 15–19

[15] Anon., *MT*, 1928, 67. It was adapted as a ballet, *Unbowed*, in 1932, which Bax disliked. See Cohen in Bacharach (ed.), 1946, 125.

[16] Bax admired his playing, writing to the editor of the *Irish Times* on 12 July 1947, "And what shall I say of Ireland's most imaginative pianist (it is superfluous to mention the sheer brilliance of his technique), except that Charles Lynch played one of my piano sonatas with a mastery that can only enhance his fame?"

A Master Musicians book on Bax was planned but had to be abandoned as Cohen kept interfering. Bax's autobiography, *Farewell, My Youth*, only covers the period of his life until 1914, because it was impossible for him to write about his later years without offending someone. Once Bax died, Cohen lent his manuscripts around the world without keeping a record as to where she had sent them, thus there is no trace of the location of the First or Fourth Piano Sonatas. Fortunately she lent many of them, including the Second and Third Piano Sonatas, to the British Library.

The first recordings of Bax's orchestral works were of *Tintagel* and *Mediterranean* in 1930,[17] but recordings of the Piano Sonatas had to wait until the 1960s. Until then, the Sonatas were never frequently performed. Over recent years, there has been more interest in Bax's music. Vernon Handley and Bryden Thomson have promoted the symphonies and Eric Parkin has recorded the complete piano works. A Bax Society was formed in the mid 1950s and in 1985 a trust was set up to finance recordings. Like Scott, Bax felt that the BBC, who continued to play uncharacteristic works, misrepresented him. The Piano Concerto for left hand became extremely popular and overshadowed his better works.

Although Bax was an accomplished pianist, the pianism in the Sonatas is derived from Chopin and Scriabin. Bax does not introduce technical innovations, although the orchestrally conceived textures and the toccata movements place tough demands on the pianist.

Bax created synthetic Celtic melodies, but did not use real folk melodies overtly in the sense that Delius or Vaughan Williams had. He was unsure whether it was possible to realise a truly native art, "unless there exists a national life upon which to found it".[18]

Bax felt that he owed a lot to Elgar in his early years, although his music shows little direct influence from any British composer. He admired Delius, and visited him with Balfour Gardiner in 1924. Through Gardiner, Bax met Norman O'Neill and Holst. It was Gardiner who had paid for a concert series that took place in 1912 and 1913, but the war prevented a series in 1914. Gardiner's concerts had been crucial in promoting the work of English composers. Here Bax met Vaughan Williams, whose *London* Symphony was premièred. They became close friends and they used to discuss each other's music. In 1926 Bax stayed with Heseltine, who probably influenced Bax's drinking habits more than his music. Of other English composers, Bax felt that

> Nearly all English composers are mightily afraid of not being idiomatically up-to-date. (Pace: John Ireland and Frank Bridge). This is no doubt

---

[17] Foreman, 1988, 271. HMV issued two 78 rpm discs, recorded in May 1928 at Queen's Hall, conducted by Goossens.
[18] Bax, *Musical Standard*, 11 April 1914, 342.

the result of the nineteenth century, and memories of those ghastly dullards, Stanford and Parry, and their deserved fate.[19]

Like Scott, Bax hated Schoenberg, as a result of discovering his Three Piano Pieces Op. 11, and considered him to be "the world's premier mathematician in sound".[20] Schoenberg's aesthetic position was far removed from his own and Bax felt that the twelve-note method was incapable of musical expression. Bax was essentially an intuitive composer rather than an intellectual one. He uses sonorities for their sensual appeal, in an impressionistic way, not because they conform to a harmonic theory. Writing in 1928, he said,

> As far as I know, the only new tendency in my style is but a modification of the manner in which I have always written. I am a brazen romantic, and could never have been and never shall be anything else. By this I mean that my music is the expression of emotional states. I have no interest whatever for sound for its own sake or any modernist 'isms' and factions.[21]

Bax's style was essentially a product of the nationalist and late romantic aesthetics. He used the sound-world of late nineteenth-century harmony, plus elements of modality. The form of his Piano Sonatas stemmed from the nineteenth-century rhetorical tradition, and ideas of thematic transformation originated in Liszt. His programmatic intentions in the First and Second Sonatas link him with the tone poem and he successfully integrated Irish, Russian, and folk influences into a pre-existing idiom. However, he represents the end of the post-romantic era and the tradition established by Dale, Bowen and Scott, in their Piano Sonatas. Despite aspects of individuality, his style led to a musical dead end that could not be continued by his successors.

John Ireland (1879–1962)

Like Bax and Bridge, Ireland wrote a vast amount of piano music, mainly short pieces with titles, but unlike them, Ireland was not attracted to the music of Scriabin. All three composers studied the piano at an early stage in their careers and although none of them performed in public, the piano was probably the instrument on which they tried out their ideas. Ireland wrote few large-scale pieces; he did not write a symphony and his largest work is the Piano Concerto (1930). Like the French composer Fauré, Ireland wrote mainly short piano solos, songs and chamber music.

Ireland's early attempts at piano writing had demonstrated influences

---

[19] Letter to Arthur Benjamin, n.d., in Misc., *ML*, 1954, 3.
[20] Bax, *ML*, 1951, 307.
[21] Bax, *Musical America*, 7 July 1928, 9.

from Brahms and other late romantic composers. This can be attributed to his studies with Stanford at the Royal College, although his teacher also made him study the music of Palestrina and strict counterpoint.

The impressionistic music of Debussy and Ravel, which Ireland discovered in 1908, proved to be one of the main catalysts for his new style. The result was the delicate sonorities, controlled dissonance and subtle use of the pedals seen in Ireland's *Decorations* (1912–13) and later works. French impressionism, the scenery of the Channel Islands and the Sussex Downs, and the writings of Arthur Machen (1863–1947), provided the liberation from Germanic music that Ireland needed. This was similar to the role that Russian and Irish influences played in Bax's music.

From 1913 to 1919, Ireland experimented with a personal idiom, with the most important pieces from this period being the Second Violin Sonata (1915–17) and *Chelsea Reach* from *London Pieces* (1917–20). Ireland's Piano Sonata was composed between October 1918 and January 1920. He may have attempted to write an earlier piano sonata, although no trace of this work survives today.[22] His published Sonata consists of a movement in sonata form, a slow and lyrical movement in ternary form and a rondo. Thus it has a classical layout, although Ireland is able to adapt this plan to suit his needs.

The exposition of the first movement contains two main themes (bars 1–21 and 34–63), linked by a bridge passage (bars 22–33). The development section (bars 64–121) is concerned chiefly with the first subject, and bars 95–7, which initially seem to indicate the start of the recapitulation, soon lead into further development. As the development concentrated on the first subject, the recapitulation begins at bar 122 with the bridge passage, continuing with the second subject. The first subject is not heard again until the coda, beginning at bar 162, where it is again fragmented and developed. This procedure is similar to that used by Chopin in his Sonata in B flat minor, Op. 35, where the first subject is used extensively in the development, and omitted from the recapitulation.

The Piano Sonata launches directly into the modal first subject [Fig. 3.14], which is accompanied by a flowing bass ostinato focusing on tonic (E) and dominant pedal notes. The melody is mainly conjunct, and any leaps are perfect fourths and minor sevenths. The tenor line provides added ninths, tenths and elevenths, in a recurrent three-note pattern. The opening bears some resemblance to Grieg's Piano Sonata, also in E minor, in 2/4, which uses a flowing semiquaver accompaniment underneath a slower-moving diatonic melody.

---

[22] Evans, *MT*, 1919, 394–6 and 457–62 lists an unpublished Piano Sonata in C minor. Anon., *MMR*, 1915, 192 indicates that it was composed between 1895 and 1906 and says that it was already discarded.

Fig. 3.14 Ireland, Sonata, Stainer & Bell, First movement, Bars 1–4

The first subject consists of three motives, the first two of which form the basis for subsequent development. Ireland uses them sequentially, in inversion and in retrograde, without every occurrence being obvious to the listener. This was a technique used later by Bax, in his Third and Fourth Sonatas.

The first phrase is sparse and almost neo-classical, but this is soon replaced by fuller textures. The second phrase imitates a fugue by repeating the first subject a fifth higher, accompanied by a counter-melody derived from it. Counterpoint is an important aspect of Ireland's style, one that his teacher Stanford had stressed. Ireland's harmonies frequently evolve from the combination of linear parts, as in the early piano music of Bax, rather than being conceived as vertical progressions. The second phrase uses more chromaticism, and the rate of harmonic change is faster. Ireland's chromaticism is used as a decoration to diatonicism and bass parts frequently use pedal notes to clarify the tonality.

Already the interval of a fourth starts to emerge as an important factor in the harmonies. This is the first occasion on which Ireland had used quartal chord structures in his piano music, although its use here remains subtle. The inner parts use perfect fourths and augmented fourths (tritones) that weaken the sense of tonality, and the section ends with a bitonal chord that superimposes the triads of B and F minor (dominant and Neapolitan chords). Ireland's Sonata uses bitonality infrequently; hence the listener does not feel that it is especially dissonant.

The bridge passage consists of a more homophonic theme that lacks a clear tonal centre. Arguably, bars 22–33 could be viewed as the second subject, as the character of this theme is lyrical. However, this would make bars 34–63 into a third subject group, whose length and thematic importance would completely overshadow the second subject. The transition section is well conceived as a link. The first subject had moved from tonality to bitonality, and the bridge passage enabled a return to tonality to be made.

The melody of the second subject consists of leaps of a fourth, like a street-cry, and conjunct motion in the bass, like the first subject. The harmony is diatonic, but includes the use of added notes in inner parts, a feature that makes Ireland's harmonies completely personal. The chords are large, spanning a tenth in the bass, and consist of seven, eight or even nine notes in total. However, the melody is centred on a restricted range of notes, a feature Ireland uses frequently, possibly influenced by Stravinsky's *Petrushka*.

From bar 42, the texture changes to another characteristic Ireland pattern in which the melody is to be found in a middle part. The down-to-earth character of this passage could represent Cockneys. The layout bears a close resemblance to *Ragamuffin* from Ireland's *London Pieces* [Fig. 3.15].

Fig. 3.15 Ireland, *London Pieces*, Augener, *Ragamuffin*, Bars 41–4

A similar passage can be seen in Debussy's *General Lavine*, from his second book of Preludes [Fig. 3.16].

Fig. 3.16 Debussy, Preludes, United Music Publishers, *General Lavine*, Bars 14–17

As already mentioned, French impressionism was an important influence in the development of Ireland's style, and he wrote a large number of short, titled works. From bar 75 there is an impressionistic section, recalling figuration used in Ireland's *The Scarlet Ceremonies*. In these sections, Ireland uses logical bass parts, and in this respect his style is closer to Ravel than Debussy. Other impressionistic traits that can be seen in Ireland's Sonata are his attention to sonorities and the spacing of chords. In the other two movements, he clearly indicates when the pianist should use the soft pedal (una corda).

The changing metres seen in this section are used to some extent throughout the whole Sonata, to allow the melodies to flow freely. Ireland's use of changing metres is more controlled and subtle than Scott's. Phrases are indicated by beaming patterns that continue over bar-lines, another individual stylistic feature.

The development is mainly concerned with the first subject, beginning in the expected dominant key. This builds up to a climax with a shift from minor to major, a small-scale replica of the whole movement's tonal plan.

The final E major section clearly illustrates the basis of Ireland's harmonic language. Octaves and triads are filled in with added notes, mainly seconds and sixths. The chord formed by a triad, with an added second and sixth, is characteristic of all movements. Unlike the harmonies that characterize Bax's or Bridge's styles, this one does not sound dissonant, being derived from diatonicism. The first movement ends with an improvisatory flourish and chords of E major with an added sixth.[23] Its chordal ending is very similar to the ending of Ireland's song *I have Twelve Oxen* of July 1918, although he does not use actual thematic quotations in his pieces until later in his career. The movement ends with a pause sign over a rest, a direction that Ireland uses in the other movements from this Sonata and in many other works.

The real achievement in this movement is the way in which Ireland is able to use short motives and contrasting themes in such a way as to transform them, whilst still retaining a sense of unity. Transitions from one idea to another seem to be effected very easily.

The second movement is in ternary form, a design common to many of Ireland's pieces, and is calm and lyrical in mood. It consists of an irregular seven-bar theme, the main notes of which are based around a restricted range (G, A flat, G, F, C). At the first appearance of the theme, pedal notes of the tonic and dominant of B flat major are present. The first and last sections of this movement are based on the variation principle. At its fourth appearance, the first two bars of the theme lead into a new chorale-like melody, which is accompanied by a quiet octave figure, suggesting timpani. This timpani figure returns in the final section of the movement, where it is combined with the main theme. The middle section, marked una corda, consists of a three-bar phrase in B minor that is varied. Flowing semiquavers provide a contrast to the slow-moving intensity of the previous section.

Like many of Ireland's slow movements, this one is expansive. He needs time to set the mood, which is deeply emotional and reflective and similar in intensity to the slow movement of Elgar's Second Symphony. The elegiac mood may represent Ireland's response to World War I, an event that had made him deeply depressed.

[23] Eric Parkin recalls asking Ireland whether he could omit the C sharp, as it made the chord extremely difficult to play, but Ireland was not keen. The added notes make Ireland's harmonies individual, but increase the complexity for the pianist. In a conversation with the author on 4 Jan. 1995, Parkin observed that in Ireland's music, no note is superfluous. However, Ireland omitted this note from his revised version of the Sonata [see p. 90].

The final movement is in rondo form, having a heroic and triumphal march-like character. It consists of a main theme in E major (bars 1–21), first episode in E flat (bars 22–50), return of main theme (bars 51–7), second episode in A and A flat (bars 58–88), main theme in B flat (bars 89–108), first episode in D flat (bars 109–22), and a coda which ends in E (bars 123–62).

The movement opens with a thick triadic texture, using rising and falling thirds, and is reminiscent of Vaughan Williams' hymn tunes. At bar 12, the accompaniment is similar to the timpani motif of the second movement, which acts as an important unifier. Thus there are incidental thematic connections between movements, although Ireland did not systematically use cyclic forms until later.[24]

The third movement contains several examples of orchestrally-conceived textures. At bar 51, a hint of the main triadic theme returns, preceded by a flourish. At this point, Ireland seems to be moving in and out of different planes of experience. The march-like theme melts in to the second episode, which is underpinned by a dominant pedal, like timpani. This section sounds retrospective, and Ireland himself described it as "looking through the wrong end of a telescope".[25] In fact the themes are new.

During the coda, there is a low bass trill on A flat, above which the main theme rises from the depths. The last twenty-one bars are to be played fortissimo, and make use of the full range of the keyboard. From bar 154, the sharpened Lydian fourth is used to add colour, and the work ends triumphantly in E major.

The final movement consists of several unrelated themes, although Ireland usually manages to make transitions from one to another smoothly. It provides a contrast with the first movement, which was mainly concerned with the organic development of short motives. The third movement contains many climaxes because Ireland is attempting to create the atmosphere of a large symphonic finale. Thus the pianist needs to ensure that the relative tone and volume of the climaxes are well judged.

The manuscript of Ireland's Piano Sonata can be seen at the British Library. It contains few alterations, and appears to be the copy used by the publishers. The title page originally said "Sonata in E for pianoforte", but the words "in E" have been crossed out. There are no metronome markings on this copy, and a few accidentals are penciled in. In the first movement, one slur originally covered bars 22–3, but this has been altered so that the last quaver beat is slurred into bar 24, as on the printed copy. In bar 160, Ireland has deleted some added notes originally present in the chords, and the four bars at the end of the first movement have manuscript paper stuck over them so it is impossible to tell how it originally ended. Similarly, in the second movement, bars 43, 45, 47, 49

---

[24] The Cello Sonata (1923) derives its material from the opening four notes.
[25] According to Parkin, in conversation with the author.

and 51 have pieces of manuscript paper stuck over the timpani motto in the bass.

Ireland took meticulous care in correcting proof sheets from the printers, as four sets of proofs can be seen at the British Library.[26] They contain alterations to slurs, accidentals, staccato and pedal marks, and include metronome marks. In the second set, Ireland urges the printers to use dots after the word rit., so that it is obvious to the performer which notes are to be played slower, and in the third set he requests that the dot at the end of the word rit. should be bigger than those that follow it. Even the fourth set of proofs contains corrections!

Augener published the Sonata in 1920 and the revised version in 1951. In the latter version there are no changes made to either notes or rhythms, only to performance directions. In bar 1 of the first movement, Ireland changes the dynamic from mezzo forte to forte and on the second beat he requests the use of an accent instead of a dash. For the second subject, he uses staccato wedges rather than dots on each quaver. The decorative figures in the right hand of bar 62 are to be played marcato. In bar 202, he requests that the word allargando should be moved to the right of the first chord, and in the final chord of the first movement he deletes the C sharp.

In the third movement he has changed the metronome mark of the main theme and the Animato, making them slightly slower. He provides metronome markings at bars 101 and 109 where none existed before. These examples demonstrate Ireland's thoroughness and attention to detail. It is difficult to understand why he should revise the work thirty years after he wrote it. Maybe he thought that it was worth changing a few details to clarify certain ambiguities for the performer.[27]

Ireland's Sonata is a late romantic work that is not revolutionary but in terms of English music contains some interesting experiments, including the use of quartal harmonies and bitonal chords. Compared to the dissonances and tonal ambiguity of Bax's and Bridge's Sonatas, Ireland's is much more approachable, and it is surprising that it is not more widely known.

Bax and Ireland differed in their use of modality. Although Ireland studied modal counterpoint, he was never attracted to the folksong school of British music. Whilst he does use sharpened fourths and flattened sevenths, it is to provide a sense of melodic colour rather than to imitate a folk melody. However, there are occasional traces of folksong influence, for instance in *Soliloquy*. Ireland's Sonata is not nationalistic, although it has a strong sense of place, having been inspired by the scenery of Chanctonbury Ring in Sussex. Unlike some composers, Ireland exhibits a remarkable consistency in his piano style from 1913 to 1943.

[26] H.403.k (1). Ireland took great care over preparing works for printing, as he realized that printing is irrevocable, according to Parkin, in conversation with the author.
[27] This theory is supported by the comments that Ireland made to Parkin and pencilled changes that he made to the printed score.

The Sonata was premièred by Frederick Lamond, a pupil of Liszt, on 12 June 1920, although this is thought to be the only performance of it that he ever gave. There are few reviews of performances of the Sonata, although Katharine Eggar reported that Howard-Jones, Winifred Christie, Lloyd Powell, Ralph Lawton and Edward Mitchell had performed it by June 1922.[28] Alan Bush performed both Ireland's and Bridge's Sonatas in a lengthy recital of all-British piano music in 1927. The reviewer noted that Ireland's Sonata was "more downright, more of the soil, and more closely in touch with life [than Bridge's]".[29] Ireland's Sonata is more directly appealing to the ear, but possibly the technical demands placed on the performer, in particular the large chords, proved problematic. Ireland played his Sonatina and several short piano pieces in radio broadcasts, but there is no surviving recording of him playing the Sonata.[30] It was not until the 1950s that his piano music was recorded by Eric Parkin.

Ralph Hill considered Ireland's Piano Sonata to be "one of the finest and most important since Liszt's in B minor".[31] According to Hill, Ireland's aim in sonata form was "the attainment of unity in diversity, without resort to mechanical and academic means", which he successfully achieved here.[32] In many respects, Ireland's Sonata can be claimed as the outstanding example of all British piano sonatas considered. It is a major contribution to the international piano repertoire, which has been shamefully neglected.

William Baines (1899–1922)

Like Ireland, Baines was influenced by impressionism. Most of his piano music consists of short character pieces, similar to those of Ireland and Bax, but there are also four unpublished Piano Sonatas. His manuscripts also include a Symphony and a single-movement Piano Concerto.

Baines attended Saturday morning music lessons at the Yorkshire Training College of Music in Leeds, where Albert Jowett taught him piano, harmony and counterpoint. This was the only musical education that he received, and he rarely travelled outside Yorkshire; two factors that make his subsequent achievements quite remarkable. His father was a cinema pianist and on occasions, Baines deputized for him, thus he developed a natural facility at the piano. Baines' first public piano recital took place in 1917. Throughout his life, Baines suffered from ill health and his period of military service was extremely brief.

Baines' Sonata No. 1 in D minor, Op. 3, was written in 1916, according to

---

[28] Eggar, *Music Teacher*, 1922, 465–7.
[29] Anon., *Manchester Guardian*, 2 December 1927, 17.
[30] Hill in Bacharach (ed.), 1946, 103–4.
[31] Ibid.
[32] Ibid.

Roger Carpenter.[33] Baines had previously written a Sonata in D minor in 1914, which relied heavily on the dominant seventh chord, but had already discarded it. The Sonata Op. 3 is dedicated to his teacher, Jowett, and it demonstrates Baines' knowledge of the classical sonata. The first movement is in the expected sonata form, the second in ternary form, the third is a scherzo and trio and the fourth is an Allegro in 6/8 metre. As in Bax's juvenilia, Chopin's pianism is in evidence in this work.

Baines' Second Sonata in A minor, written in 1917, is more interesting. It is a five-movement work, lasting approximately forty-five minutes, dedicated "to all those whose aims and ideals are high". The ostinato introduction over a chromatic bass is used as a cyclic theme, which recurs as a coda to the first movement and to the finale [Fig. 3.17].

Fig. 3.17 Baines, Sonata No. 2, Manuscript, First movement, Bars 1–4

The influence of impressionism is evident in the annotations made to the music, as well as the resulting sonorities that Baines uses. The introduction contains the instruction "Imagine a tranquil, moonlight [sic] night, by the sea" as well as "very slow, and with beautiful expression". In the third movement, Baines requires the performer to "imagine a beautiful cave". He knew piano music by Scott – another composer who was influenced by impressionism and who attached short texts to some of his piano works. An entry in Baines' diary in September 1920 reveals that he practised both Scott's and Ireland's Piano Sonatas, although he admitted preferring Scott's.[34] Scott's use of arabesque and his multimetricism influenced Baines. This is demonstrated in Prelude No. 4, which does not use a time signature and is rhythmically free. The second movement of the A minor Sonata, a scherzo, is well written for the piano and it successfully captures the spirit that Baines wishes to convey. The parallel movement of triads in the third movement sounds archaic, and recalls Debussy.

The copious amount of performance directions also bears comparison with Scriabin. Baines knew much of Scriabin's music, as his friend John E. Kennedy owned a complete library of his piano works. Later, Baines made great use of tritones and ostinati. This is seen in the Sonata in F sharp minor, written originally in 1918, which Carpenter describes as being

---

[33] Carpenter, 1977. The manuscripts in the British Library have been dated incorrectly.
[34] Ibid., 55.

"written under the spell of the first three Scriabin sonatas".[35] Thus, simultaneously with Bax, Sorabji and Bridge, Baines began to synthesize aspects of Scriabin's style into his piano music.

Baines' F sharp minor Sonata is a long and virtuosic work, in a romantic-impressionistic style. It was revised in 1919 and again in 1921, and Carpenter suggests that Baines may have been trying to prepare the work for publication.[36] Some of Baines' shorter piano solos were published and Eaglefield Hull promoted his music. Despite the recording of a selection of Baines' solos by Parkin in 1972, the most famous of which is *Paradise Gardens* (composed in 1918), Baines remains virtually unknown today. He died at a tragically young age, but his Piano Sonatas were ambitious. This is quite remarkable, given that he did not study at a major institution, and he remained for most of his life in Yorkshire. The lack of formal musical education allowed Baines to synthesize his own personal style at an early stage in his career, and we can only speculate how this would have developed had he lived longer.

Alan Bush (1900–95)

The pianist and composer Alan Bush has already been mentioned in Chapter 2 (p. 52), owing to his training at the Royal Academy of Music, where his piano teachers included Tobias Matthay, Benno Moiseiwitsch and Artur Schnabel. Subsequently, he studied with John Ireland from 1921 to 1927. Bush's Piano Sonata Op. 2 is not mentioned in the *New Grove*, and Warner Chappell, who took over its copyright from Murdoch, do not possess an archive copy. The only extant score is held in the British Music Information Centre in London. Bush decided to withdraw all the works that he had written before his period of study with Ireland, with the exception of the Sonata Op. 2 and a Suite for two pianos, both of which were out of print anyway. I have included a discussion of Bush's Sonata to illustrate that stylistic trends observed in the major works of the period are reflected also in less significant works. Nevertheless, it was hailed by Corder as "a second Benjamin Dale Sonata".[37]

Bush's Sonata is a single-movement work in B minor, like Liszt's, although it ends in B major. It is in ternary form, and the themes of the opening section are recapitulated in the final one, the central section providing a slower and more lyrical contrast in F sharp major. The pianism is grounded in Chopin, using arpeggio accompaniment figures that weave throughout the texture. The themes follow one another without being sectionalized, using ideas of free flow as in the music of Delius and Scott.

---

[35] Ibid., 97.
[36] Ibid.
[37] Stevenson (ed.), 1981, 39.

The harmonies and textures of the Sonata are influenced by the music of Liszt, Wagner and Strauss, although Bush denied this.

> ... Wagner was rather a dangerous composer to be influenced by ... Wagner was a composer who dominated many people then. I did not want to be one of them.[38]

Bush acknowledged the influence of Brahms, especially in matters of orchestration. He had analysed the sonatas of Beethoven and Brahms besides having performed them and thought that the word sonata still conveyed certain implications.

> Well, I think that if you want to get your works performed, you have to provide the performer with some structure that is to a certain extent imposing. That's why I chose a sonata.... it suggests a composition of some magnitude.[39]

There is one theme, having the character of a folk melody, which is diatonic and is harmonized with seventh chords [Fig. 3.18]. It illustrates Bush's flexible metres and irregular rhythmic accentuation, features that anticipate Tippett's First Sonata, as demonstrated in Chapter 5 (pp. 140–58).

Fig. 3.18 Bush, Sonata No. 1, Murdoch, Bars 42–7

Bush felt that folksong was an important influence upon his compositions.

> ... A composer betrays the fundamental principle of musical art when he writes in a way which contradicts essentially the mode of expressing the particular feeling in song. It also vindicates very strongly our folk music. Music ought to have a national character. If it has not got a national character then it will mean that the composer is artificially imposing a barrier between himself and the culture of which he is an exponent.[40]

Later, Bush studied English folk music systematically and tried to derive modes and scales from it. This parallels the use of folk music by Bax, who composed synthetic Irish folk tunes, as in his Third Sonata. Bush's

---

[38] Interview with author: see Appendix 1, pp. 175–6.
[39] Ibid., p. 178.
[40] Schafer, 1963, 57.

conscious use of nationalism in music was part of a wider musical movement that included Holst and Vaughan Williams.

Bush's Sonata uses some chromatic harmonies, but this is a very early work. From the composition of *Dialectic* (1929) and during the 1930s, Bush developed his own form of thematicism in music, whereby all notes were organized melodically, rhythmically and harmonically. This was partly a result of his period of study at Berlin University. Bush studied musicology and philosophy there, and although he knew Schoenberg's music, he did not study with him. By 1940, Bush's thematic techniques dominated his compositions.

As in the case of Bax, Ireland and Bridge, the effects of World War I took their toll. Bush's eldest brother was killed in action and the experience led Bush to think about his political beliefs. In 1925 he became a member of the Russian Communist Party with his fellow composer Rutland Boughton, and in 1936 he founded the Workers' Musical Association. During World War II, the BBC considered banning Bush's music because he had signed the People's Convention, but Vaughan Williams supported Bush by threatening to sever his relations with the BBC if they did not lift the ban. Bush believed in the theories of the Russian Asafyev, that political beliefs are reflected by music. This is most obvious in the subject matter of his operas and song texts. Bush has always identified with the working class, despite not being born into it.

Bush's greatest contribution to the British piano sonata in the 1920s was as a performer. He included Ireland's and Bridge's Piano Sonatas in his repertoire, besides some of their shorter works.[41] He performed pieces by Bax – but not the Sonatas – and his repertoire included piano and chamber works by Bennett, Delius, Goossens, Michael Head and Moeran.

Bush and Tippett were part of a minority of British composers whose Piano Sonatas spanned their careers. Even at the age of 93, Bush was able to work on his Fifth Piano Sonata, with the aid of wide-ruled manuscript paper and a magnifying glass. He wrote prolifically for piano, and remembering that his Fourth Piano Sonata is Op. 119, it is understandable that he categorized the Op. 2 Sonata as juvenilia. His Second Piano Sonata, Op. 71, was written in 1970 and premièred by his close friend Ronald Stevenson, who has championed Bush's works in recent years. Leslie Howard has performed the Third Sonata. Bush's music has not been widely appreciated in Great Britain, and in the 1940s and 1950s his works had more performances in East Germany and the Soviet Union than in this country.

---

[41] Stevenson (ed.), 1981, 205.

(Edward) Benjamin Britten (1913–76)

Benjamin Britten wrote surprisingly little for the piano, considering that he was such a proficient pianist. His output includes a Piano Concerto (1938, revised 1945), *Holiday Diary* (1934) and *Night Piece (Notturno)* (1963), which was written as a test piece for the first Leeds piano competition. He began writing a piano work for Richter in 1965–6, but this remains unfinished. Several works for two pianos were written for Ethel Bartlett and Rae Robertson. Britten tended to write chamber music for friends, and was not inclined to write for himself, although he performed his Concerto.

Although the piano parts of Britten's songs are imaginative and idiomatic, requiring a talented interpreter, he seems to have found only limited potential in the instrument.

> I like the piano very much as a background instrument, but I don't feel inclined to treat it as a melodic instrument. I find that it's limited in colour. I don't really *like* the sound of a modern piano.[42]

Britten's chamber music is concentrated in his early and late years, the middle period being mainly devoted to operas and orchestral works. It is not surprising that the young Britten, who played classical piano works including those of Beethoven and Brahms, should start by imitating them in his own Sonatas. These are merely curiosities, included here to compare Britten's attempts at sonata writing with the juvenilia of other composers. It also illuminates Britten's stylistic development throughout the 1920s.

Britten's twelve Piano Sonatas date from 1923 to 1928, and all are unpublished. The surviving manuscripts are held in the Britten–Pears Library at Aldeburgh. The three Sonatas written in 1922 and 1923 are incomplete. The opening of the E minor *Sonata Fantasti* is reproduced by Mitchell and Reed.[43] This Sonata, as well as the A flat Sonata, contains the direction "forth [sic] movement".

Sonata in B flat (1925) is a four-movement work, following the classical plan of fast movement, slow movement, scherzo and trio, and fast movement. The third movement contains a theme subsequently used in the *Playful Pizzicato* from the *Simple Symphony* (1934) [Fig. 3.19]. A footnote to the published score of the latter work traces its origin to a Scherzo of 1924. It is possible that this movement existed independently, before the writing of the Sonata, but I have been unable to trace it. The piano original was transposed to F major for the *Playful Pizzicato*, and a 6/8 time signature replaced the fast 3/4. The Sonata uses two-part textures throughout, whereas the string version uses imitation more effectively. There are some minor changes made. The *Playful Pizzicato* does not use triplets, but

---

[42] Carpenter, 1992, 433.
[43] Mitchell and Reed (eds.), 1991, 77.

generally the piano original is reproduced for the first twenty-two bars. The trios of the two works are quite different.

Fig. 3.19 Britten, Sonata in B flat (1925), Manuscript, Third movement, Bars 1–44

Unpublished excerpts from Benjamin Britten's Sonata in B flat (1925) are © copyright the Trustees of the Britten–Pears Foundation, and may not be further reproduced without the written permission of the Trustees.

The *Simple Symphony* adapts many different themes from Britten's student compositions, and the *Frolicsome Finale* uses material from the Sonata in C sharp minor (1926). The third movement of this work begins with an introductory rising fifth figure, as does *Frolicsome Finale* [Fig. 3.20]. The string parts begin with a repeated note, which keeps them within the required range. Britten transposed the piano version from C sharp minor to G minor. The ensuing melody is also the same, although the accompaniment in the later version is sparser.

Fig. 3.20 Britten, Sonata in C sharp minor, Manuscript, Third movement, Bars 1–4

Unpublished excerpts from Benjamin Britten's Sonata in C sharp minor (1926) are © copyright the Trustees of the Britten–Pears Foundation, and may not be further reproduced without the written permission of the Trustees.

Following the writing of the Sonata in C sharp minor, Britten had an eighteen-month break before returning to this genre. The last three Piano Sonatas show a considerable advance in his musical language, and coincide with the beginning of his education with Frank Bridge. His previous sonatas had been clearly diatonic, using frequent arpeggio and alberti bass patterns, classical key relationships and modulations. The Sonata in B flat (September 1927) shows the advance in his language clearly [Fig. 3.21]. The harmonies are more adventurous and the structure of the work is more episodic. Britten abandons the expositional repeat, and the sonata form is more heavily disguised.

Fig. 3.21 Britten, Sonata in B flat (1927), Manuscript, First movement, Bars 1–14

Unpublished excerpts from Benjamin Britten's Sonata in B flat (1927) are © copyright the Trustees of the Britten–Pears Foundation, and may not be further reproduced without the written permission of the Trustees.

Its second movement uses the irregular time signature 7/4, possibly influenced by Britten's knowledge of the music of Holst [Fig. 3.22]. This movement is concerned with exploiting sonorities, and it follows directly from the end of the previous movement without a break.

Britten's unpublished works do not play an important part in the development of the British piano sonata. However, it is interesting to consider why a composer who wrote a considerable number of piano sonatas whilst very young, became dissatisfied with the form and failed to

Fig. 3.22 Britten, Sonata in B flat (1927), Second movement, Bars 1–6

Unpublished excerpts from Benjamin Britten's Sonata in B flat (1927) are © copyright the Trustees of the Britten–Pears Foundation, and may not be further reproduced without the written permission of the Trustees.

develop the genre. Britten felt that the piano lacked the emotional intensity of other instruments, and to a melodist, this was a major disadvantage – although Schubert, Schumann and Chopin did not find it a problem. Britten considered music to be a social event. His music was mainly designed to be communal and participatory, and consequently he wrote few pieces for soloists. The other major British composers, Delius, Elgar, Holst, Vaughan Williams and Walton, did not write piano sonatas. Nevertheless, Delius, Elgar, Vaughan Williams, Bax and Britten all wrote piano concertos. Britten was unusual in that he was the only proficient pianist who wrote very little solo music for the instrument.

Scott-Sutherland once asked Scott why it was that few British composers wrote significant piano works. His answer was that, to write good piano music, one must be a good composer and a good pianist.[44] All the above-mentioned British composers played the piano as children, yet they did not consider themselves to be proficient pianists. The situation of Elgar has already been discussed at the end of Chapter 1 (p. 31). Delius, Holst, Vaughan Williams and Walton all wrote at least one piano work, but their orchestral music has overshadowed these pieces. However, with the resurgence of interest in the English musical renaissance, there has been an influx of recordings of piano music.

The major works discussed in this chapter illustrate the importance of impressionist influences upon the British piano sonata. This influence had first manifested itself in Scott's First Sonata, but during the subsequent decade the appeal of impressionist harmony to the British composer became overwhelming. This influence resulted both from the performance of French music in Britain, including Debussy and Ravel, and through Scriabin. Scriabin's music was the result of an exaggeration and intensification of impressionist ideals. His interest in mysticism and his Eastern European nationality provided a lure for British composers seeking an exotic influence. Scriabin's pianism, harmonic techniques and formal schemes

---

[44] Scott-Sutherland, 1973, 104.

became the most important influences upon the development of the British piano sonata between 1909 and 1925. The British composer had at last found an alternative to the Austro-German tradition. The way in which Sorabji and Bridge used the discovery of Scriabin's style is now of major importance.

4

Piano Sonatas by Sorabji and Bridge

In this chapter, my discussion concentrates on two sonatas: the First Sonata by Sorabji (1919) and the Sonata by Bridge (1921–4). These works, like the Second and Third Piano Sonatas by Bax (1919–20 and 1926), and the Sonata by Ireland (1920), were composed in the post-war period. Taken as a group, these sonatas form the climax of my study. Sorabji and Bridge have been included in a separate chapter in order to compare the influence of Scriabin on their respective harmonic languages.

Kaikhosru Shapurji Sorabji (1892–1988)

Sorabji wrote six piano sonatas between 1917 and 1935. The earliest was neither performed nor published and appears to have been discounted by Sorabji, who called his subsequent Piano Sonata of 1919 No. 1. The first three Piano Sonatas were published and the Fourth and Fifth remain in manuscript.

I have decided to concentrate my study on Sonata No. 1 and mention the others only in passing. This corresponds to my treatment of other composers who have written several sonatas – they tended to make their impact with the first one. This has already been seen in the case of Cyril Scott. Bax's Second Sonata made a greater impact than his First, owing to the on-going revisions of the First in the decade after its composition. The compositional techniques that are described here are representative of Sorabji's First Sonata, and are also demonstrated in his Second and Third Sonatas.

Sorabji's sonatas are virtuoso works, following in the Lisztian tradition. They make almost impossible demands upon the technique of the pianist and require a great deal of stamina. At approximately twenty minutes, the First Sonata is the shortest. All are single-movement works, like Liszt's B minor Sonata and most of Scriabin's. They encompass a wide range of moods and textures. Nevertheless, the demands placed upon the pianist in Sorabji's Piano Sonatas are not quite as gruelling as those in his *Opus*

Clavicembalisticum, which lasts more than three hours, nor his three-volume Symphonic Variations for piano, which last eight hours in total. Sorabji had heard the first performance of *Sonata Teutonica* Op. 24 by John Powell on 7 March 1914, which may have been the first piano sonata to last more than one hour.[1]

Sorabji's style is an intensification and exaggeration of romantic ideals. He embraced those of large-scale conception, structural and textural complexity and virtuosity. Sorabji believed that all the great musical works had been complex, citing Bach's Mass in B minor, Beethoven's Hammerklavier Sonata and Wagner's *Ring* cycle as examples.[2] He thought that simple works were merely academic and non-stimulating, so Sorabji followed these principles in the hope that he would create great works of art.

Sorabji was an eccentric outsider. Instead of living in an ivory tower, he envisaged himself in a granite tower, with plentiful supplies of boiling oil that he could pour on unwelcome visitors.[3] He was homosexual, the only child of a Parsi father who had married bigamously and of a dominant, Spanish-Sicilian mother. Throughout his life he suffered with racial and sexual identity problems. Although he spent most of his life in Britain, he did not consider himself to be a British composer, and referred to himself as a Spanish-Sicilian Parsi.[4] Thus he was alienated in all aspects of his lifestyle, not only from the traditional musical mainstream like Scott. Perhaps Sorabji's love for the piano can be viewed as a reflection of his solitary existence. He is the most extreme example of the composer as recluse, writing advanced and difficult music with very limited performance opportunities and virtually no audience.

Although his mother gave him his first piano lessons and he received elementary instruction in Western music theory and harmony from Charles Trew at the London Organ School before 1915, Sorabji was largely a self-taught composer. Despite his initial training, he soon grew to hate Germanic music with a vengeance and his style owes more to the impressionism and mysticism of Scriabin, coupled with an interest in Eastern music.

Sorabji's First Piano Sonata opens with a descending flourish, presenting an important seven-note motif that appears in semiquavers in the highest part, with a simultaneous presentation in rhythmic augmentation in the middle part [Fig. 4.1]. This descending melodic motif recurs throughout the

---

[1] John Powell (1882–1963) was an American pianist, composer and ethnomusicologist. He wrote three piano sonatas, of which this is the last, written between 1906 and 1913. Sorabji heard a performance by Moiseiwitsch at the Bechstein Hall. The Sonata was recorded in 1977 and published in a shortened version edited by Roy Hamlin Johnson, New York and London, OUP, 1983.
[2] Sorabji, 1932, 115.
[3] Sorabji, 1947, 141–8.
[4] Ibid., 76–9.

Sonata. The first recurrence of the melodic motif is in bar 3, where it is transposed down a fourth and slightly modified, with every note harmonized. The harmonizations consist mainly of altered dominant chords, with the occasional triad. The modification of melodic ideas occurs immediately, rather than being saved for a special development section. This continues the principle of thematic transformation, demonstrated previously in the Sonatas of Dale, Scott and Bax.

Fig. 4.1 Sorabji, Sonata No. 1, London & Continental, Bars 1–4

Meanwhile, the bass part accompanies the motif with a dominant ninth and thirteenth chord built on A. Sorabji admitted being obsessed by the sonority of Scriabin's mystic chord, which can be described as a dominant thirteenth with the addition of an augmented eleventh (or tritone) [Fig. 2.19].[5] Comparison of Sorabji's chord with Scriabin's mystic chord reveals that Sorabji omits one note from the accompaniment, but the missing D sharp appears at the end of the bar in the melody. Also in the manner of Scriabin, Sorabji's spacing of the chord exposes the fourths. It is used to accompany the main presentations of this motif and its frequent use as a

[5] Sorabji, *The New Age*, 19 July 1934, 141–2.

characteristic sonority throughout the Sonata has led me to use the term quasi-mystic chord when referring to it. Thus the impact of the opening bar is both horizontal and vertical. Fig. 4.2 illustrates the numerous recurrences of this motif, in both harmonic and melodic forms. The continual transformation of the melodic motifs and the harmonies provide the listener with a sense of the music moving in and out of focus.

Fig. 4.2 Recurrences of Sorabji's quasi-mystic motif

Bar	Harmonic	Melodic	Comments
1	Y	Y	First presentation
1–2		Y	In augmentation
3		Y	Transposed down perfect fourth
5	Y		Transposed up minor second. Non-chord note in bass. Identical to mystic chord
11	Y	Y	
13	Y	Y	Fragmented
17		Y	
18	Y	Y	Transposed down major second
25	Y		
38		Y	
53	Y	Y	
61	Y	Y	
65	Y	Y	Same pitch as opening
88	Y	Y	
105	Y	Y	Same as bar 1
113–14		Y	cf. bar 3
128	Y		
149	Y	Y	

Bar	Harmonic	Melodic	Comments
156	Y	Y	
167		Y	
177		Y	
191	Y		
204	Y	Y	
205		Y	
209		Y	
236	Y	Y	cf. bar 1, D sharp explicit
254	Y		
255	Y		
259	Y		

Sorabji's harmonies are usually built from the bass upwards, and generally follow logical root progressions. Thus the bass A from bar 1 is reiterated in bar 2, below a dominant seventh arpeggio on D. This note is already contradicted by the D sharp octave above, and augmented triads in the upper part of bar 2 negate any tonal implications of the D7 arpeggio. This rising arpeggio adds an increasing number of chromatic notes as it approaches its peak. These are like upper partials, and it is a characteristic Sorabji technique. His low bass notes tend to be prolonged like pedal notes, and provide stability, whilst upper parts move rapidly through chromatic areas. Also in this bar, G sharp acts as an important focal note, which is a tritone above D. Tritone relationships, used both melodically and harmonically, are important in Sorabji's Sonata, as in the music of Scriabin. The following excerpt from a letter to Philip Heseltine illustrates Sorabji's obsession with Scriabin's music:

> Scriabine is to my mind a colossal genius and there is, to me at any rate, nothing in the whole range of music quite so wonderful and strangely, wierdly [sic] <u>beautiful</u> as his marvellous music.[6]

---

[6] Lbm Add MS 57963 (Heseltine papers). This example is taken from collection H1, 3 October 1913.

Bar 5 uses Scriabin's mystic chord built upon B flat with the addition of the non-chord note F in the bass. The relative stability of altered dominant chords and quasi-mystic chords connected by a logical bass are contrasted and negated by the instability of tritones and free atonality. This accounts for the fascination of Sorabji's harmonic technique.

Sorabji was influenced by impressionism and uses chords for their sonorities and sensual effect. He described his use of harmony as metadiatonic.[7] This means that isolated chords can be explained within the diatonic system, but their relationship to one another cannot be analysed in terms of any particular key. His fondness for the impressionism of Debussy and Ravel is seen in early piano works such as *Le jardin parfumé* and in his song settings of Baudelaire (*Correspondances*, 1918) and Verlaine (*Pantomime*, 1919). This influence is also illustrated by Sorabji's hypersensitivity to sonority. The score of his First Sonata is littered with voluptuous expression marks and performance directions, mostly in French. These are derived, through Scriabin, from Symbolist poetry.

In bar 23 of Sorabji's Sonata, the outer parts of the right hand remain on A whilst the inner parts oscillate. This creates the effect of a constantly changing shimmer of sound. This climax is similar to bars 144–7 of the second movement of Scriabin's Fourth Sonata, where the Andante theme of the first movement returns above a succession of changing dominant chords. Sorabji also appears to anticipate some of the pianistic sonorities of Messiaen, such as using second inversion triads with added tritones. He spaces dominant thirteenth chords by placing the seventh above the thirteenth, resulting in a minor second at the top.

Another important harmonic resource is bitonality, both in chords and as a result of the superimposition of individual musical lines. Sometimes, Sorabji uses both major and minor thirds simultaneously, as in the music of Stravinsky and Bartók. At other times, chords result from the superimposition of unrelated triads. Harmonic saturation is relieved by the periodic use of triads. For example, in bar 19, right hand F major triads are accompanied by an ostinato of conflicting perfect fourths (E flat and A flat). The use of rhythmic displacement to the repetitions is interesting. The resulting rhythm is 4:3, but the right hand has three repetitions of each triad whilst the left hand has a syncopated pattern in triplets oscillating between two notes. This passage illustrates that despite initial appearances, the work is by no means entirely improvisatory.

The second section, from bar 29, is quieter and more lyrical in character. The widely spaced arpeggio accompaniment and lyrical melody are a reminder of Chopin's Nocturnes [Fig. 4.3]. The left hand pattern even repeats an octave higher. There is a misprint in bar 30 of the published score. The first note of the right hand should be a crotchet, not a dotted crotchet. The main melodic idea is again a descending one, now consisting

[7] In Chisholm, *c*. 1938.

of a chromatic descent. Thus it may be related to the end of the quasi-mystic motif, in inversion.

Fig. 4.3 Sorabji, Sonata No. 1, Bars 29–30

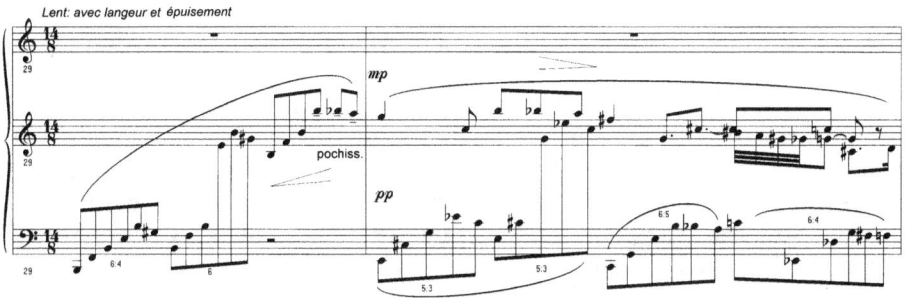

This second section is athematic but it can be distinguished from the first section by its contrasting character. Musical material associated with the first subject includes virtuoso displays of repeated chords and, later in the Sonata, bravura octave passages and trill-tremolos. The second section is more introspective and static. Thus the differences between the two sections are textural rather than thematic.

The frequent changes of time signature and flexible groupings of beats give the impression that the Sonata is a written-out improvisation, although some aspects of the music were carefully planned. Additionally, the use of irrational rhythms such as 6:4 and 5:3 give the impression of spontaneous flow. This rhythmic technique is a logical development of Chopin's piano writing and early Scriabin, where irregular groups of notes in one hand are required to fit against a regular accompaniment in the other. Sorabji, however, frequently combines two irregular groups, and by taking this principle to an unprecedented degree of complexity he anticipates the techniques of Michael Finnissy and Brian Ferneyhough by approximately fifty years.

The two main ideas, the virtuoso and static textures, are increasingly fragmented and juxtaposed, so that climaxes become successively closer together as the work progresses. Unusually for Sorabji, the work ends quietly. The whole work has moved from A to B flat, a large-scale replica of the tonal shift in the first section that began on A and ended on B flat. Sorabji's coda summarizes the main harmonic principles used throughout the work: the quasi-mystic chord, tritones, and bitonality. The bass pedals form harmonic anchors to the chromaticism above. Thus the end indicates the relationships that have been operating and helps to prove the hierarchies established.

Sorabji, driven to fever pitch in a unique musical language, assimilates many diverse influences. The style of Sonata No. 1 was unprecedented, and it demonstrates Sorabji's individuality. The First Sonata works successfully, owing to its concise length. It is a well-paced work, and its improvisatory character is given a sense of direction owing to the recurrence of the opening motif.

The type of pianism employed by Sorabji is appropriate to the instrument. The spatial separation of the hands provides a contrast between the low and high registers of the piano. Most of the music is written on three staves for clarity, and each stave overflows with notes. Other piano works by Sorabji use up to seven staves simultaneously. Sorabji invented his own notation to prevent the pianist struggling to read leger lines. He used the symbol I/VIII at the beginning of a system to indicate that the notes are to be played an octave higher than written in the First and Second Sonatas.[8] The piano was his favourite means of expression; Sorabji considered the instrument to be part of him and it therefore follows that he composed at the piano.[9]

Note clusters illustrate Sorabji's physical pianism. The full potential of the fingers is utilized, playing up to seven notes simultaneously. Elsewhere, right hand chords frequently contain the interval of a second at the bottom, which the thumb plays by striking two keys simultaneously. Tremolos, a pianistic device influenced by Scriabin and ultimately derived from Beethoven's Piano Sonata Op. 111, are used frequently. Repeated octaves are used to relieve harmonic saturation. These motoric sections provide the work with unexpectedly conventional but effective displays of brilliance.

Although this work is titled Sonata, it is far removed from the conventional Western concept of this genre. It can be compared to musical prose. The content creates the form owing to a succession of climaxes and there is a sense of narrative evolution. Sorabji hated systems of composition, hence the work took shape intuitively. Improvisation is used as a counter to sonata structure.

Sorabji's music flows freely and can be compared to Ives' *Concord Sonata* (1911–15), Scott's First Sonata and the works of Delius. Scott's and Sorabji's first sonatas are of similar lengths. Whereas Scott subdivides his continuous sonata into movements, Sorabji does not. Both Scott and Sorabji were interested in the occult and separated themselves from the musical mainstream. They were more interested in subjective expression than modern abstraction, either twelve-note or neo-classical. Sorabji's Sonata is more successful than Scott's because he builds the whole movement upon figures and gestures derived from the opening motif and its accompanying harmonization. He has a well-paced rate of harmonic and textural change throughout and he deliberately avoids repetition.

Like Scriabin, Sorabji's interest in mysticism and the occult influenced aspects of his compositions. He frequently used number symbolism to

---

[8] In the Third, he used a Roman I with a ^ above (Î) or below (I̬) to indicate that the notes are to be played an octave higher or lower.
[9] Ibid., 34.

determine in advance the number of pages or variations that there were to be in a work, although there is no evidence to suggest that his First Sonata was conceived to a numerical plan. His Second Sonata consists of 49 pages (seven squared), Sonata No. 4 consists of 111 pages (he was fond of repeated digits) and in Sonata No. 5, which is heavily influenced by tarot, the significance of the number 343 (7 cubed) is preserved by numbering the final page 343a instead of 344.

Thus from Western music, Sorabji synthesized elements from the impressionists and Scriabin. These influences affected his use of harmony, tonal centres, sonority, piano technique and some aspects of form. Nevertheless, his Sonatas are original contributions to the genre. However, there is another aspect to consider, that of Eastern music. His immediate ancestry embraced both Western and Eastern elements.

Eastern visual art uses intricate patterning, and extemporisation upon a simple motive is a feature of its music. Sorabji blends Western-derived harmonies with Eastern principles of decoration. Despite their decorative function, these notes are an essential part of Sorabji's unique sound-world. His music has a melodic basis, and much of it results from the combination of linear parts. He uses ostinati to provide stability. Following another Eastern principle, Sorabji's music is improvisatory in character, although notated and fixed as in Western music. Indian music has a much larger conception of time than European music and it is not uncommon for a single work to fill a complete evening.

Thus, there is a blend of Western and Indian influences in Sorabji. The only other composer to have attempted to synthesize both aspects was the British composer John Foulds (1880–1939) who taught Indian musicians to read and notate music, in order to create an orchestra consisting of both Western and Indian instruments. However, other composers, especially the French, used non-Western elements in their music, such as the evocation of the gamelan and pentatonic modes. Holst was influenced by the oriental tunes that he had heard whilst on holiday in Algeria, as seen in his orchestral suite, *Beni Mora* (1909–10). Like Scott and Sorabji, Holst was also interested in astrology and Indian philosophy, although he was discreet about his mystic influences, whereas Scott and Sorabji were not. Sorabji can be considered to belong to a post-Debussy, pre-Messiaen era.

Sorabji hated modern music, but he championed the music of European composers who were considered unfashionable at the time.[10] He praised the works of Mahler, Busoni, Szymanowsky, Chausson, Rachmaninov, Delius and Medtner, whose Piano Sonata No. 2 in E minor he felt was one of the greatest piano works.[11] Sorabji's admiration for Bowen (see Chapter 2) may be explained by regarding Bowen's music as a continuation of the Chopin-Scriabin pianism that Sorabji adopted. Bowen, like

[10] Rapoport, 1988, 263–5.
[11] Sorabji, 1932, 59.

Sorabji, was neglected, and even at this time he was a survivor of a past age.

Sorabji met Busoni in 1919 and became a great admirer of his music. He dedicated piano works to him, including the First and Second Sonatas.[12] Busoni's *Fantasia Contrappuntistica* was a profound influence upon Sorabji's style, seen especially in *Opus Clavicembalisticum* (1930).[13] By this time he was writing massive fugal sections clearly influenced by his love of Bach, Busoni and Reger.

Bernard van Dieren, a close friend of Sorabji's, had settled in London in 1909. His anarchic harmony was unprecedented. Heseltine was also a close friend, and Sorabji wrote articles for Heseltine's journal, *The Sackbut*. Through him, Sorabji knew Lambert and the Sitwells. Thus Sorabji was more allied to the British avant-garde than to the mainstream. He was never connected with any British institution, unlike most of his contemporaries.

The complexity of Sorabji's Piano Sonatas has deterred most pianists from attempting them. As Sorabji was a pianist, he was able to perform his own works, following in the tradition of the romantic composer-pianists such as Liszt and Scott. However, he never had any desire to perform the standard repertoire. Sorabji could create his own performance opportunities, and he made his recital debut at the Mortimer Hall with a performance of his First Piano Sonata.[14] Sorabji performed his First and Second Sonatas in Vienna in 1922, but the first performance of the Second Sonata in England did not take place until 1924.[15] He performed his Fourth Piano Sonata in Glasgow, at a concert organized by Erik Chisholm's Active Society for the Propagation of Contemporary Music, on 1 April 1930.[16]

Sorabji's father funded the printing of his son's compositions from 1921 until his death in 1932.[17] In the first review of the published score of Sonata No. 1, the editor of the *Musical Times* noted that "not often is one so baffled by the printed page" and that "Mr. Sorabji would have done better

---

[12] He played his First Piano Sonata to Busoni in November 1919, in Maud Allen's studio in Regent's Park. See Rapoport, 1988, 254. The dedication to Busoni appears only on the manuscript of the First Sonata, not the published version.

[13] Sorabji reviewed a performance of the Busoni, performed by Egon Petri, in London, 1929.

[14] 2 November 1920. *The Sackbut* promoted this concert. Forty-four copies of this Sonata were sold in the first three weeks according to Sorabji's letter to Heseltine, 8 November 1921, Lbm Add MS 57963.

[15] 13 January 1922, Musikverein, Kammersaal; 13 May 1924, British Music Society concert at the Contemporary Music Centre.

[16] Sorabji, *The New Age*, 17 April 1930, 284. Sorabji noted the "concentrated and sympathetic attention" paid by the audience. He appreciated the loyal championship of his music by Chisholm, who expended considerable energy on the promotion of contemporary music.

[17] Due to the efforts of Norman Peterkin, a friend of Sorabji's, the fourteen works that were published between these dates by three different publishers became available from OUP in 1938, the company of which Peterkin was Chief Music Editor. OUP remained the sole selling agent for Sorabji's works until 1988.

to publish it straight away as a player-piano roll."[18] On most of the published scores appears the sentence "All rights, including that of performance, reserved by the composer." Sorabji did not allow recordings of his work to be made, even by himself, as he realized that under the existing copyright law, he would lose his exclusive rights to the work if he did so. Thus his later works were in danger of being paper music. Sorabji gave his last public piano recital in 1936.

Sorabji became increasingly dissatisfied with concert procedures and c. 1940 he imposed the notorious ban on performances of his works. This seems to have been prompted by a poor performance of *Opus Clavicembalisticum* by John Tobin in 1936 that lasted about ninety minutes as opposed to fifty. Sorabji felt that both performers and audiences mishandled his music and so he stipulated that his consent was needed before a performance could occur. Sorabji needed to be in complete control of his life, and the performance ban is one example of this. Also, he was secretive about details of his birth date, because this could reveal astrological information about himself that could be potentially damaging and would make him vulnerable to curses.

Sorabji had an idealistic and almost religious attitude towards his music. His chief concern was with composition rather than performance, and he felt that "no performance at all is vastly preferable to an obscene travesty".[19] He wanted to make his music available only to a selected audience and he had no sympathy for the masses. Just as other composers wrote music for a specific performer, Sorabji considered his music suitable only for its dedicatee. Like Alkan, whom he admired, Sorabji withdrew his works. He condemned all popular and commercial music, viewing music as a serious art form rather than entertainment. This illustrates the gulf between the British composer and his public then. The general public wanted popular music as entertainment, and the composer who continued to write serious music for a committed audience found the size of that audience dwindling. Sorabji was fortunate in having a private income. He did not need to earn a living as a composer or performer, although he was a critic for *The Sackbut* (1920–1), *The New Age* (1924–34), and *The New English Weekly* (1932–45). He was grossly self-opinionated and his writings are provocative, damning those who could not accept him as he was. His attitude towards music was extraordinarily elitist.

During the 1950s, Frank Holliday wrote a letter, obtaining signatures from sympathetic musicians worldwide, in an attempt to persuade Sorabji to make recordings. They were unsuccessful in their attempt, although during the 1960s Holliday made private recordings of Sorabji playing his own works.[20]

---

[18] Grace, *MT*, 1921, 781.
[19] in MacDiarmid, 1966, 39.
[20] Six recording sessions took place between May 1962 and April 1968 at Sorabji's home in Corfe Castle, Dorset.

By this time, Sorabji was in his seventies and the tapes are full of mistakes. It was not until 1976 that Yonty Solomon was granted permission to perform his works, as Solomon was a pupil of Sorabji's close friend, Erik Chisholm.[21] In 1977, Sorabji allowed London Weekend Television to record an interview at his home, which was broadcast as a documentary and included Solomon playing examples of his piano music.[22] Solomon performed Sorabji's Third Sonata in June 1977, which was received warmly by critics.[23] They disagreed widely over its duration, three reviews timing it at 90, 75 and 65 minutes, although it actually lasted about 73 minutes.[24] Like the First and Second Sonatas, this is a single movement work but it is notated without barlines.[25] It is organic in construction, growing out of the initial rising sequence of quavers that Sorabji called a radix, which pervades the entire work in some form or other. Canonic and fugato sections are used as a contrast to the freer ones, and a fugal section is used towards the end to bring the work to an impressive climax.

Also in 1977, Sorabji granted the American pianist Michael Habermann permission to play his music in public. Initially this was to exclude performances in England, for Solomon's benefit, although Sorabji later lifted this restriction.

One of the chief problems hindering performances of Sorabji's works today, is that in 1988 all of his music went out of print. Additionally there are many errors in his published scores, which are not immediately obvious. Sorabji could see no benefit in reissuing error-ridden copies of his scores. His manuscripts are held at several locations around the world, but Alistair Hinton has established the Sorabji Archive in Bath, which keeps microfilms of some of them and acts as a co-ordinating centre for research.[26] Sorabji frequently made several versions of the same work, or called a piece by several different titles, causing many problems in the attempt to catalogue a full list of his works. Fortunately, compact disc recordings of Sorabji's music are becoming more common, and his Piano Sonatas may soon become familiar to a wider public.

[21] Solomon's performance at the Wigmore Hall in December 1976 included *Le jardin parfumé*, Two Piano Pieces (*In the Hothouse* and *Toccata*) and *Fantaisie espagnole*.
[22] Transmitted June 1977. Derek Bailey was the producer, Russell Harty the presenter.
[23] This was the first documented public performance. There may have been an earlier one, owing to the availability of the published score.
[24] Chisholm, *c*. 1938, states that it lasts about 45 minutes. Sorabji says it lasts about 75 minutes in a letter to Heseltine, 19 June 1922, Lbm Add MS 57963.
[25] The Fourth Piano Sonata (unpublished) is in three movements with a complicated finale that is almost self-contained. See Browne, *ML*, 1930, 6–16.
[26] The Sorabji Archive, Easton Dene, Bailbrook Lane, Bath, BA1 7AA, England; tel. 01225 852323, Fax 01225 852523, Website http: //www.music.mcgill.ca/~schulman/sorabji.html)

Frank Bridge (1879–1941)

Before World War I, Bridge had composed easily and prolifically, but he produced no large-scale works between his Cello Sonata (1913–17) and Piano Sonata (1921–4). He sketched an opera, *The Christmas Rose*, in 1919, but it was not completed until 1929. There were several factors contributing to his small output during this period. The war had led to a reduction in piano sales whilst the gramophone was gaining in popularity. The wireless was first used for time and weather reports in 1919, the British Broadcasting Corporation was formed in 1922 and the wireless boom commenced in 1923. As a consequence, Bridge's royalties from sheet music declined and despite some income from his viola playing and conducting, it became necessary for him to teach. Thus he had little time to compose.

Bridge's financial crisis coincided with a period of stylistic crisis. He felt that his old and mainly nineteenth-century diatonic musical language was no longer appropriate, as nothing in life could ever be the same again. Unlike most British composers who had studied under Stanford at the Royal College, Bridge had not reacted against his training in the Austro-German tradition, essentially derived from Brahms. His stylistic development was a gradual process, in which the war acted as a catalyst. This was not consistent; Bridge, like Schoenberg, frequently looked back to a previous style whilst experimenting with a new one.

The war affected Bridge, a committed pacifist, deeply and personally. In 1915, he wrote *Lament* for strings, dedicated to Catherine, a nine year old who had lost her life during the sinking of the Lusitania. In 1918, Bridge wrote Three Improvisations for Left Hand for Douglas Fox, a pianist who had lost his right arm in the war. Bridge's fellow musicians Thomas Morris and Frederick Kelly were killed in action, and he dedicated his Piano Sonata to Ernest Bristowe Farrar, an English composer lost in the war. Bridge mainly wrote abstract music, although he did write some evocative pieces for orchestra. The experience of war enabled him to make a major statement in the form of an abstract piano sonata that nevertheless appears to depict images of war and his personal reaction to it.

In 1922, Bridge met the American music patron Elizabeth Sprague Coolidge, who gave him a regular stipend and organized performances of his chamber works. In return, he dedicated works to her. Coolidge also commissioned works by Stravinsky, Schoenberg, Bartók and Hindemith, hence Bridge might have met them and heard their music at the annual Berkshire Festival in Pittsfield, Massachusetts, which Coolidge had inaugurated in 1918.[27] Certainly he was present in 1923 to hear Hindemith's Third String Quartet. The most important influence upon Bridge's style, as

---

[27] Pears, *Recorded Sound*, 1977, 666, quotes Britten recalling that Bridge had introduced him to Schoenberg, after Berg's death (1935).

in the case of Sorabji, was that of Scriabin. It is impossible to ascertain exactly which pieces by Scriabin Bridge knew, or whether the two composers had ever met when Scriabin visited London in 1914.

Bridge had always placed the public first, writing music that was accessible to performer and audience, but now he was faced with reacting to the war. Coolidge's patronage had widened his outlook, and he realized that it was necessary to become less provincial if he was to be recognized internationally. The first work that exemplified this new style was the Piano Sonata.

The Sonata is in three movements, to be played continuously. It is written on an epic scale, and is of consistent emotional intensity. Bridge had been a keen contributor to Cobbett's one-movement Phantasy competitions, writing a Phantasy Quartet in 1905, Phantasy Trio in C minor in 1907 and a Phantasy Quartet in F sharp minor in 1910. One-movement works tend to express unity in diversity and in Bridge's Piano Sonata there is an organic unfolding of themes. Schoenberg also uses this technique in his early works, for instance in the String Quartet in D minor (1904–5) and String Quartet No. 2 (1907–8).

The first movement of Bridge's Sonata is in arch form rather than sonata form, therefore the recapitulation of ideas occurs in reverse. At the end of the movement, the listener is returned to the starting point. Themes are rarely repeated exactly; recurring motifs act as static pillars around which the other material is shaped. As early as 1906 Bridge had written a Dramatic Fantasia for piano (originally called Sonata), which was also in arch form.[28] The harmonies of the Piano Sonata are ambiguous and frequently bitonal, so Bridge needed to find a method for articulating form without relying on tonal relationships. Like Sorabji, Bridge used the principles of thematic transformation, although his Piano Sonata has much more in common with a traditional sonata structure than Sorabji's.

The first movement begins with an introduction, a common feature in Bridge's music, in which the main motifs are presented. This immediately conjures up images of war, the high G sharp octaves sounding like the tolling of bells. It recalls Wilfred Owen's poem, *Anthem For Doomed Youth*, beginning, "What passing bells for these who die as cattle?". The G sharps are reiterated above chorale-like low bass chords (A min, C min, B min, D min), creating a stark bitonal opening. Throughout the movement, G sharp (and its enharmonic equivalent, A flat) acts as an important focal note.

Like Scriabin, Bridge characterizes themes by giving them individual tempo markings. Bridge's themes are short and fragmented, juxtaposing rhythm, mood, pace and intensity. An important phrase, which will be called the compassion motif, begins at bar 11 [Fig. 4.4]. The melody consists of a descending scale and a perfect fourth, which is repeated with the addition of an ornamental figure in the next bar. This melodic motif is

[28] MacDonald, sleeve notes to Continuum CCD 1018.

closely related to one in Bridge's *Summer* (1914) [Fig. 4.5].[29] This type of melodic decoration seems to be derived from the vocal ornamentation of folksong.

Fig. 4.4 Bridge, Piano Sonata, Stainer & Bell, First movement, Bars 11–15

Fig. 4.5 Bridge, *Summer*, Stainer & Bell, Oboe 1, Bars 13–21

Following the compassion motif, the bell and chorale motifs return in modified form and are extended. The rising perfect fifth, descending semitone appoggiatura in bars 18–19 and the accompanying chord sequence prove crucial later in generating the first subject, marked Allegro energico. In a similar manner to the piano part of *Speak To Me, My Love*, the second of Bridge's Four Songs (1925), the dirge-like chorale of the introduction uses a dotted rhythm and is accompanied by a pedal [Fig. 4.6].[30] The high G sharps continue throughout this section, eventually being notated enharmonically as A flats. A flat seventh chords descend and resonate like pealing bells, culminating in an unusual cadenza-like passage which never recurs.

Like Beethoven's use of a bare fifth in his Ninth Symphony, the two motifs from Bridge's introduction recur at points of structural importance. The compassion motif recurs at the end of the exposition (bar 113) and at the end of the development (bar 228), transposed, whilst the bell and chorale motifs are heard at the start of the coda (bar 291), unchanged in pitch. This can be compared to similar procedures in Scriabin's Fifth, Ninth and Tenth Piano Sonatas, whose introductions recur at the end of their

[29] Palmer, sleeve notes to Unicorn RHS 359.
[30] Banfield, 1985, 348.

Fig. 4.6 Bridge, Four Songs, Augener, *Speak to Me, My Love*, Bars 10–20

expositions and as conclusions. Like Liszt, Scriabin was capable of deriving everything in a sonata structure from motifs, although his sonatas are on a small scale. Bridge also attempts to write a sonata using a small number of motifs that are modified or superimposed on their recurrence, but his conception of a sonata is on a much larger scale than Scriabin's. The combination of musical ideas illustrates Bridge's organic technique, which he uses throughout the movement.

When the compassion motif returns in the introduction section, it is faster and rhythmically contracted from 4/8 to 3/8. Like Scott, Bridge uses flexible metres, allowing themes to be expanded or contracted fluidly, although later in the movement, metrical changes are used to juxtapose contrasting material rather than for smooth transitions. The compassion motif formed the starting point for my harmonic investigations, because the harmonization of this motif in the Piano Sonata is considerably more dissonant than that in the earlier orchestral work, *Summer*. There are two ways in which the harmonies can be analysed. The score indicates enharmonic triads underpinned by major seconds [Figs. 4.4 and 4.7]. Alternatively, by rewriting the chord in close position, the resultant sonority could be heard as a major seventh chord with added major second and minor sixth. It will be referred to as the Bridge chord version 1. This chord contains an augmented triad, and four of its five notes are present in the whole-tone scale beginning on C. It descends chromatically to accompany the compassion motif, and it is used at a resting-point at the close of the introduction, highlighting its tonic function. This is similar to the way in

Sorabji and Bridge

which Scriabin used his mystic chord as a substitute tonic. The bass note is G sharp, the note with which the introduction began.

Fig. 4.7 Bridge chord

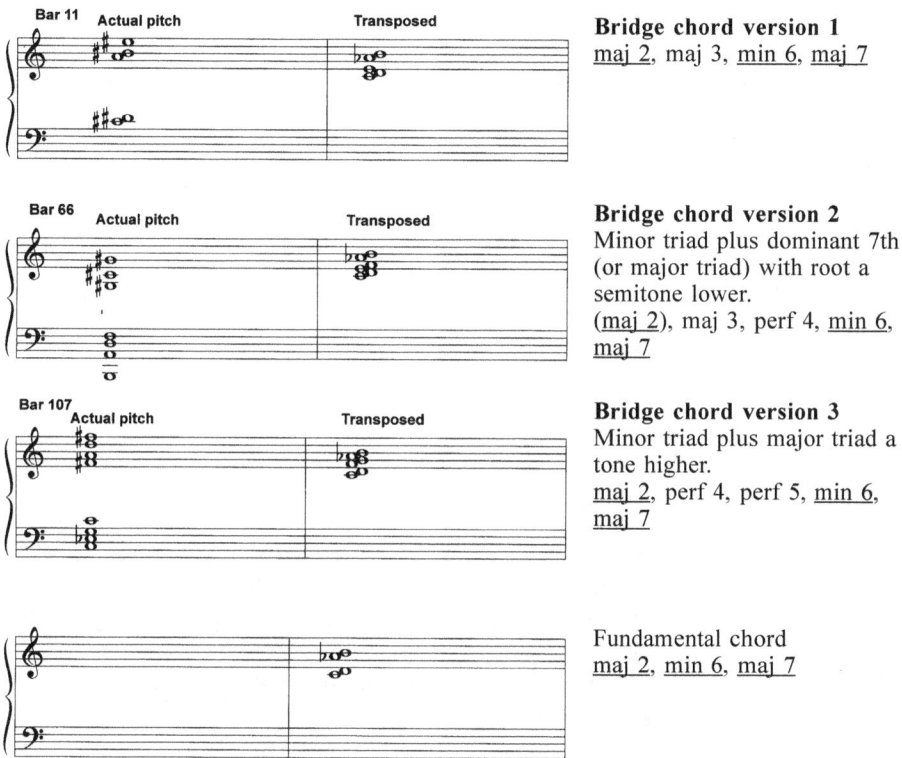

Bridge chord version 1
maj 2, maj 3, min 6, maj 7

Bridge chord version 2
Minor triad plus dominant 7th (or major triad) with root a semitone lower.
(maj 2), maj 3, perf 4, min 6, maj 7

Bridge chord version 3
Minor triad plus major triad a tone higher.
maj 2, perf 4, perf 5, min 6, maj 7

Fundamental chord
maj 2, min 6, maj 7

Bridge must have heard the opening of Scriabin's Sixth Piano Sonata [Fig. 4.8], in which the sonority of bars 5 and 7 is similar to Bridge's. Scriabin's chord is identical to the Bridge chord version 2 [Fig. 4.7].

Consistent bitonality is the main feature of Bridge's harmonic language and is usually similar to that of Milhaud, although in places the two hands play in different keys, having more in common with Stravinsky's *Petrushka*. In bar 45 there are bitonal chords created by the superimposition of two major triads with roots a tritone apart. Bar 66 begins with the superimposition of C sharp major and D minor triads, which have a shared mediant. They are underpinned by a pedal B, a significant focal note with which both the first and last movements end. This chord can be described in two ways. Either it is a chord formed from the superimposition of a minor triad and a dominant seventh chord with its root a semitone below (e.g. D minor + C sharp 7), or alternatively it can be written in close position as a major seventh chord with added major second, perfect fourth and minor

Fig. 4.8 Scriabin, Sixth Piano Sonata, Dover, First movement, Bars 1–9

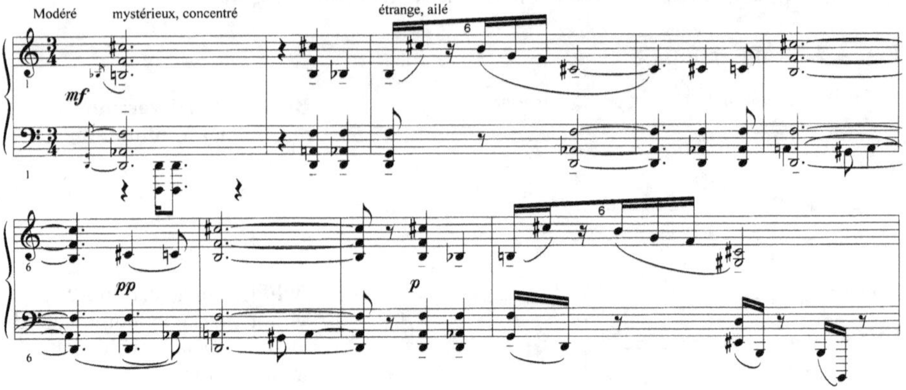

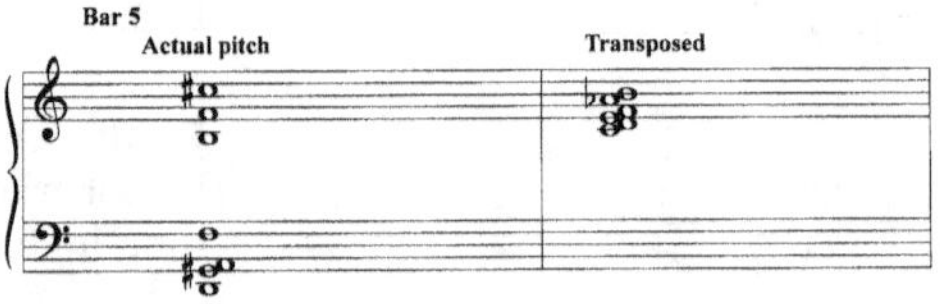

sixth [Fig. 4.7] and shall be called the Bridge chord version 2. If the pedal B in bar 66 was ignored, it could more simply be described as a bitonal chord resulting from the combination of a minor triad plus a major triad a semitone below (e.g. D minor + C sharp). The Bridge chord version 2 appears throughout the first main section and the middle section of the movement.

The expressive second subject, marked Allegro Rubato, is closely related to the first subject, beginning with a descending tone followed by a rising perfect fourth in a dotted rhythm. It develops the interval of a major seventh by doubling the melody in it. The prominence given to this dissonant interval is a result of Scriabin's influence, whose Etude Op. 65/2 is based solely upon the major seventh. The use of major sevenths as a basis for harmony makes Bridge's Sonata almost consistently dissonant.

Another important sonority is heard at bar 107. Bitonality resulting from the combination of a minor triad with a major triad a tone higher (e.g. C minor + D major) is characteristic of the harmonic technique of Bridge's new style. Analysing it in the manner of previous chords reveals that it contains the intervals of major second, perfect fourth, perfect fifth, minor sixth and major seventh, and is referred to as the Bridge chord version 3 [Fig. 4.7]. All three versions of this chord use the intervals major second, minor sixth and major seventh, illustrated by the fundamental chord in Fig. 4.7. The third version of the Bridge chord is the most important. As well as its use in the first movement, it is heard as the final sonority of the last movement of the Sonata.

To contrast with the intense bitonality of the previous sections, when the compassion motif returns at bar 113, it is interrupted by a new answering phrase in bars 114–17. This sounds very English, akin to John Ireland, and recalls Bridge's old diatonic harmonic language, owing to the fact that its harmonies are built upon thirds and sixths, rather than fourths and sevenths. However, the bass notes move through tritones from G sharp to D and back, a progression typical of Scriabin and Sorabji.

The middle section of the arch form (bars 153–227) is an extended section, remaining at constant tempo. The bass oscillates from G sharp, this note being a focal note of the movement. Previous motifs are modified and developed. The first part of this section uses the Bridge chord version 2, both harmonically and melodically, but the third version of the Bridge chord dominates the latter part. The recapitulation of themes in reverse begins with the compassion motif, now combined with the third version of the Bridge chord. Repeated G sharp octaves herald the return of the bell and chorale motifs, now fortissimo forzamente, which are extended. The final Allargando also uses the third version of the Bridge chord, contrasting high and low registers in the manner of the introduction.

The second movement has the typical introspective mood of Bridge's shorter solos such as *Solitude, Ecstasy*, and *Retrospect*. Bridge was a retiring and modest person, who expressed himself most fully through chamber music. This movement represents a private world, which seems to have caused him tremendous problems. The first movement was written between Easter 1921 and 5 May 1922, and the whole work was completed on 3 March 1924.

> At the moment I have renounced that damn slow-arriving slow movement. Yesterday and this morning I got going with an unaccompanied three part song. Words by Thomas Decker [*Golden Slumbers*]. I am thankful I have completed even those few bars. Quite a relief not to have fought for a fortnight over it.
>
> ... the pressing need of the moment is what to do in the next bar. I don't suppose the 'blissfuls' trouble themselves much about such a problem. That's why there is such an output of Melée and Fantasque.[31]

The second movement consists of two themes that alternate and are varied on each presentation. The first theme, Andante ben moderato, is elegiac and bitter, and the harmonies are based on decorations of dominant ninths, sevenths, elevenths and thirteenths, in a similar manner to Scriabin. Descending semitone appoggiaturas in inner parts impart a sense of longing, and can be related to the chorale melody of the first movement.

Bridge's chordal spacing exposes the fourths between upper parts and sevenths in the bass. Despite the advanced bitonality, Bridge's bass lines are

---

[31] From letters to Marjorie Fass dated 22 May 1922 and October [1922] respectively. The reference is to Bliss' early work, *Melée Fantasque* (1921).

often dominant functioning, and resolve in the manner of Berg or Scriabin. A bass ostinato emerges underneath the second version of the Bridge chord in bar 9. Ostinati were characteristic features of Russian music, and the previous chapter demonstrated how Bax used them in his Piano Sonatas.

The second theme begins at bar 14. It contrasts with the first, providing a glimpse back to a pre-war age, similar to the way in which the compassion motif was contrasted with its answering phrase in the first movement. Whereas the first theme was based around flat keys, the second introduces the sharp area. Although the tonal centre is elusive, the chords of the second theme have a diatonic basis and use added sixths and seconds, which are reminiscent of the music of John Ireland.

The two main themes are alternated and reharmonized throughout the movement. Bridge provides thematic unity with the outer movements of the Sonata, by recalling and vaguely hinting at some of their main themes. For example, the melody of bars 31–3 and 36–40 seems to anticipate the main Allegro non troppo theme from the third movement, in rhythmic augmentation. Bar 41 recalls the Allegro animato from the first movement (bar 125). The left hand of bar 50 recalls bar 18 from the first movement, and in the left hand at bar 52, transferring to the right at bar 53, the compassion motif appears. This is a heavily disguised treatment of the motif. Bar 71 anticipates the main theme of the third movement. The second movement ends with the reiteration of low bass chords containing the notes D and A, mirroring the opening of the first movement, which had a high pedal and low melody.

The third movement is in ternary form with a coda. It opens with a Lento introduction, presenting the main march-like theme (Allegro non troppo) in rhythmic augmentation, with G sharp as a focal note, as in the first movement. It consists of a falling semitone (an interval common to all three movements) and low bass chords A min, C min, B min (D min), which were the bass chords of the first movement's chorale motif.

A tritone appoggiatura resolving onto the third of the triad is a feature used regularly, acting as a tonic equivalent for the movement. This motif may be identifiable as a response to war; it is a motif also used by Bridge's pupil Britten in his *War Requiem* (1962), especially in the fifth movement, *Agnus Dei*. Tritones had also been important in *Mars, the Bringer of War*, and *Mercury, the Winged Messenger*, from Holst's *Planets* (1914–16). Bridge's voicing of his chord in the right hand (G–C–F sharp) combines a perfect and augmented fourth, the triad spanning a major seventh. It is similar in structure to the chord at the end of the first movement (bar 329, C–F sharp–B–C) and is identical to the concluding chord of Holst's *Mars*. Composers of the Second Viennese School regularly used this atonal triad as a method of avoiding tonal implications.[32] Later, Bridge uses the atonal

---

[32] It may not sound atonal to someone attuned to the double-leading-note cadence typical of fourteenth-century vocal music.

triad dissonantly as part of a rising melodic sequence, without resolving it. When the Allegro non troppo theme returns in bar 98, the atonal triad harmonizes it.

The third movement recalls motifs and harmonies from the previous movements, such as the compassion motif and the second version of the Bridge chord. Bitonal chords with their roots a tritone apart are also common. As in previous movements, the third movement contrasts dissonant harmonies based on fourths and sevenths with dominant-derived, diatonic chords.

As in the coda to Sorabji's Sonata, the coda to Bridge's Sonata summarizes the main compositional techniques that have been operating throughout. At bar 120, the chordal setting of the first movement's chorale is applied to the march theme, emphasizing its organic derivation. The coda begins at bar 127 with a direct quotation from the first movement (bars 44–9). The chorale motif returns at bar 141, but on this occasion the G sharp repeated octaves are replaced by major triads in the right hand and the left hand's chorale is transposed up a tone to climax on B. Now each bar sounds the third version of the Bridge chord. On the first beat of bar 151, the triad plus tritone sonority characteristic of this movement is heard and a bass pedal B begins, continuing to the end. The compassion motif is heard again, now in a more relaxed triplet rhythm, before sinking into the bass region. It is harmonized with the third version of the Bridge chord and is briefly interrupted by the first theme of the third movement before dying away. The presence of the Bridge chord as the final sonority of the Sonata confirms its importance.

Two versions of the manuscript exist, one at the Royal College and the other at the British Library. The latter probably was the copy used by the printers, as it contains fewer alterations. The one at the Royal College is more interesting. The first six bars of the second movement are written out twice. The first version is very similar to the recapitulation of the first theme at bar 75 [Fig. 4.9]. Additionally, four sets of proof sheets can be seen at the British Library.[33] They have been thoroughly checked by Bridge, as evidenced in a comment on the first set, "These sharps! I think the ♯ to C is too high and not straight." Considering the volume of notes in this sonata, to question the placing of one accidental in a dense chord demonstrates meticulous observation!

The piano featured prominently in Bridge's output from 1905 to 1928. The early pieces followed in the salon tradition of Chopin and Liszt and were accessible to amateurs. The piano was Bridge's original subject of study at the Royal College, although he soon swapped to viola and the piano was relegated to his second study.

Several of the stylistic features observed in the Piano Sonata were anticipated in earlier piano works. *Solitude* from *Three Poems* (1913)

---

[33] H. 403. w.

Fig. 4.9 Bridge Sonata, Second movement, Manuscript (RCM), Original version of Bars 1–6

used chromaticism and showed Bridge's interest in Berg, and the opening of *Ecstasy* from the same set was atonal. The other piece from this set, *Sunset*, used the Bridge chord and the octatonic scale. The first use of pedal notes under unrelated chords could be seen in *Fragrance* from *Four Characteristic Pieces* (1917). In 1924, *Dainty Rogue* from *Three Lyrics* and *Retrospect* from *In Autumn* both illustrated his new chromatic language. The latter expressed anguish through consistent use of seconds and sevenths. As Kennett observes, Bridge's harmonic language in the Piano Sonata is an intensification of bitonal, whole tone and octatonic ideas that were already in evidence in his previous pieces.[34] The Piano Sonata is a virtuoso piece, and Bridge continually strove to expand the potential of the instrument, as Beethoven did in his Hammerklavier Sonata Op. 106. The extrovert character of the Piano Sonata seems to have prepared the ground for Britten, whose Piano Concerto (1938) treats the instrument similarly.

Bridge's aim in the Piano Sonata seems to have been to create a unique harmonic language to express a particular reaction to bereavement and sacrifice. It was ostensibly an abstract work and Bridge adapted traditional forms to suit his own purpose. Whereas Sorabji's Sonata can be considered to be impressionistic, Bridge's Sonata is expressionistic and clearly based on Germanic principles. Bridge's Sonata is in three distinct movements, retaining formal divisions, as opposed to Sorabji's more

[34] Kennett, 1995.

flexible, improvisatory approach. Sorabji went further than Bridge in deriving his piano style from the most bombastic elements of Scriabin.

Bridge's depiction of war permeates all aspects of the Sonata, through its constant harmonic tension. Unlike Sorabji, Bridge did not use Scriabin's mystic chord, preferring to create his own harmonic fingerprint in the Bridge chord. However, both composers use harmonies emanating from the use of decorated dominant sevenths, ninths, elevenths and thirteenths. Sorabji and Bridge use tritones to confuse the tonality in addition to chromatic harmony and bitonality. The spacing of chords by both composers exposes the fourths.

Sorabji found Bridge's Piano Sonata derivative of John Ireland, a composer whom Bridge admired.[35] Added-note harmonies in certain passages of the first two movements may suggest the influence of Ireland, and the heroic mood of the third movement links it to some of Ireland's marches. Like Ireland, Bridge was extremely concerned with sonority, but Bridge's Sonata is much more dissonant than Ireland's and it is hard to understand why Sorabji found it derivative. Bridge's training in the Brahmsian tradition meant that his harmonies had to provide a linear argument, hence his bass parts are always functional. Although both Ireland and Bax had occasionally used short bitonal passages, Bridge was the first British composer to develop bitonal textures consistently on such a large scale.

Berg, Schoenberg and Scriabin influenced Bridge, but it was works of the previous decade (*c.* 1905–15) that provided the stimulus for his new style, rather than the contemporary developments of the 1920s such as the use of the twelve-note technique. Even though Bridge's harmonic language was bitonal and sometimes polytonal, it was never completely atonal. To British musicians, his music seemed radical, but placed in the context of contemporary European developments (Schoenberg, Webern, Berg, Bartók and Hindemith), it was not. Bridge's cosmopolitan and eclectic outlook enabled him to prove that a British composer could ultimately be enriched by an appreciation of foreign developments.

Bridge originally wanted Harold Samuel to première his Sonata, but the work did not appeal to him and he declined the invitation. Howard Ferguson recalled the circumstances.

> ... I don't particularly like the Bridge [Sonata]. I knew it from its earliest days, because Frank wanted Harold Samuel to play it. He was an old friend of Harold's as they were at college together. Frank came when the work was in manuscript and played it to Harold; he was a good pianist himself. I heard this going on, and said to myself that I know Harold will never play that! Sure enough, he wriggled out of it and the first

---

[35] Sorabji, 1932, 64.

performance was given by Myra Hess, both in England and America. She said that she lost more of her American friends by playing it than anything else![36]

Hess performed the Sonata in New York and Alan Bush championed it at home and in Berlin.[37] It received a mixed reaction. The general public did not understand Bridge's new style, which did not appeal to the critics either. His new harmonic language alienated the public. It was the acoustical density resulting from the all-pervasive major seventh interval that would have put listeners off. They were by now used to British music tinged with the modernism of French impressionism, but Bridge was the first British composer to employ consistent bitonality. Nevertheless, some reviewers praised the work.

> The drawback of the modern elaborate treatment is that ideas are apt to get lost in the welter of sound. But there is a great deal of beauty in individual incidents, particularly in the more restrained and reflective slow movement. The vigorous theme from which the *finale* is generated stands out boldly, and by contrast the soft ending after its energy has subsided is made peculiarly impressive. Miss Hess's playing showed extraordinary grip of the musical detail, and convinced us of the rightness of much of which looked inexplicable to the eye beforehand.[38]

Retrospectively, Frank Howes regretted that Bridge "began to uglify his music in order to keep it up to date".[39] Bridge's music entered into a vicious circle of being unpopular, therefore not performed and thus never able to be popular. In 1934, he wanted his pupil Britten to study with Berg in Germany, but the Director of the Royal College, Sir Hugh Allen, vetoed this plan as Berg was considered an unsuitable influence.[40]

Bridge seems to have remained positive, despite the hostile reaction to his new style by some critics, and Augener published the Piano Sonata in 1925. Bridge continued to write piano music until 1928, when his publishers rejected *Gargoyle*, owing to its advanced language. It remained in manuscript until 1977. Bridge more fully developed his new style in the Third String Quartet (1926). The third version of the Bridge chord is common, as are intervals of the fourth, tritone and seventh. He used the principle of developing variation to compensate for the absence of tonality, following

---

[36] Interview with author: see Appendix 1, pp. 187–8. Hess first performed it at the Wigmore Hall, 15 October 1925. See Anon., *Daily Telegraph*, 16 October 1925, 15.
[37] Hess, Aeolian Hall, New York, 18 February 1926. Bush, Wigmore Hall, London, 1 December 1927, and Berlin, 29 January 1931.
[38] Anon., *The Times*, 16 October 1925, 12b.
[39] Howes, 1966, 160.
[40] Kennedy, 1993, 12.

the ideas of the Second Viennese School, and integrated horizontal and vertical aspects of his music.

The *Musical Times* of 1934–41 barely mentioned Bridge's name. One reason that his name was less well known to the general public than other British composers was that he wrote very little choral music. His death went almost unnoticed, occurring during World War II. Britten did something to promote Bridge's music by including performances at Aldeburgh in the 1960s. It was not until the early 1970s that a serious assessment was made of his work.[41] The first recordings of the Piano Sonata date from 1974 and 1979 and during the 1990s his complete piano music has been recorded on compact disc. Music written by Bridge in the 1930s remained unknown until the 1970s, and even today, there is no collected edition of his piano music, as there is for Ireland's. Nevertheless, the situation is improving. The Frank Bridge Trust, administered by the Royal College of Music, maintains an archive. It gives grants for performances of large works and it sponsors recordings, books and publications of Bridge's music. During Bridge's centenary in 1979, some scores, including the Piano Sonata, were reissued. The Sonata makes an outstanding original contribution to the repertoire, and deserves to be performed more frequently.

The period from 1919 to 1925 saw the production of many important piano sonatas, including the First Sonata by Sorabji, the revision of the First Sonata and the composition of the Second and Third sonatas by Bax, and the Sonatas by Ireland and Bridge. The sudden increase in quantity and quality of the repertoire may be accounted for by the impact of World War I, which had provided a stimulus to artistic creativity and changed Europe irrevocably. Bax was declared medically unfit for active service, whereas Ireland and Bridge were pacifists. Their response to the war manifested itself in their music. The Second Sonata by Bax depicts conflict between good and evil; the Sonata by Ireland uses low repeated notes to symbolize drums, and both Bax's First Sonata and Bridge's Sonata depict bells. Bridge even dedicated his Sonata to a composer lost in the war. It would appear that the British composer needed extra-musical influences or a sense of protest as a goad. The situation of war had reawakened national identity in the public, and in this period some composers turned to the British heritage of folk and modal music. This is demonstrated by all the above, with the exception of Sorabji, who came from a mixed-race background. Also, the anti-German feelings towards Bruckner, Mahler, Wagner and Strauss, resulted in a wider appreciation of French and Russian music.

The inspiration from the war, combined with an existing predisposition towards the impressionistic music of the French composers and Scriabin, resulted in these highly expressive and rhetorical piano sonatas. The Sonatas by Sorabji, Bax, Ireland and Bridge exhibit a high level of technical

---

[41] Pirie, 1971. Also Payne, Foreman and Bishop, 1976.

command in comparison with the feeble attempts of the nineteenth-century British composers. An enormous advance had been made in only a couple of generations. This situation was paralleled in France and the United States of America, as the composers broke away from the Teutonic stranglehold.

5

The African–American Influence

After 1925 subjective emotion as the principal driving force behind the rhetorical piano sonata was replaced by modernism, neo-classical economy and African–American idioms. The term African–American music is used to include the melodic and rhythmic characteristics of spirituals, blues, ragtime, dance music and jazz. It is useful to consider how this affected Britain's cultural life in general before embarking on a more detailed scrutiny of the piano sonatas by Constant Lambert and Michael Tippett that exemplify this.

African–American influences in Britain

Historically, the development of jazz can be traced back to the negro spirituals of the nineteenth century. According to Van der Merwe, the blacks integrated influences from European hymn tunes as well as African call and response patterns,[1] so that spirituals were largely of European origin. Their melodies were based upon modal scales, the blue notes of the mode being slightly flatter than the corresponding major ones, evoking a sense of longing or nostalgia. The most usual notes to be flattened were the third and seventh, as in British folk music, but fifths and sixths were not uncommon,[2] the flat versions of the notes often being used alongside the major or perfect ones. Having begun as a vocal technique, the blues was subsequently used in instrumental music and consisted of two essential characteristics, the mode and syncopation. Syncopated rhythms had been used in cakewalks and ragtime, which were published in America from the 1890s, although improvised versions existed before this time.

Dance music that contained syncopated rhythms was commonly referred to as jazz. After World War I, American dance bands, including The Original Dixieland Jazz Band, travelled to Britain to perform. Dance bands

---

[1] Van der Merwe, 1989, 75–9.
[2] Ibid., 119.

played at London hotels and jazzy arrangements became popular with the public. The British novelty pianist Billy Mayerl performed with the Savoy Havana Band, giving five sell-out concerts at the Queen's Hall in 1925. Louis Armstrong and Duke Ellington visited London in 1932 and 1933.

The BBC broadcast dance bands from 1923, and by 1928, it formed its own resident band. Radio was a crucial factor in bringing dance music to a wider public.[3] By the 1930s, jazz was taken seriously and Stanley Nelson's *All About Jazz* became the first jazz textbook to be published in Britain in 1934. The Jazz Society was formed, and by 1940 the BBC presented the jazz programme Radio Rhythm Club for thirty minutes each week. Although this met with public success, it was disliked by the establishment.

Symphonic jazz, as exemplified by Gershwin's *Rhapsody in Blue*, developed in the 1920s. It attempted to cross the divide between classical music and jazz, with limited success. The audiences who were interested in classical music did not like the infiltration of jazz, and those who enjoyed the spontaneity of improvisation disliked the use of notation and the more formal concert venues.

The first European piano pieces to have been influenced by ragtime were Satie's *Le Picadilly* (1904) and Debussy's *Golliwog's Cake-walk* (1908). Lambert commented on Milhaud's *Le Boeuf sur le toit* (1920), *La Création du Monde* (1923) and Satie's *Parade* (1917) in *Music Ho!*, regretting that the French were generally too facetious in their attempts to integrate jazz.[4] However, Ravel used the blues in the slow movement of his Violin Sonata (1927) for expressive purposes. Stravinsky's jazz-inspired works, *Ragtime* (1918) and *Piano Rag Music* (1919), were written as a result of obtaining copies of sheet music, and he only later realized that jazz was essentially an improvised music. There are also examples of jazz-inspired compositions by Kurt Weill and Hindemith, but Lambert considered the Germans to be too serious to appreciate jazz.[5] In Britain, William Walton had studied jazz in the early 1920s, but he withdrew his *Fantasia Concertante*, a jazz-inspired concerto, as a result of hearing the first performance of Gershwin's *Rhapsody in Blue* in 1924.

> On the concert platform at the Queen's Hall, it had no success and worse on the provincial tours. There was no interest then in that type of music and I feared for the *Fantasia*.[6]

[3] London, Marconi House transmitter 2LO, 363.5 metres. First broadcasts by Savoy Havana Band (13 April 1923, 10–10.30 p.m.) and Savoy Orpheans (11 Oct. 1923, 9.05–10.45 p.m.).
[4] Lambert, 1945, 158.
[5] Ibid.
[6] Walton, letter to S. Craggs, 9 Feb. 1976. Quoted in Kennedy, 1990, 40. *Rhapsody in Blue* was composed in 1924, originally for jazz band and piano, and was first performed by Gershwin at Queen's Hall in 1924. Paul Whiteman played it at the Royal Albert Hall on 11 April 1926. Gershwin was there and did not approve of the interpretation.

Newspaper reviews suggest that *Rhapsody in Blue* was in fact very successful, and all five concerts at the Queen's Hall sold out. It may have been that Walton worried about the effect the jazz composition would have on his reputation as a serious classical composer. His *Sinfonia Concertante* (1925–6), *Portsmouth Point* overture (1932) and *Façade* suites (1921–2) use syncopated rhythms. Additionally, Arthur Bliss' *Rout* (1920) for soprano and chamber orchestra, *Bliss – A One Step* (1923), and *Rout Trot* (1927), show the influence of early jazz and ragtime. The two composers who first assimilated African–American influences into their piano sonatas were Constant Lambert and Michael Tippett.

Constant Lambert (1905–51)

Lambert came from a cosmopolitan and artistic family, describing himself as a "francophil [sic] English composer-conductor born to an Australian painter from St. Petersburg".[7] His family background clearly laid the foundations for Lambert's art, and he was able to assimilate diverse influences. He became attracted to the music of Stravinsky and the Russian ballet through Diaghilev, with whom he was well acquainted. Lambert was the first British composer to be commissioned to write music (*Romeo and Juliet,* 1926) for Diaghilev's company.

Lambert's immediate circle of musical friends consisted of Cecil Gray, Bernard van Dieren and Philip Heseltine (Peter Warlock). Sorabji was also linked to this group. These composers were interested in the other arts, including painting, sculpture and ballet, and shared a self-satisfied isolation from the musical mainstream. Like the Sitwells, they were opinionated and wrote for periodicals, and all except Heseltine wrote books of critical essays. The establishment viewed them as radicals, and they were considered to be a group somewhat like Les Six in France.

Lambert's three-movement Piano Sonata was written in Toulon and London between 1928 and 1929. It marks a significant step in the development of the British piano sonata, as it was the first to be influenced by African–American music.

Lambert had been interested in jazz since his school days, but the catalyst for further explorations of the style was provided by a performance by the Plantation Orchestra in a revue called *Dover Street to Dixie* at the London Pavilion in May 1923. His *Elegiac Blues* for piano was written in memory of the coloured singer, Florence Mills, who had made a profound impression on Lambert at this performance. The orchestra returned to London for performances in 1926 as The Blackbirds, and was more widely acclaimed. Unfortunately, Florence Mills made no recordings, and only four by The Plantation Orchestra exist, so it is difficult to cite direct influences on

---

[7] Shead, 1986, 11. Motion, 1987, 121.

Lambert.[8] Lambert was sympathetic towards American negroes, especially women. He wrote *Eight Poems of Li Po* (1926–9), inspired by the screen star Anna May Wong, and his disastrous marriage was to a woman of partly oriental ancestry, Florence Chuter.

Lambert admired Duke Ellington, and in *Music Ho!*, he mentions Ellington's *Black and Tan Fantasy*, *Swampy River*, *Hot and Bothered*, *Creole Rhapsody* and *Mood Indigo*.[9] The first three pieces were recorded in 1927 and 1928; hence it is virtually certain that Lambert had heard them before writing his Piano Sonata. The others were recorded in 1930 and 1931. Lambert's general style moved further towards that of hot jazz after *The Rio Grande* (1927).[10]

The piano has an extremely important role in Lambert's output. He was trained as a pianist, and although he never performed as a concert pianist, he did accompany ballet rehearsals. The piano has a solo role in *The Rio Grande*. Lambert wrote a Concerto for nine players (1930–1) as a memorial to Heseltine, and a Piano Concerto (*c.* 1927) that received its première in 1988.[11] He also wrote *Elegiac Blues* (1927) for piano solo, and *Trois Pièces Nègres pour les Touches Blanches* (1949) for piano duet.

Lambert realized that to create a Piano Sonata with contemporary relevance, he must impart new ideas to the established form.

> I am a great admirer of the classics, but the young composer cannot be expected to express himself in dead forms. He must get away from the classical tradition. He must not be weighed down by the responsibility of trying to be another Brahms or Beethoven. You might as well expect an artist to work in a museum.[12]

This had been the problem with the nineteenth-century British composers, who had been too ready to adopt German styles without bringing their individuality to bear on them. Typically, a sonata would be a complex, highly organized and intellectual work, which in some sense continued an established tradition. In contrast, the use of jazz suggests impulsive and instinctive music that makes a direct and immediate impact on the listener. Lambert presented himself with the challenge to fuse the serious form of a sonata with the spontaneous and improvisatory character of jazz. He manages to retain a coherent sonata structure, using established principles

---

[8] Recorded in London, 1 December 1926. *Silver Rose* WA–4519–2, Col 4185. *Arabella's Wedding Day* WA–4543–1, Col 4238. *Smiling Joe* WA–4544–1, Col 4185. *For Baby and Me* WA–4545–1, Col 4238. See later comments on the Plantation fanfare (pp. 135–6).

[9] Lambert, 1945, 150–2.

[10] Broadcast 1928. First public performances: Manchester, 12 December 1929, and Queen's Hall, London, 13 December 1929 by Lambert, Sir Hamilton Harty, Hallé Orchestra.

[11] 2 March 1988. Redcliffe concerts presented this concerto, scored for chamber ensemble, with Jonathan Plowright as soloist. It exists only in manuscript.

[12] Lambert, *The Star*, 14 December 1929.

of repetition and development, whilst using the rhythms, melodies and harmonies of African–American music.

The first movement of Lambert's Piano Sonata follows the outline of sonata form, consisting of an exposition (bars 1–43), development (bars 44–141), recapitulation (bars 142–90) and coda (bars 191–202). However, the recapitulation begins with the second subject, which is interrupted by a cadenza passage before leading to the return of the first subject. The exposition and recapitulation are concise; therefore the main weight of the movement is in the development section.

The rhythms of the opening bars suggest that Lambert was trying to notate improvising practices that he had heard. Despite being mainly in 4/4, syncopated and anticipatory rhythms disguise the metre and a mixture of crotchets, quavers, triplets and demisemiquavers is used. Peter Dickinson has classified syncopation under three headings: mid-beat, mid-bar and cross-bar.[13] The terminology was originally devised for rags and Dickinson suggested the term mid-beat diminished for a fourth type of syncopation found in the Sonata [Fig. 5.1].

Fig. 5.1 Dickinson, types of syncopation

The first theme, from bars 1 to 21, uses mainly mid-beat and mid-bar syncopation, with the exception of the mid-beat diminished syncopation in bar 16. The mid-bar category can be considered a special type of mid-beat syncopation. It is not as appropriate to consider here as in rags that remain in regular metre.

Lambert contrasts phrases where both hands play different rhythms, with more homophonic phrases where the hands play the same rhythms. He sets up polyrhythms and repeats them in the manner of secondary ragtime, as in bars 5 and 13. The repetition of small patterns is used to build the first subject to a climax at bar 21, not with a cadence, but with the jazz technique

---

[13] Dickinson, 1979, 63–76.

of stop time. The absence of cadences can also be compared to the free flow of Delius' music.

Bars 14–16 and 18–21 are effectively divided into 3+3+2 quavers. This grouping, characteristic of a rumba, forms the basis of much of the subsequent material. The rumba was common in black Africa, and later became typical of Latin American music. Novelty piano pieces by Zez Confrey (1920) and Billy Mayerl (1925 onwards) used 3+3+2 interpolations to create rhythmic uncertainty and therefore excitement.

These rhythmic techniques form the basis of the style of Lambert's Piano Sonata, contrasting with the style of previous British piano sonata composers, such as Sorabji and especially Bridge, whose harmonic techniques have been of more significance. In Lambert's Sonata, the rate of harmonic change of the first subject is very fast, and the opening D minor tonality is only briefly established. Bar 10 demonstrates the parallel movement of chromatic ninth chords in close position, typical of Duke Ellington.

The second subject, characterized by running quavers, begins at bar 22 in F, the relative major. Lambert uses modal contradiction, with both the natural and blue version of notes appearing in close proximity or juxtaposed. The melody is highly chromatic, and there are increasing dissonances between the hands, which play in parallel minor sevenths in bar 35. Chords built upon perfect fourths are also important, as seen in bar 30.

The use of modal contradictions is a characteristic feature of the second subject, and in bar 38 the right hand plays in F sharp minor, whilst the left hand uses F sharp major. Thus there is a constant tension resulting from the use of major and minor (i.e. blue) thirds. Bitonality, a feature of the music of Milhaud and Stravinsky also, is present in the following bars, where D major and minor are superimposed, followed by D flat major and D minor.

Like the first subject, the second uses mid-beat and mid-bar syncopation, and also some cross-bar syncopation. The exposition ends without a cadence. The effect of slowing down is written into the music; bar 43 is extended to 5/4 metre and the instructions indicate a ritenuto. The double bar lines confirm the end of the section.

The development commences in A minor, the dominant minor. Arpeggio patterns and triplets characterize the development of the first subject, whereas the second uses running and syncopated quavers. The first subject is briefly treated in the manner of a fugato, with the addition of a countermelody, before leading into a descending sequence of major seventh chords in rumba rhythm. The two subjects are fragmented and increasingly juxtaposed, both being harmonized bitonally. The jazz techniques of stop time and polyrhythmic secondary ragtime are again used. The spacing of chords is pianistic, at times using the thumb striking keys sideways to play intervals of a second.

From bar 102, the second subject is developed. The left hand accompaniment combines dotted and ordinary quavers in the manner of a habañera, which, like the rumba, is a Latin American dance rhythm.

Bars 132–40 are virtually identical to bars 13–21, providing elements of a recapitulation. Bars 140–1 use cluster chords in stop time, amplifying the chords in bar 21. The use of the double barlines indicates the commencement of the recapitulation proper, beginning with the second subject. This is played more slowly and harmonized by full chords, including the augmented chord. The left hand now plays the habañera rhythm slowly, in stride style, and the two hands explore a wide range of the piano.

A Presto section leads into an unbarred passage, similar to a jazz break or a cadenza, typical of a classical concerto, but not sonata. The hands begin playing in sevenths, and the rhythms explore various groupings of 2, 3 and 4 quavers, demonstrating the virtuosity of the pianist. The cadenza is used by Lambert as a climactic device, rather surprisingly, in the midst of the recapitulation.

This is followed by a return of the second subject. After a rare perfect cadence, using the dominant seventh chord, the first subject returns in the original key, D minor, although it is modified after two bars. The passage slows down into the lyrical coda, using longer note values to suggest a ritenuto. The movement ends with the opening theme over an F major chord, its notation indicating a controlled rubato. Thus the movement, which began in D minor, ends in the relative major, the key of the second subject, although the brief final gesture adds C sharp and D.

The first movement uses elements of traditional sonata form in an individual way. The two subjects have their own identities; one is declamatory and the other more lyrical, but they are both fast. Thus they can be easily fragmented and juxtaposed. The climax of the development is provided by a recapitulation of the two themes and their interruption by a cadenza. The recapitulation of themes in reverse was a structural principle also used in Bridge's Piano Sonata, to create arch form. Lambert uses this device to assert the importance of the second subject, in F major, above that of the D minor first subject.

The second movement, Nocturne, has the structure of a rondo (ABABA), alternating the slow main theme with two faster episodes, between bars 32–64 and 100–130. The main theme uses chromaticism and the blues, whereas the faster episodes are more diatonic. Like the first movement, the second begins with a six-bar phrase, providing an introduction based on impressionistic chords. It uses the rhythm of threes against twos, which alternate between the hands. The tonality of the opening is ambiguous, and there are enharmonic changes in the first two bars, from A sharp to B flat.

Arpeggiated chords, which may have been inspired by Duke Ellington, accompany the main blues melody. The middle section of his *Mood Indigo* uses a trumpet solo accompanied by repeated banjo chords. Although this piece was not recorded until 1930, Lambert may have heard earlier works by Ellington that used the same sonority. The melody is typical of the blues in that it spans a restricted range of notes and both natural and blue versions of notes are used simultaneously. The melody slides down chromatically from F sharp to F natural, the major and blues sevenths of G. The harmonization of this theme is similar to that of the second subject in the first movement. Bitonal thinking is in evidence, and the interval of a tritone becomes increasingly common. Lambert attempts to imitate the sounds of the jazz band in bar 26, by writing dissonant parallel seconds, like brass smears, in the right hand.

The syncopation of the rondo theme can be categorized as a mixture of mid-beat, mid-bar and cross-bar. As in the first movement, the 3+3+2 rumba rhythm is heard, becoming an essential part of the first episode, which follows without a break or cadence. Its running and syncopated quavers make it similar to the second subject of the first movement.

The texture in bars 40–5 is very reminiscent of ragtime. The left hand uses a stride bass, and the right hand is syncopated in quadruple metre. The rhythm soon returns to that of the rumba, with alternate bars of D flat7 and G7 chords, another tritone relationship. Parallel descending triads lead to a return of the opening of the first episode. As in the first movement, Lambert rarely repeats themes exactly and now the accompaniment is sparser and has changed register. Thirds are piled up to create seventh chords and sustained tremolandos lead into a variant of the opening theme, using chords in the original triplet rhythm, but adding a new melody and a sustained bass note to the texture. The new blues melody moves around the focal note B flat. This seems vocally inspired, as it uses ornaments and chromatic glissandos. The thirds in the inner parts slide chromatically.

The second episode, characterized by running semiquavers, begins at bar 100. This is the most highly syncopated theme in the whole Sonata, using all four types, as illustrated in Fig. 5.1. Semiquaver rests are used frequently, to create short, percussive sounds. The figuration is similar to the piano part of bars 39–40 in Lambert's *The Rio Grande* [Fig. 5.2]. In this section, major and minor seventh chords and perfect fourths are used extensively.

The main theme returns from bar 131, at the same pitch as the opening, but only fragments of the previous themes are recalled. There are extreme dynamic contrasts. Bars 151 to the end provide the rhythmic essentials of the movement – the contrast of triplet and ordinary crotchet rhythms. The movement ends on an open fifth from C to G.

Fig. 5.2 Lambert, *The Rio Grande*, OUP, Bars 39–40

The African–American Influence

The third movement begins with a chorale-like introduction in C major. Lambert subsequently used this theme in the Saraband (*Adieu, Farewell, Earth's Bliss*) in *Summer's Last Will and Testament* (1932–5) [Fig. 5.3]. The descending thirds of bars 1 and 2 are used as a fugue subject later in the movement, and will be referred to as a motto. The introduction is very slow moving, using semibreve beats, and consists mainly of triads, sevenths and ninths. From bar 5 there are bell-like octaves, and the six-bar introduction ends on a C major triad.

Fig. 5.3 Lambert, *Summer's Last Will and Testament*, OUP, Saraband, Bars 29–32

The main part of the movement begins Presto, in the Aeolian mode on D [Fig. 5.4]. This mode uses a flattened seventh, and it thus relates closely to the blues. The theme, which initially uses only mid-beat syncopation, is presented in octaves. In bars 14–20, mid-bar syncopation is used also, but the syncopation fails to transcend the regularity of the four-bar phrases, even though the metre is changed to 4/4. At bar 15, the tonality shifts to F major and blue notes are used. As in the previous movements, Lambert avoids cadences. Unfortunately, the syncopated theme has little potential for development. The main ways in which Lambert extends his material include adding an accompaniment either above or below the theme, changing the metre, or changing the key.

Lambert's discovery of jazz as played by the Plantation Orchestra has already been mentioned.

> After the humdrum playing of the English orchestra in the first part [of the revue] it was an electrifying experience to hear Will Vodery's band playing the Delius-like fanfare which preluded the second. It definitely opened up a whole new world of sound.[14]

This rising fanfare [Fig. 5.5] was pentatonic. It is virtually identical to a characteristic Delius phrase, seen in *Appalachia* (1903) [Fig. 5.6] and *The Walk to the Paradise Garden* from *A Village Romeo and Juliet* (1900–1901). At bars 15 and 17 of Lambert's third movement [Fig. 5.4], the rising pentatonic motif recalls the main theme of *The Rio Grande* [Fig. 5.7].

[14] Lambert, *The New Statesman and Nation*, 1932. See Palmer, *ML*, 1971, 173–6.

Fig. 5.4 Lambert, Sonata, Third movement, Bars 7–18

Fig. 5.5 Pentatonic fanfare [See Palmer, 1971]

Fig. 5.6 Delius, *Appalachia*, Universal Edition, Bars 43–4

Fig. 5.7 Lambert, *The Rio Grande*, Bars 14–16

Bars 101–4 provide an introduction to the ensuing fugal section. Major seventh intervals are important in the right hand, fourths in the middle part, and fifths in the bass. The fugue begins with the motto, based on descending thirds, in E flat major. It is repeated from bar 110, a major third higher in G major, with a countersubject. The next key change is to B major, a major third above G, continuing the key sequence established by the previous modulation. Unusually, bars 115–18 use a diatonic motif that is unrelated to the fugue. The next entry of the fugue subject appears in the right hand at bar 119, accompanied by the countersubject in the bass and an inner part, based on the subject. Freer development occurs from bar 124, with fragments of the subject appearing in augmentation and the syncopated theme also being recalled.

Bar 162 is a climactic point and its importance is stressed by its slow tempo and use of homophonic chords in contrast to the fugal style of the previous section. It uses the fugue subject in altered rhythm, initially over a G pedal. From bar 163, the left hand uses a stride bass in octaves in polyrhythmic three-beat units, whilst the right hand has syncopated ragtime rhythms. Further development of the fugue subject and syncopated theme follows.

The coda, from bar 248, delivers the triumphant motto in C major, although it is interrupted by the syncopated theme. The motto is again repeated, but instead of ending on a C major chord as before, the last chord is D major. Thus the introduction's tonality shift from C to D is replicated by the coda and the Sonata, which began in D minor, ends in the major mode.

The third movement is the weakest of the three, as its syncopated theme offers limited potential for development and the movement is rather long. Nevertheless, Lambert tries harder with his fugue than in the first movement, and this section is successful. Despite its occasional shortcomings, the Sonata is an impressive work and it provided a basis on which Lambert could build for his Piano Concerto (1930–1).

The Sonata was dedicated to Thomas W. Earp, an art critic, who was a friend and drinking companion of Lambert's. It was premièred at the Aeolian Hall on 30 October 1929. The critic of *The Times* was unimpressed.

> There was nothing vague about Lambert's Sonata for pianoforte, which was played by Mr [Gordon] Bryan. This was utterly uncompromising in its hardness of outline and made the more so by the emphatic performance, which, one supposes, had the sanction of the composer. As pianoforte music, the harsh dissonances and jumbled rhythms, apart from being unpleasant to the ear (which may have been intended), resulted in obscurity. The work might show its strength and originality more plainly in an orchestral version.[15]

---

[15] Anon., *The Times*, 1 November 1929.

It is possible that the performer, an enthusiastic champion of British music, did not do justice to the work. Alan Frank recalled that Bryan was "a nice enough chap, but not a particularly distinguished pianist".[16] Angus Morrison (Lambert's brother-in-law) and Louis Kentner also performed the Piano Sonata. Its technical demands deterred all but the most accomplished pianists.

Edmund Duncan Rubbra, reviewing the publication of the Sonata, found the rhythms monotonous.

> By avoiding the straight four beats in a bar, with the normal accents on the first and third beats, and by fixing attention on the normally unaccented portions of the bar, the composer has merely jumped from the frying-pan of rhythmic dullness to the fire of rhythmic breathlessness – and it is difficult to say which is the lesser evil.[17]

The whole point of Lambert's technique was to provide rhythmic interest, something that he saw as a major shortcoming of romantic composers. In the fast music there is constant rhythmic variation – Lambert does not rely too heavily on any one rhythm. The musical argument depends upon this continual displacement of accents, as in African music or Stravinsky's *Rite of Spring*. Lambert defended his technique:

> It is often suggested that jazz rhythm, though exhilarating at first, ends by becoming monotonous through its being merely a series of irregular groupings and cross-accents over a steady and unyielding pulse. This is true in a way, and certainly nothing is more wearisome than the mechanical division of the eight quavers of the foxtrot bar into groups of three, three and two; yet in the best negro jazz bands the irregular cross-accents are given so much more weight than the underlying pulse, that the rhythmic arabesques almost completely obscure this metrical framework, and paradoxically enough this 'bar line' music often achieves a rhythmic freedom that recalls the music of Elizabethan times and earlier, where the bar line was a mere technical convenience like a figure or letter in a score.[18]

It is crucial that the performer maintains a regular pulse, so that the full effects of Lambert's syncopations and cross-rhythms are experienced. Improvisatory passages are written into the music by changing metres, and ritenutos are notated by longer note values.

Reviews of *The Rio Grande* had been much more positive than those of the Sonata, and Richard Gilbert, reviewing the first recording for an American journal, regretted that it had not been written by an American composer.[19]

---

[16] Interview with author: see Appendix 1, p. 195.
[17] Rubbra, *MMR*, 1930, 356. This is the British composer.
[18] Lambert, 1945, 155.
[19] Gilbert, *Disques*, 1930, 201–2.

Rex Harris' comments on *The Rio Grande* could equally well apply to the Sonata.

> Apart from the rhythms, which are obviously of jazz origin, he subtly combines those two characteristic elements of Negro music: a yearning nostalgia and sudden unbounded boisterousness.[20]

This is illustrated particularly well by the second movement, which alternates between slow sections using the blues and rag-scherzo. Lambert claimed to deplore the folksong school, especially Vaughan Williams, although in later life he began to appreciate his music. Lambert may have thought that he had avoided the folk influence, but he has synthesized elements, including modality, from a variety of different folk cultures.

Lambert's sympathy for the negro and love of French culture can be compared to Delius'. Of all the major British composers, Delius seems to have had the most significant influence upon the British piano sonata. Interestingly, he wrote very little for the piano, with the exception of his Piano Concerto (1897, revised 1906). It was his orchestral textures and continually flowing forms that British composers attempted to imitate. His influence has been the strongest upon Scott, Sorabji and Lambert – three composers who deliberately distanced themselves from the musical establishment. These composers were keen to discover a replacement for the rhetorical piano sonata. Sorabji attempted to notate improvising practices, but his metres are always irregular, whereas Lambert tends to use more regular ones. Lambert's music is derived from popular and dance music, a type of music that Sorabji rejected.[21]

Lambert's most important contribution to the development of the British piano sonata was his rhythmic innovation. The works that preceded it, Ireland's and Bridge's Sonatas, had developed harmony and form, but paid little attention to rhythm. Like Sorabji's and Bridge's, Lambert's harmonies seemed dissonant to the audiences of the 1920s. Bax and Bridge anticipated Lambert's bitonality, but he was the first composer to attempt to bridge the gap between popular and classical culture.

Lambert's compositions, with the exception of *The Rio Grande*, were not taken seriously by the public, owing to the jazz idioms that his music employed. Despite articles by Alan Frank, this attitude remained until the 1970s, when Richard Shead made a study of Lambert's life and music. Andrew Motion made a study of Constant Lambert's life, which draws parallels with his father's and son's lives, in 1986. However, these studies do not provide detailed scrutiny of Lambert's music. One article that discusses the music dates from 1970.[22] There has been a recent upsurge in the release

---

[20] Harris, in Hill (ed.), *Penguin Music Magazine*, Vol. 2, 1947.
[21] The chapter titled "The Modern Piano Sonata", in Sorabji, 1932, 52, does not mention Lambert's work.
[22] McGrady, *ML*, 1970, 242–58.

of compact discs of the Piano Sonata. At last, Lambert's music has been subject to a reappraisal through performance at a time when the barriers between classical and popular styles are less emphatic.

Lambert wrote little music after 1935. He was concerned that he was known only for *The Rio Grande* and felt that the attention given to it distracted the public from other, and in his opinion, better works. Both Geoffrey Bush and Alan Frank confirm that Lambert considered *Summer's Last Will and Testament* to be his magnum opus, yet it only received a couple of performances during his lifetime.[23] Lambert made his name as a composer early, without a struggle, and during the 1920s he was as well known as Walton. By 1931, the year of *Belshazzer's Feast,* Walton's popularity was increasing whilst Lambert's was declining. Lambert made a significant impact as a conductor, bringing hitherto unknown works by French and Russian composers to the public. He also contributed to a revival of interest in earlier British music. Geoffrey Bush recalled that Lambert made a suite for the Vic-Wells Ballet out of movements from Boyce's symphonies, which he edited for publication.[24] Bush was influenced by Lambert, and his First Symphony (1954) quotes an extract from *The Rio Grande*.

In the 1920s, Lambert was considered to be a radical composer, but his later music looked backwards for its inspiration. Like Scott and Sorabji, he was a polymath – a pianist, composer, conductor, critic and fluent in French, and consequently the British were sceptical. His intense activities in his younger years left him little time to compose and he subsequently burnt out. This parallels the situation of Benjamin Dale, another composer who, having established his reputation with a Piano Sonata early in his career, subsequently failed to fulfil his potential and died in virtual obscurity. Lambert's lack of popularity with the public, persistent ill health and increasing alcohol consumption meant that his death in 1951 went practically unnoticed.

Sir Michael Tippett (1905–98)

There is much common ground between Lambert and Tippett, although nine years separate Lambert's Sonata from Tippett's Sonata No. 1 (1936–8). Like Lambert, Tippett came from a cosmopolitan family and his travels in Europe broadened his outlook. Both composers spoke fluent French. Their period of study at the Royal College overlapped, Lambert attending 1922–5 and Tippett 1923–8. Tippett was also interested in African–American music, sharing Lambert's admiration for Duke Ellington.

Tippett's first acquaintance with the syncopated music of Tin Pan Alley

---

[23] Interviews with author: see Appendix 1, pp. 182, 194.
[24] Ibid., p. 182.

had been c.1911, when he heard two girls singing Irving Berlin's *Alexander's Ragtime Band* and *Everybody's Doing It*.[25] These songs were not authentic ragtime pieces, but they immediately intrigued and interested the young Tippett. Thus his interest in African–American music dates from his childhood, to a time when jazz was considered morally unacceptable.

Gershwin's *Rhapsody in Blue* was a work that Tippett heard whilst attending the Royal College of Music.

> There was a great deal of argumentation between critics about it, whether it belonged in music, and what was it? I can remember it and was fascinated by it, but I couldn't analyse it.[26]

Tippett's attitude towards Gershwin's symphonic jazz contrasts with Lambert's, who thought that American composers were too close to the origins of jazz to integrate it successfully into their serious music.[27] Tippett was obviously impressed by it, and it may have been the catalyst for the assimilation of African–American influences into his own works. Subsequently, Tippett heard Lambert's *The Rio Grande* (1927), which also uses African–American idioms.[28] The person who helped Tippett to understand jazz idioms was Jeffrey Mark, a contemporary at the Royal College.

> He went to America and he had experienced jazz. I remember asking him what it was and he said it was really a piano technique. The main thing was an anticipation of the beat, which was unlike the straight classical style.[29]

Presumably, Mark would have heard jazz bands in America, rather than simply ragtime pianists, as jazz is not exclusively associated with piano technique. In 1938, Winthrop Sargeant's book, *Jazz: Hot and Hybrid* was published, although it is unlikely that Tippett had obtained Sargeant's book before writing his Sonata No. 1. Tippett recalled

> It was an extraordinary book, written by Winthrop Sargeant, whom I later met. These were all part of my explorations to find out what it was and what it meant.[30]

The blues became a significant influence on Tippett's later music. His first contact was through recordings made by Bessie Smith and Louis Armstrong.[31]

---

[25] Tippett, 1959, 37.
[26] Interview with author: see Appendix 1, p. 209 and footnote 6, p. 128.
[27] Lambert, 1945, 158.
[28] Interview with author: see Appendix 1, p. 208. First performed December 1929.
[29] Ibid., p. 209.
[30] Ibid., p. 209.
[31] Bessie Smith's recordings date from 1923 to 1933. She recorded *St Louis Blues* with Louis Armstrong on 14 January 1925.

In the fourth movement of Sonata No. 1, Tippett is influenced by negro spirituals. He needed to develop a style that created a light-hearted mood for a finale, and African–American music ideally suited this purpose. Tippett's early interest in the music of Tin Pan Alley, later knowledge of dance music and the symphonic jazz of Gershwin and Lambert, provided a foundation on which the spirituals could easily be assimilated. The techniques of ragtime and spirituals overlap. Both use syncopation and have a sense of forward momentum, rhythmic aspects that Tippett was keen to exploit. He was able to assimilate such rhythmic influences easily, owing to his interest in the word-setting of Purcell and the metrical irregularities of the Elizabethan madrigalists. His mature rhythmic style stems from the common ground between madrigals, ragtime, spirituals, symphonic jazz and dance music.

The first movement of Sonata No. 1, a set of variations, was composed in 1936 with the intention of being a self-contained piece, but Tippett later decided to incorporate it into his Fantasy Sonata. The Fantasy Sonata was first recorded by Phyllis Sellick and issued privately by Rimington, van Wyck, in 1941. Subsequently, Tippett made some modifications and it was published with the title Piano Sonata by Schott in 1942, and reprinted as Piano Sonata No. 1 in 1954.[32]

Some confusion exists over the dates of composition and first performance of the Sonata. Kemp and Bowen give the date of composition as 1936–7 and the first performance as November 1937 in their studies of 1965 and 1982 respectively.[33] However, Kemp gives the date of composition as 1936–8 and the first performance as November 1938 in his study of 1987.[34] 1938 is confirmed to be correct by the inclusion of the programme and subsequent review of the first performance in *A Man of our Time*, and the manuscript of Sonata No. 1 is dated July 1938.[35]

Tippett's initial reticence to name his work Sonata was due to the fact that the first movement was a set of variations, not a movement in sonata form. Tippett recalled, "later, I grew to learn more about Beethoven and I realized it was no problem".[36] Sonata No. 1 was one of Tippett's earliest compositions.

[32] Schott Edition 10123. Kemp (1987, 52) is incorrect in his assertion that the work was published with the title Fantasy Sonata. The latter publication differed from the former only in its title and appearance. The 1954 version prints notes at their actual pitch, rather than using 8va signs, and it contains metronome markings, which the 1942 version did not.

[33] Kemp, 1965, 234. Bowen, 1985 (reprint of 1982), 179. The same date is given in Whittall, 1990, 34.

[34] Kemp, 1987, 499.

[35] Schott, 1977, 30–1. Kemp, 1987, 499. Only the completion date is given on the score. The extant version is a photocopy of the copyist's which is currently kept by Kemp, the original manuscript having been sent to Mainz during World War II and subsequently destroyed.

[36] Interview with author: see Appendix 1, p. 206.

Mind you, in the early days you are derivative and you have to find your own style. In a sense, the First Piano Sonata is the first work that is really free, not totally, but then nothing can be.[37]

Tippett's aim in Piano Sonata No. 1 was to "steer clear of a heavy, Germanized and too serious work".[38] Certain features are inherited from the Beethovenian tradition, but to counterbalance Germanic formal structures, Tippett assimilated influences from folk music of different nations, including Scotland, Indonesia and America.

The first movement opens with a declamatory phrase, its octaves progressively accumulating added notes. The melody of the first four bars is repeated with a flowing quaver harmonization, and the second part of the theme (from bar 9) is also repeated with quaver accompaniment. The second part is longer than the first, but they are united by their common rhythmic identities.

The theme begins in 3/4 + 2/4 metre. This type of rhythm, where the beat remains constant whilst its interior construction is assymetric, is referred to by Kemp as "fixed-additive rhythm".[39] This relates to the primitive and irregular rhythms of Stravinsky and Holst, whose *Hymn of Jesus* Tippett cited as an important influence.[40] Holst made much use of quintuple and septuple rhythms. Despite his irregular five-beat pulse, Tippett uses regular four-bar phrases. Kemp, however, considers them to be "five-bar groups disguised by overlap", a statement with which I disagree.[41] Tippett's syncopation is of the mid-beat type. It is different to Lambert's in that he displaces all the beats by one quaver rather than anticipating certain ones.

R. O. Morris' *Canzoni Ricertati* (1931) for strings, uses cross-rhythms and mid-beat syncopation in a similar manner to Tippett [Fig. 5.8]. Here, as in much of Tippett's first movement, barlines are used for notational convenience rather than to imply accentuation. Tippett took lessons from Morris after leaving the Royal College, to improve his understanding of harmony and counterpoint.

The 3/4 + 2/4 metre continues to the end of the theme, with the exception of bars 21 and 22, which are extended by one crotchet. The first variation begins in bar 26, retaining the G major tonality of the theme but modifying the metre to 3/4 + 5/8. Each subsequent variation uses a different metre, and Kemp describes the effect that these various metres have, taking into account the tempo changes.[42]

---

[37] Interview with author: see Appendix 1, p. 207.
[38] Kemp, 1987, 86 cites *The Gramophone*, August 1941. I have been unable to find the quote in this publication.
[39] Ibid., 102.
[40] in Kemp and Rayment, *Audio and Record Review*, 1963, 27.
[41] Kemp, 1987, 102. Similarly, I disagree with his subsequent assertion that the second part of the phrase consists of nine-bar groups divided 4 + 5.
[42] Ibid., 103. In the third variation, the tempo is approximately one third of the original, and so the effective duration of each bar must take this into account. Here, my

Fig. 5.8 Morris, *Canzoni Ricertati*, OUP, No. 1, Bars 98–105

The first variation explores conventional piano figurations, repeating passages at different octaves, and begins with a quintuple motif that uses the Lydian sharpened fourth as an appoggiatura. The number five is significant throughout; the theme began in quintuple metre and there are five variations. Unlike the theme, variation one begins on the downbeat but it retains the bipartite structure. Bars 26–9 are equivalent to the first part, which is repeated with modified textures and flowing accompaniment from bars 30 to 33. The second part begins at bar 34, and when it is repeated from bar 42, it explores the flat side of the circle of fifths.

The second variation (bars 51–75) retains many features of the original theme. It uses octaves in each hand in the manner of Schumann and Brahms, and the contrapuntal theme begins on the second quaver of the bar. This variation imparts great rhythmic energy, with each hand filling in the rhythmic gaps left by the other. Both parts of the theme use invertible counterpoint, and the counterthemes are melodically inverted, appearing first descending and then ascending.

> calculations differ from Kemp's. I think that this is equivalent to a dotted semibreve + dotted semibreve (rather than Kemp's dotted minims). Both readings make the first and second halves of the bar equal.

The third variation (bars 76–90) is written in the style of Elizabethan virginal music and increasingly elaborate scales accompany the theme. This variation marks the central point in the movement and it is the slowest. Unlike the previous two variations, this one does not follow the established layout, but uses a ternary structure instead. Bars 76–80 (beat 1) relate to the first part of the theme. The second part, beginning in bar 80, modulates to the flat side again, and is reduced in length. The return of the first part occurs in bar 86, where it is again decorated by scalic figurations that lead directly into the fourth variation.

The fourth variation (bars 91–115) is a lively scherzo-like movement, in B flat major. This is the first variation to depart from the G major of the theme. Modulation to the flat third was an unusual choice by classical standards, but it illustrates Tippett's interest in modality and the blues. The style is influenced by Scottish pibroch (classical bagpipe music), which Tippett had learnt about from Jeffrey Mark. Traditional pibroch is usually in variation form and consists of a modal melody of increasing complexity accompanied by a drone. Clearly, Tippett does not attempt to imitate its style precisely, but he uses its typical dotted rhythms. The dotted rhythms can also be related to those in the variations of Beethoven's Piano Sonata Op. 111, a composer to whom Tippett is indebted.

This variation is closely related to the second one, as it is another two-part invention. Despite Tippett's frequent use of two-part textures, in this Sonata he does not write a fugue. This is unlike Lambert, whose textures are mainly homophonic, but who includes a brief fugato in the first movement and a fugue in the third. As in the second variation, this one consists of a first part (bars 91–4), which is repeated with invertible counterpoint (bars 95–8). The second part (bars 99–105) is also inverted in bars 106–15. As in the theme and first two variations, the second part of the theme is longer than the first. The second part uses interesting cross-rhythms to contrast with the repetition of dotted rhythms, as in bars 100, 102, 107 and 109. This type of offbeat accentuation is typical of jazz, and requires precise execution from the pianist.

The fifth variation, again in two parts, uses the most innovative sonorities. It evokes the sound of the Indonesian gamelan, which Tippett had heard on 78 rpm records during the 1930s.[43] It is the least tonal variation, owing to the rapid alternation of octaves a semitone apart, which evoke the bell-like sonorities of the gamelan. It can either be considered to be in G minor or the Lydian mode on E flat, and its irregular accents give it an improvisatory feel. In this variation Tippett dispenses with the repetition of sections, the first part lasting from bars 116 to 119 and the second from 120 to 133, leading to free development. It was this variation that Tippett modified between 1941 and 1942. In her recording, Sellick repeated bars

---

[43] The National Sound Archive holds recordings dating from 1932. (Columbia GJ 116, 119, 120).

116–19 two octaves higher and the second part was also extended. Kemp gives the original version of bars 126–7.[44]

The recapitulation of the original theme begins in G major at bar 134. Bars 134–7 use arpeggio octaves to accompany the theme, but it is essentially a direct repetition of the opening section.

Tippett deliberately juxtaposes different textures to exploit the contrast between variations. The main theme is used as material to generate the variations, but its elements are fragmented and then varied. Certain features are maintained throughout, such as the repetition of each part of the theme with variation. The use of two-part textures and octaves also provides a sense of unity. However, preconceived plans yield to the individual demands of each variation, which are all dominated by rhythm.

The second movement is in five parts (ABCB´A´). It begins with a simple folk theme, a variant of *Ca' the Yowes to the Knowes*, in the Aeolian mode. A similar melody was also used by Tippett in the violin part of the slow movement of his Concerto for Double String Orchestra (1938–9). Tippett uses the melodic contour of the folk melody, without repeating it exactly. He evens out the rhythms, which in the arrangement given here consisted of quavers followed by semiquavers and the reversal of this rhythm, the Scotch snap. The arrangement of this folk tune uses mainly chords I, III, IV and VII [Fig. 5.9]. Tippett uses these chords as the basis of his harmonization [Fig. 5.10]. The opening D–E–A of the melody is an inversion of the beginning of the first movement, which used the notes D–C–G.[45]

Fig. 5.9 *Ca' the Yowes to the Knowes*, from G. F. Graham *The Folksongs of Scotland*, Wood & Co.

The use of folk tunes and modality relates Tippett to the English pastoral tradition and works by Bax, Holst and Vaughan Williams. Unlike Bax in his Third Piano Sonata, Tippett did not attempt to compose a pastiche folksong, he adapted an existing melody. Tippett recalled the use of folk music by British composers.

> [Jeff Mark] believed, as was common at the time [1930s], that folksong had some reality in the music of any particular place. Vaughan Williams

---

[44] Ibid.,133–4.
[45] Ibid., 134.

felt this very strongly, and that so much of the music we played in concert halls was derivative of German folksong. He thought that you could begin again and produce another music but I knew perfectly well you couldn't.[46]

Fig. 5.10 Tippett, Sonata No. 1, Second movement, Schott, Bars 1–16

Tippett's harmonic technique is interesting. The essential sonority of this section is that of a triad with an added second. The use of added seconds may indicate that Tippett was familiar with some of John Ireland's works. Ireland was fond of using modes and chords of this type permeate his harmonic language. The first two bars contain the notes D, E, F and A – a D minor triad with a passing note, E. Added seconds are introduced either as passing notes or else appear as suspensions. Tippett was familiar with the rules of sixteenth-century counterpoint, but he uses features of the style in an individual way. For instance, the added second (D) in bar 3 has been prepared by implication in the tenor voice in bar 2. Its resolution onto C is anticipated in the bass part, something that the sixteenth-century composers would not have done. The preponderance of 9–8 and 4–3 suspensions in this section hint at associations with the style of Parry and Stanford. In bar 4, the supposed C major chord has a root, three thirds and no fifth. Doubling the third would have been unusual, but trebling it highlights Tippett's idiosyncratic handling of harmony.

Tippett uses root progressions in his harmonization, rather than parallel chords in the manner of Vaughan Williams. In bars 5–6 he moves from E to A, followed by G to C in bars 7–9. In bars 1–16 the harmony is particularly exposed, whereas in other movements the driving rhythms and syncopations command more attention and Tippett's harmonic insecurities are therefore less evident.

---

[46] Interview with author: see Appendix 1, p. 210.

The second section (bars 17–35) contrasts with the first in its use of contrapuntal textures, chromatic lines and variable metres. Like those in the first movement, it is another two-part invention, although the imitation is not strict. The semiquavers give it a sense of flow, and it contrasts with the first section by using limited chromaticism. Kemp has noticed similarities between the intervallic structure of the folk and invention themes, and suggests that Tippett may have been influenced by the Prelude and Fugue Op. 9 (1928) by his contemporary Alan Bush.[47] Tippett later recalled how his approach to harmony had been learnt from Bush.

> ... I was shown long ago by Alan Bush how to make use of a kind of neo-romantic harmony (which you will find in the slow movement of the first quartet) in which the harmony is markedly dissonant in order to propel the parts against each other and make them more exciting harmonically. This comes from early Schoenberg, who was thus shown to me by an Englishman. It was never direct, by looking at a Schoenberg score.[48]

Hence Tippett must have held his discussions with Bush before writing Sonata No. 1, and he was likely to have been familiar with Bush's works. Like Tippett, Bush was a non-conformist and both developed their own musical language, based on diatonicism [see pp. 93–5].

Tippett attempts to combine the two different styles in the central section beginning at bar 36. This can be compared to a similar procedure in the second movement of Bax's Third Sonata, where Bax uses the A and B themes in the concluding section of the ternary form. The semiquaver rhythm of the invention is used as an accompaniment to the modal tune, which is fragmented and decorated. The melody is transposed up a semitone to the Aeolian mode beginning on B flat. Tippett preserves its essential harmonic structure, although the end is slightly modified.

The fourth section (bars 53–66) returns to the chromatic style of the invention and its changing metres. This is followed by the folk theme, differently introduced (bars 67–83). After a two-bar introduction, the opening section is repeated, although now an extra bass part provides imitation in octaves. Thus the contrapuntal textures of the second section are successfully integrated with the opening modal theme. In the 1942 edition of the Sonata, this section was printed on three staves. It was therefore easier to compare it with the original statement and see the addition of the imitative bass part.

The third movement is like a scherzo, although it is in sonata form. As such, it is the movement that attempts to carry the greatest weight in the Sonata, but its dual purposes of being serious and providing light-hearted relief are not entirely reconciled. It uses virtuosic pianism and opens with

---

[47] Kemp, 1987, 134.
[48] Kemp and Rayment, 1963, 27.

The African–American Influence

dissonant octaves between the hands in a gesture similar to the opening of Vaughan Williams' Fourth Symphony (1931–4).[49] Fig. 5.11 illustrates the structure of the movement and its associated tonal centres.

Fig. 5.11 Tippett, Sonata No. 1, Third movement

1–112 Exposition

1–10	First subject: Theme 1	B minor
11–21	First subject: Theme 1 modified	
22–4	First subject: Theme 2	A major
25–7	First subject: Theme 2 repeated	
28–62	First subject: Theme 3	
63–71	Second subject: Theme 1	F sharp major
71–7	Second subject: Theme 1 repeated	
78–84	Second Subject: Theme 1 inverted	
85–92	Second subject: Theme 2	F sharp minor
93–106	Second subject: Theme 3	A major
107–12	Second subject: Theme 2	F sharp minor

113–94 Development

113–17	First subject: Theme 1	F sharp minor
118–22	First subject: Theme 1	A minor
123–34	First subject: Theme 1	C sharp minor
135–46	First subject: Theme 1	E minor
147–57	First subject: Theme 1	D minor
158–65	Second subject: Theme 1	E flat major
165–74	Second subject: Theme 1	
175–87	First subject: Theme 1	A major
188–91	First subject: Theme 2	
192–4	First subject: Theme 3	

195–296 Recapitulation

195–201	First subject: Theme 1	B minor
202–37	First subject: Theme 3	G major
238–46	Second subject: Theme 1	F major
246–52	Second subject: Theme 1	
252–7	Second subject: Theme 1	
258–65	Second subject: Theme 2	B minor
266–79	Second subject: Theme 3	B major
280–96	Second subject: Theme 2	B minor

---

[49] Kemp, 1987, 136.

Kemp compares Tippett's approach to modulation with Vincent d'Indy's, although he notes that Tippett only discovered d'Indy's treatise *Cours de Composition Musicale* (1912) in 1938 and by July of that year the Sonata was complete. Tippett was particularly interested in the chapter titled "La Sonate de Beethoven", and in May 1938 he wrote a report for the festival of the International Society of Contemporary Music.[50] This describes how Beethoven used modulations using tonal centres rising in fifths to produce a sense of struggle, whereas those that descended implied resignation. Thus tonality could be used to define the structure of a work, and at the same time, could evoke an emotional response from the listener.

Hindemith's use of tonal centres covers similar ground to d'Indy's, although Tippett found Hindemith's *Unterweisung Im Tonsatz* "as unrewarding as Schoenberg's theoretical works", owing to its "exclusively harmonic atmosphere".[51] Tippett maintains tonal centres throughout the Sonata, and saw their use as part of

> the back-to-the-primitive longing (negroid jazz, Indonesian gong music, etc.), whose devotees can pass several hours in one key as long as the rhythm is elemental and the timbre exotic.[52]

Whittall notes that Tippett has "a tendency to prolong single chords rather than to compose 'in progressions'. The linear motion around the chords is what matters, even when cadential definition is relatively clear."[53] This is demonstrated by the second theme (bars 22–7) which uses filled in octaves. Octave As are used as pedal points whilst the melody weaves in the middle of the texture. Octaves are the most important type of pianistic figuration in this movement – it is only the lyrical first theme of the second subject group that does not employ them. They are a unifying texture throughout the whole Sonata, and are clearly influenced by Tippett's love of Beethoven's piano music. The finale of Chopin's Sonata in B flat minor Op. 35 also uses running quavers in octaves, and the piano parts in Tippett's songs use octaves frequently. This texture has similarities with the finale of Lambert's Sonata [Fig. 5.4, see p. 136], which Tippett claimed he did not know.[54] In addition to octaves, running quavers help to unify the movement, although occasional crotchet-quaver rhythms provide welcome relief. Repetition and sequence are important constructional principles in this movement. Tippett sustains the quaver momentum to the end of the movement and it ends without a coda. The 1942 score contained the instruction "V. S. to IV".

---

[50] Tippett, *MMR*, 1938, 176–7.
[51] Tippett, 1980, 98.
[52] Ibid., 33.
[53] Whittall, 1990, 35.
[54] Interview with author: see Appendix 1, p. 208. Sixty years on, it is unlikely that he would be able to recall whether he knew Lambert's Sonata before writing his own.

The African–American Influence

The fourth movement is influenced by African–American music. Tippett acknowledged this in his programme note to Paul Crossley's recording.

> There are hints in the rondo theme of an interest in American popular music, as heard always through the ears of someone whose ancestors took English, Scottish and Irish songs with them to the new land.[55]

Tippett felt that the use of popular idioms was essential if the public was not to be alienated. Jazz was a language that all audiences could understand.

> Because jazz is a musical vernacular, it has attracted many serious composers, thinking to find in it a way through to the big public – or just a means to refresh serious music by the primitive.[56]

The syncopated rhythm of the main theme of the fourth movement is a cakewalk, a genre that was very old-fashioned and virtually forgotten by 1938. Tippett's rhythm is almost identical to that of the Trio from *Eli Green's Cake Walk – Characteristic March* by Sadie Koninsky (1896) [Fig. 5.12]. Like Koninsky, Tippett also uses a decorative grace-note figure.

Fig. 5.12 Koninsky, *Eli Green's Cake Walk – Characteristic March* (in *Ragtime Rarities: Complete Original Music for 63 Piano Rags*, ed. Trebor Jay Tichenor, Dover), Bars 1–16

Tippett's choice of ragtime as an element in his finale was unusual, although classic rags were originally written for the piano and ancestors of ragtime included the march and jig, both of which were common forms for a finale. Tippett chose rondo form (ABACABA) for the finale, to contrast with the seriousness of the preceding sonata form movement. Although Tippett's choice of form for the finale was traditional, the ragtime-derived content was not.

Tippett's fourth movement is related to ragtime by the use of duple metre,

---

[55] Philips 6500534, 1974.
[56] Tippett, 1959, 40.

major tonality and secondary ragtime as in bars 10–12. Some ragtime exploits subdominant relationships to a greater extent than dominant ones, and in the first phrase, Tippett tends towards C major rather than D.

Tippett does not attempt to imitate classic ragtime techniques, instead he extracts various features and uses them within his own style. In bar 1, the left hand plays the same syncopated rhythm as the right hand, instead of providing a regular pulse on each downbeat. Tippett's frequent doubling of the melody in octaves is not typical of ragtime, although Scott Joplin sometimes used octaves in his introductions. This technique provides unity with the previous movements of the Sonata. Each main theme uses a different type of syncopation, the rondo theme using the mid-beat type. Tippett mostly avoids the cliches of dominant-tonic progressions. The opening twelve bar phrase is repeated, with the cakewalk in the bass, accompanied by semiquaver decoration in the right hand. At bar 22 there is an extraordinary cadenza-like flourish, which elaborates the diminished seventh chord.

The first episode, beginning at bar 24, combines mid-bar syncopation with the semiquaver decoration of the previous section. Semiquaver octaves and descending arpeggios lead to a more lyrical phrase, using mid-bar, mid-beat and cross-bar syncopations (from bar 33). This soon leads to more octaves before the cakewalk returns at bar 51. This is a brief appearance of the second half of the phrase only, now in E major.

At bar 57 the second episode, consisting of fantasia-like flourishes, begins. It is repeated, a fifth lower, at bar 69. This theme uses octaves in the outer parts, decorated by semiquavers in the middle of the texture. The outer parts use syncopated rhythms, beginning on the second quaver of the bar.

The cakewalk returns in bar 85, transposed to E flat major. It is presented by the left hand, decorated by right hand semiquavers. At bar 94, the expected diminished seventh chord is replaced with components of dominant and diminished sevenths. The first episode returns at bar 97, and the opening of it is repeated at bar 124. This effects a return to the tonic for the cakewalk at bar 139. The end of this theme is modified, using chromatically altered dominant-derived harmonies that are influenced by Delius and the blues.

The possible influence of d'Indy's theory of modulation is more strongly in evidence in this movement than in the third. D'Indy thought that modulations to the first and second fifth, either ascending or descending, were weak, but modulations to the third and fourth fifths were strong.[57] The first part moves through ascending fifths, from G (rondo theme) by way of D and A (first episode) to E (recurrence of rondo theme). This is a decisive modulation, to the third fifth, highlighting the importance of the main theme. After the central section, the themes return through the descending

---

[57] See Kemp, 1987, 89–90 and 136.

cycle of fifths, beginning with the fourth one, E flat. This powerful modulation is used for the rondo theme, again stressing its importance. The first episode uses B flat and F, and finally the cakewalk returns in G major.

It is often assumed that the influence of negro spirituals upon Tippett's music first manifested itself in *A Child of our Time* (1939–41). During 1938, Tippett first heard negro spirituals in a radio broadcast, and was completely bowled over by the impression made by the singer in *Steal Away*.[58] He subsequently obtained a copy of James Weldon Johnson's *The Book of American Negro Spirituals*, five of which were later arranged in *A Child of our Time*.[59] If Tippett had heard the radio broadcast in the early part of the year, he would have had sufficient time to obtain the score and assimilate the style before writing the fourth movement of the Piano Sonata. Also, before writing *A Child of Our Time*, Tippett had heard spirituals sung by the Hall Johnson choir in the film *Green Pastures*.[60] It is possible that he had also seen this film before writing the final movement, and absorbed the idiom intuitively.

Gershwin had used quasi-spirituals in *Porgy and Bess*, although he absorbed the idiom and composed original tunes, rather than setting existing versions. Although Tippett was interested in Gershwin's music, it is unlikely that he would have had a chance to study the music of *Porgy* before writing his Sonata, as it was first performed in September 1935 and did not gain widespread recognition until 1941.

The spiritual *Somebody's Knocking at your Door* begins with a rhythm identical to Tippett's first bar, but notated at half the speed [Fig. 5.13]. *Peter, Go Ring Dem Bells* also uses syncopated rhythms, and in bar 8, climaxes on a diminished seventh chord [Fig. 5.14]. Tippett also uses a diminished seventh in bar 10, as the theme draws to its climax. The use of a diminished seventh chord, especially in the final phrase, was a feature also common to ragtime and countless popular songs. This connection may appear rather tentative; diminished seventh chords appear in many genres of music from Beethoven to Victorian song. However, further examples will illustrate similarities between Tippett's music and those of the spirituals.

In bar three, Tippett uses a flattened seventh (F natural), harmonized by an F major chord. Blue notes are not typical of ragtime, but a flattened seventh is used in the melody of *Hallelujah!* Here it is treated as part of a

---

[58] Bowen, 1985, 46–7. The first broadcast of negro spirituals during 1938 was at 9.35 p.m. on 8 May, entitled "Mississippi Nights". This may have been the broadcast referred to.
[59] James Weldon Johnson (ed.), *The Book of American Negro Spirituals*, New York, The Viking Press, 1925 (London, 1926). Tippett, 1980, 143, note 16. See also Dickinson, *ML*, 1985, 245–7, although he incorrectly states that only four of the spirituals can be found in Johnson's book. In fact, all five appear in the same keys.
[60] Warner Bros., 1936, directed by Marc Connelly and William Keighley. The choral music was arranged and conducted by Hall Johnson.

Fig. 5.13 arr. Johnson, *Somebody's Knocking at your Door*, Viking, Bars 4–9

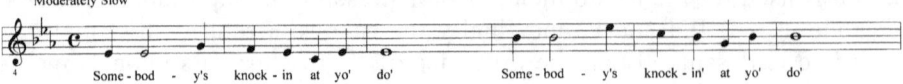

Fig. 5.14 arr. Johnson, *Peter, Go Ring Dem Bells*, Viking, Bars 1–10

dominant seventh chord [Fig. 5.15]. *John saw the Holy Number* illustrates the type of rich chromatic harmony that was used, for instance dominant sevenths and ninths [Fig. 5.16]. Chromatic harmony was very common in dance music and popular songs of the 1930s.

The last three spirituals are notated in G major. *Peter, Go Ring Dem Bells* has a pentatonic melody, and *Hallelujah!* is also mainly pentatonic. Tippett's theme begins pentatonically, and then deviates.

In Johnson's book, the majority of spirituals are in the major mode (50 major, 11 minor). G major is the most frequently used key (12 spirituals), closely followed by F major (10 spirituals). Of the G major spirituals, eight use pentatonic melodies, and seven are lively in mood. Tippett's use of G major, the pentatonic mode and similar syncopated rhythms provides evidence that he was probably aware of these pieces. When Tippett arranged the spirituals for *A Child of Our Time*, he maintained the keys used in Johnson's book. Additionally, he used certain features of their harmonization, for instance borrowing the supertonic major chord in the first phrase of *Deep River*.

Tippett's opening phrase bears a striking resemblance to the pentatonic melodic contour and syncopated rhythm of the spiritual *Do Don't Touch-a my Garment, Good Lord, I'm Gwine Home* [Fig. 5.17]. However, this spiritual is published in Johnson's *Second Book of American Negro*

Fig. 5.15 arr. Johnson, *Hallelujah!*, Viking, Bars 1–10

Fig. 5.16 arr. Johnson, *John saw the Holy Number*, Viking, Bars 1–8

Spirituals.[61] It is unclear whether Tippett possessed a copy of the subsequent volume and this spiritual is not sung in the film *Green Pastures*. The melodic contour of the opening also suggests comparison with Stephen Johnson's *Camptown Races* (1850).[62] Hence, the final movement is a hybrid of

---

[61] James Weldon Johnson, *The Second Book of American Negro Spirituals*, London, Chapman & Hall, 1927.
[62] Noted by Stephen Banfield in private correspondence.

African–American influences, both rhythmic and melodic. Tippett uses the syncopation of ragtime and spirituals, and the modality of pentatonic and blues melodies.

Fig. 5.17 arr. Johnson, *Do Don't Touch-a my Garment, Good Lord, I'm Gwine Home*, Chapman & Hall, Bars 5–12

The first performance of Tippett's Piano Sonata received a favourable review.

> Here is someone who did not insult the piano either by treating it as an overgrown dulcimer in the modern manner or by writing merely pianistic piano music as virtuosos do.[63]

Tippett considered himself to be a mediocre pianist, but this enabled him to reconsider the potential of the piano from a more distant standpoint. He studied the piano at the Royal College, and became familiar with the repertoire, including music by Scarlatti, Beethoven and Ravel. Possibly he had problems with the co-ordination of two independently moving hands, which may give a clue to his over-reliance on the use of octaves in this Sonata. The use of octaves was a standard part of Austro-German piano technique and was used by composers from Beethoven to Brahms. Tippett's fondness for two-part textures is influenced by Baroque music, and it

[63] See Schott, *A Man of our Time*, 1977, 31. No reference is made to the source of the cutting.

exploits the individuality of the two hands. It was in Tippett's Third Sonata (1972-3) that he developed this idea further, where the two hands mirror each other in moving outwards to the extremities of the piano. In this Sonata, as in subsequent ones, Tippett did not limit what he wrote to what he could play. He was the antithesis to Britten, who was a good pianist, yet wrote virtually no large-scale works for piano solo.

Mellers' review of Sellick's recording of the Fantasy Sonata observed

> It is therefore a pleasure to be able to announce that English music has in Michael Tippett a composer whose music is as airy, gracious and unteutonic as could be, yet is unmistakably the expression of a sensibility of real distinction.[64]

Sackville-West had some reservations, chiefly that the jazz snippets did not seem to fit comfortably in Tippett's style and that sometimes he became so fixated by a figuration that it had the effect of note-spinning.[65] The latter comment is appropriate to parts of the third movement, but the former seems unjustified. Tippett eventually succeeds in assimilating jazz idioms into his own style more successfully than Lambert. Lambert's Sonata uses African-American idioms throughout, whereas the jazz influence is less overt in Tippett's Sonata. Tippett is more selective in his use of African-American idioms, and his style is a result of a much wider variety of influences than Lambert. This was the reason that Lambert was unable to develop his style further whereas Tippett turned his African-American derivations into the basis of much of his mature work and was able to continue exploring the many possibilities that this music opened up to him.

Unlike many of the British composers, including Lambert, who wrote piano sonatas early in their careers, Tippett took time to mature as a composer, writing his first published works when he reached the age of thirty. In this respect he was similar to Lennox Berkeley, whose Sonata is mentioned in the following chapter (pp. 168-70). Tippett had been able to develop a personal style that could be used as a basis for subsequent compositions. He was able to follow this Sonata with a further three piano sonatas that are more important in terms of his overall output.

In the previous two chapters, the impact of World War I was noted as a particularly important stimulus to creativity. Tippett's Sonata was not written as a response to war, but his pacifist beliefs led him to be imprisoned as a conscientious objector during World War II. His musical response to the war came in *A Child of Our Time*, and subsequent operas have depicted racial tension and the alienation of individuals.

Despite being a hybrid of wide-ranging influences, Tippett's Sonata No. 1 forms a coherent whole. He manages to retain a link with the Germanic tradition by including movements in variation, ternary, sonata and rondo

---

[64] Mellers, *Scrutiny*, 1942, 309.
[65] Sackville-West, *The New Statesman and Nation*, 1941, 397-8.

forms. Tippett's use of traditional forms links him with the neo-classical approaches of Stravinsky and Ravel. Like Stravinsky, Tippett uses irregular metrical patterns. Both composers' rhythms were influenced by their respective languages, Russian and English, and they incorporated elements of their modal folk traditions. Stravinsky's contrapuntal textures are related to neo-Baroque ideas, and he was also influenced by ragtime.

Tippett's music shows some similarities with the neo-classical approach of Hindemith, who advocated the use of tonal centres. Hindemith used counterpoint frequently, but unlike Stravinsky and Tippett, paid comparatively little attention to rhythm. Hindemith tended to use regular metres, even if their division was irregular. Hence Tippett's neo-classicism is closer to Stravinsky's than Hindemith's. The tendency towards a neo-classical style is also exhibited by Bax's Fourth Sonata (1932) and Arnold Cooke's First Sonata (1938), a composer who studied with Hindemith [see Chapters 3 and 6].

Tippett's harmony is anti-romantic; he rejects the extravagance of ninth, eleventh and thirteenth chords that typified the harmonies of Scriabin, Bridge, Sorabji and to some extent, Lambert, and instead favours the neoclassical economy of resources. Tippett's harmony is tonal or modal throughout, and consequently his Sonata is considerably less dissonant than Bridge's. Unlike that in Lambert's Sonata, Tippett's harmony is a result of contrapuntal textures; he tends to think linearly rather than vertically. Tippett's linear approach also leads to the independence of rhythms in each voice. The rhythmic impetus is the main transmitter of Tippett's personal style, and as a consequence he does not need harmonic innovation. Whilst acknowledging the Austro-German tradition, he revitalized it by placing an emphasis on rhythm, as Lambert had done. However, Tippett's consistent use of irregular syncopated rhythms that are not restricted by harmonic constraints makes even this early Sonata more original than Lambert's.

The integration of jazz and classical music to form symphonic jazz had been common in the 1920s, but in the 1930s there were fewer attempts to synthesize these two elements. Perhaps this can be accounted for by the English temperament. The jazzy works of Walton and Lambert were seen as part of the extravagance and witticism of the 1920s, but the typical Englishman was reserved and discouraged from expressing unrestrained emotions. There were two different markets, one for popular music and jazz, the other for serious classical music, and there was little overlap between them. Also, jazz idioms were incapable of expressing a wide range of emotions, which Copland found. The only way in which jazz could form the basis of a future musical language was by a complete stylistic integration with classical music, which in Tippett, came later on. However, Sonata No. 1 proves more than any other that to write an original British piano sonata, a variety of influences from outside the Austro-German tradition needed to be synthesized.

6

Observations Drawn from Selected Sonatas 1930–1945

The purpose of this chapter is to confirm earlier observations and to carry the discussion forward to another unstable war period. Minor figures are included merely to cast light on the overall scene; no attempt is made to conduct a comprehensive discussion of the sonatas.

The period 1930–1945 was a significant one for the British symphony, including the composition of Walton's First Symphony, Vaughan Williams' Fourth and Fifth Symphonies, Bax's Fourth, Fifth, Sixth and Seventh Symphonies and Havergal Brian's Second, Third, Fourth and Fifth Symphonies. There appeared to be a greater interest in the composition of large-scale orchestral works than solo and chamber music. This was unusual, because chamber music provided a means of developing new styles on a small scale. In fact, there were many attempts at writing piano sonatas, although most of them were juvenilia. Composers of such works include Arnold Cooke, who destroyed a Piano Sonata written when he was fifteen, John Gardner, who withdrew all of his compositions written before World War II, Elizabeth Lutyens, Malcolm Arnold and Harold Truscott.

As we have already observed, the Royal Academy of Music had been the most significant institution in the training of pianists and composers of piano sonatas, including Dale, Bax, Bowen and Bush, in the first two decades of the twentieth century. Despite this, Ireland and Bridge, both educated at the Royal College of Music, produced a large corpus of works for the piano. From the 1920s onwards, the Royal College, with its piano professors Harold Samuel, Cyril Smith and Angus Morrison, became a more significant training ground for composers of piano sonatas. Its pupils included Lambert, Tippett, Britten, Arnold, Truscott, Howard Ferguson, Antony Hopkins and Mervyn Roberts. The only composer to write piano sonatas between 1930 and 1945, having been educated at the Royal Academy, was Joseph Holbrooke (1878–1958). He had studied under Corder in the early years of the twentieth century, but his piano sonatas, written in 1936 and 1938, were late works.

Since the early years of the English Musical Renaissance, the Royal College had been associated with traditional methods of teaching, including a thorough grounding in sixteenth-century counterpoint and Austro-German musical forms. In 1934, Sir Hugh Allen, the Director of the Royal College, refused Britten permission to study with Berg, despite the encouragement of his teacher, Frank Bridge, considering serialism to be an unsuitable influence. Hopkins, who was educated at the Royal College between 1939 and 1943, recalled that

> Dyson was the director, and he didn't like modern music, so little was performed. There were no twentieth-century music courses, and I never heard a note of Stravinsky when I was there. Neither did I hear a note of Purcell. It was just mainstream nineteenth-century music.[1]

This view of Dyson seems rather harsh. His *The New Music*, written in 1924, formed a landmark in serious musical criticism, in which he discussed music by Debussy, Scriabin, Schoenberg and Bartók. He was well aware of contemporary developments, even if his own compositional style remained traditionally grounded in the Parry–Stanford tradition. Ferguson had been a contemporary of Lambert and Tippett, studying at the Royal College with R. O. Morris and Vaughan Williams from 1925. He recalled knowing a great deal of contemporary music, including Stravinsky, although he was not greatly influenced by him.

> Most of the others were more interested in the progressive trends of modernism than I was. Betty Maconchy was interested in Bartók ...[2]

Rubbra, who wrote in 1938 that the Royal College was a revolutionary place, supported Ferguson's view; piano players would perform Stravinsky's *Rite of Spring* and Prokofiev's *Chout*.[3]

Nevertheless, the Royal College's emphasis on classical forms and methods of construction of piano sonatas did not go unheeded by its pupils. Ferguson's Piano Sonata (1938–40) is a fine example of a classically constructed work that stems directly from the rhetorical tradition of Beethoven and Brahms.

Ferguson was unable to devote long periods of time to composition, because he had many musical activities, like Lambert. He performed in chamber ensembles, accompanied soloists and enjoyed editing. During World War II he assisted Myra Hess in organizing a daily series of concerts at the National Gallery, and it was Hess who premièred his Piano Sonata at one of these concerts in April 1940.[4]

[1] Interview with author: see Appendix 1, p. 204.
[2] Interview with author: see Appendix 1, p. 187.
[3] Rubbra, *MMR*, 1938, 100–103.
[4] The first broadcast of this work occurred at 11.30 a.m., 27 October 1940. Hess also recorded the Sonata.

Observations Drawn from Selected Sonatas

The work is published as Piano Sonata in F minor and Ferguson retains a strong feeling for tonality. Both the first and third movements use conventional sonata form, although Ferguson shortens the recapitulation of his second subjects in both cases, to allow for a coda. The published score contained a discussion of the structure of the work by Denis Matthews. Unfortunately it was included on a loose-leaf sheet, which may be lost easily.

The Sonata was inspired by the sudden death of Ferguson's teacher, Harold Samuel, with whom he shared a house. Samuel was admired as an interpreter of Bach, Beethoven and Brahms, and it was he who helped to foster Ferguson's love for this repertoire. Just as Bridge had been inspired to write a Piano Sonata in memory of his friend who had been killed in action during World War I, Ferguson's inspiration came from the loss of Samuel and his pessimism at the start of World War II. Paul Spicer noted this connection in an interview with Ferguson in 1988, but he did not elaborate on their common harmonic language.[5]

The opening of Ferguson's Sonata, which presents an important motto that recurs in every movement, conveys a sense of anger and despair [Fig. 6.1]. The motto contains a falling semitone, recalling the opening of Vaughan Williams' Fourth Symphony (1934), also in F minor. Ferguson's C major and D flat minor triads of bar 1 contain overlapping thirds. This bitonal technique was also used in Bridge's Sonata, and the harmonies can be analysed as the combination of a minor triad plus a major one a semitone lower [See Fig. 4.7 (p. 117), Bridge chord version 2]. Bar 4 uses the combination of B flat minor and C major triads. This chord, a minor triad plus a major one a tone higher, is the third version of the Bridge chord, the sonority with which his Sonata is saturated.

Unlike Bridge, Ferguson does not consistently use this chord throughout his Sonata. He contrasts the outer dissonant movements with a diatonic central one in D flat, which owes more to the lyricism of the early nineteenth century than the twentieth. The contrast of old and new harmonic languages was also a feature of Bridge's Sonata, but the effect of Ferguson's is too dramatic and indicates an incongruity in his style.

Ferguson played Bridge's *Rosemary* in a competition in Belfast at which Samuel discovered him. He had heard later piano and chamber works by Bridge, including the Piano Sonata, in which the Bridge chord is used. I questioned Ferguson about these connections, but he replied that he did not like Bridge's Sonata.[6] He was extremely reluctant to divulge any information about influences on his music, claiming that

> I don't think that one can ever tell about influence in one's own works. They obviously must be there, but one can't identify them. Other people have to do that.[7]

---

[5] Ferguson, Eightieth Birthday talk, 28 October 1988, BMIC Cassette 584.
[6] Interview with author: see Appendix 1, p. 187. See also Chapter 4, pp. 123–4.
[7] Interview with author: see Appendix 1, p. 187.

Fig. 6.1 Ferguson, Sonata, Boosey & Hawkes, First movement, Bars 1–6

The resonant sonorities of the first movement's introduction are succeeded by the main Allegro inquieto, consisting of lighter textures and two-part counterpoint. Successive entries are carefully worked out, using transposition and inversion. His use of two-part counterpoint and octaves bears some comparison with Tippett's Sonata No. 1. However, Ferguson was content to continue in a romantic tradition, derived from Brahms and

Observations Drawn from Selected Sonatas

Bridge, whereas Tippett was more experimental and able to integrate diverse influences. Unlike Tippett, Ferguson was not influenced by jazz or folk music, despite his Irish ancestry. Interestingly, by 1946, the only British piano sonatas to have been recorded were those by Tippett and Ferguson.[8]

Another composer who was educated at the Royal College was Malcolm Arnold. His Sonata was written two years after he left the College, in 1942, remaining in manuscript for fifty years, until Roberton reproduced it for publication. Benjamin Frith has recently recorded Arnold's complete piano music, which spans his composing career.

The Sonata was written as a birthday present for Arnold's mother.[9] Arnold has always been a fluent composer, performer and conductor. With Lambert he shared a hatred of the folksong school of composition, but more significantly, a love for jazz. The playing of Louis Armstrong made a significant impact upon the young boy and he received a trumpet for his sixteenth birthday. Although he was principally a trumpeter, he studied the piano at the Royal College.

Arnold's Sonata is in three concise movements, lasting about ten minutes. He retains a strong sense of tonality throughout, using the key of B minor. This is primarily achieved by ostinati and pedal points in the first movement, in sonata form. Arnold makes no harmonic innovations and chords are almost exclusively triadic. The melody of the second movement is more chromatic, and the third is a lively and ironic Alla marcia. This movement uses more two-part writing and harmonic clichés [Fig. 6.2]. Bitonality results from using different keys in each hand. This may be influenced by Prokofiev, a composer who was becoming an important influence upon the British composer, owing to his development of the piano sonata genre. Like Hindemith's, Arnold's piano writing is practical and not virtuosic.

Fig. 6.2 Arnold, Sonata, Roberton, Third movement, Bars 62–75

[8] Bacharach (ed.), 1946, 235–56.
[9] Burton-Page, 1994, 11.

Like Ferguson's and Arnold's, Hopkins' education at the Royal College encouraged an acceptance of sonata form, and his three piano sonatas, written in 1944, 1945 and 1946–8, are text-book examples of this form.[10] Like Arnold, another composer who has written numerous film scores, Hopkins found composition easy, and wrote his Second Sonata in two and a half days. Most of his output was written in response to commission rather than for posterity. The exceptions were the piano sonatas, which Hopkins wrote to form a centrepiece to his own piano recitals. However, he lacked a solid technical foundation to his piano training and found them challenging to perform.

The syncopated rhythms of Hopkins' First Sonata are influenced by ragtime. Although he claimed not to have known any other British piano sonatas whilst writing his own, he had admired Lambert's *The Rio Grande* since he was a schoolboy. The opening of the Sonata uses a syncopated rhythm in octaves. Fig. 6.3 shows the beginning of the second subject, with the syncopated theme returning in bars 23 and 24. It is similar to the finale of Lambert's Sonata, illustrated in Fig. 5.4 (p. 136). Hopkins uses a curious mixture of chromatic and diatonic harmonies.

Fig. 6.3 Hopkins, Sonata No. 1, Chester, First movement, Bars 12–24

[10] The dates given in *The New Grove* differ from the above, which are taken from Hopkins, 1982, 213–14. Details regarding dates of revisions are clarified in my interview with Hopkins in Appendix 1, pp. 199–200.

Observations Drawn from Selected Sonatas

Hopkins sang in Morley College Choir, which Tippett conducted, and occasionally deputized for him. He occasionally stayed with Tippett in Oxted, and Tippett gave Hopkins advice about composition. Hopkins' Second Sonata is dedicated to Tippett, and its language is indebted to him. The second movement is a two-part invention, and the third uses a recurring motif that is almost identical to part of the third movement of Tippett's Sonata No. 1 [Figs. 6.4 and 6.5].

Fig. 6.4 Hopkins, Sonata No. 2, Manuscript, Third movement, Bars 1–5

Fig. 6.5 Tippett, Sonata No. 1, Schott, Third movement, Bars 93–9

Hopkins must have known Tippett's Sonata by 1945, because it had been recorded by Sellick and published by Schott. Like Tippett's, Hopkins' piano writing relies heavily on octaves. This may be a result of his poor performance technique, or a result of the influence of Beethoven on both composers. Like Tippett, Hopkins uses irregular accentuation, which is achieved in both examples by multimetricism.

Hopkins' Third Sonata, written for the pianist Noel Mewton-Wood, is indebted to Hindemith.

> He played things like Hindemith's *Ludus Tonalis* and his Piano Sonatas in such a way that it made you feel that they were the greatest music that had ever been written.[11]

Tragically, Mewton-Wood committed suicide before Hopkins had shown the piece to him. Hopkins felt that it echoes Hindemith, "especially in the first movement, where there are chunky chords going out in opposite directions".[12] The existing third movement, written in 1948, replaced the

---

[11] Interview with author: see Appendix 1, p. 199.
[12] Ibid., p. 200.

original. Hopkins knew Hindemith, and had read his theories. Like Hindemith, Hopkins rejected serialism, retained tonal centres, and used contrapuntal textures in preference to harmonic ones, features that Tippett's Sonata No. 1 also displayed.

Hopkins' First Sonata received a favourable review by the *Yorkshire Post*, which praised its qualities of lyricism, melodic line and straightforwardness.[13] It appealed to the average concert-goer, but its style was old-fashioned and it is unsurprising that it has not remained in the repertoire. Hopkins performed his Second Sonata at the Salle Gaveau in Paris in 1946. As a result, the reviewer thought that Hopkins deserved to stand at the head of the young British school of composers, beside Britten.[14] This flattering opinion seems quite incredible. Unlike Hopkins' First and Third Sonatas, the Second was never published, possibly because of its attempt to recreate pastiche Tippett.

Hopkins observed that recently there has been a revival of British music previously considered imitative, and wondered whether his Piano Sonatas would soon become popular.

> I would love them to be considered more seriously by pianists. Someone played one at the Wigmore Hall about three years ago. It had a criticism saying that this is an admirably written piece, and I'm sure that it served its purpose in its time, but it's of little interest now. It's unfashionable, but if there's hope for Parry now, maybe there's hope for the Hopkins Sonatas![15]

Hopkins' main failing was his inability to cultivate a personal musical style. Pastiche composition was ideal for film scores, but not for serious musical works. If audiences wanted to listen to Hindemith or Tippett, they would go to listen to their piano sonatas, not a pale imitation of them.

Like Lambert and Tippett, Arnold and Hopkins were influenced by African–American syncopation. There have always been inherent difficulties in combining jazz with classical music, in that classical musicians are reluctant to take it seriously, whereas audiences who prefer jazz expect to hear improvisations and displays of virtuosity. Jazz works are performed differently by individual musicians, and are varied at each performance, whereas for classical music, the performer strives to give a faithful interpretation of the score.

The influence of Hindemith has been mentioned in connection with the neo-classicism of Tippett and the musical language of Arnold and Hopkins. Like Tippett, Arnold Cooke studied with Charles Wood, although at Cambridge, and subsequently went to Berlin between 1929 and 1932 to study with Hindemith. This was a relatively unusual choice for a British

---

[13] See Hopkins, 1982, 123.
[14] Ibid., 130.
[15] Interview with author: see Appendix 1, p. 206.

composer, although Walter Leigh and Franz Reizenstein were also educated by Hindemith. Reizenstein performed Cooke's piano works, and wrote piano sonatas that demonstrate Hindemith's influence.

Cooke's First Piano Sonata (1938) remains in manuscript, although it was performed in Manchester in 1939. The majority of Cooke's music was written to commission, but he usually had a performer in mind when he composed. However, there is no indication for whom he wrote his First Piano Sonata.

The music of the First Sonata is mainly tonal, and the intervals of the fourth and fifth are important in the construction of melodies and harmonies. The first movement uses a rondo structure rather than sonata form, although when the themes recur they are subject to development. Like Hindemith, Cooke uses contrapuntal sections and his piano writing is practicable and accessible.

Cooke was the Professor of the Royal Manchester College of Music from 1933 to 1938. He was replaced by Richard Hall, a prolific composer of piano sonatas dating from the mid 1930s, which all remain unpublished. Both Cooke and Hall tried to encourage young composers to keep abreast of contemporary European musical developments, but the provincialism of the college reflected the national attitude that was aggravated by the war. It was not until the 1950s that things changed, when Hall taught the composers Peter Maxwell Davies, Alexander Goehr, Harrison Birtwistle and John Ogdon.

Unlike Stravinsky and Prokofiev, Bartók did not make a significant impact on British composers. He made his British début in 1904, having been invited by Richter to perform in Manchester, but his subsequent visit in 1922 was more widely acclaimed. Periodical articles had prepared the public for his second visit, but his folksong compositions were generally better received than his abstract music. Henry Wood did much to promote Bartók's orchestral music, Cecil Gray was a keen supporter and Philip Heseltine corresponded with Bartók and performed his works. Edward Clark resigned his position at the BBC in 1936 in protest at the removal of Bartók's Four Orchestral Pieces from a concert by the BBC Symphony Orchestra. However, the general public received a poor impression of Bartók from the press. Percy Scholes, the first music critic at the BBC and the critic for the *Observer*, hated Bartók's Violin Sonatas and although his view was extreme, it was widely disseminated.

Bartók's piano music was of two types – pieces suited to amateurs and those for professionals. In 1923, George Woodhouse, a piano teacher, organized concerts at his studio that led to interest in Bartók's pre-war piano pieces as ideal teaching material. Bartók's Piano Sonata (1926), which he performed as part of a BBC concert of contemporary music on 4 March 1929, uses the piano percussively. Only the first hour of the concert was broadcast, and Bartók deliberately left the Sonata until the second part, considering it too difficult for the radio audience. Ferguson described how

Bartók's memory failed him twice during the performance.[16] By 1933 Bartók preferred to play it with the score, and in 1934 he tried to leave the Sonata out of a programme as he was worried that it would frighten the audience![17] The percussive use of the piano was not influential in Britain.

The final important British work to demonstrate the influence of neo-classicism is Lennox Berkeley's Sonata (1942–5). His neo-classicism stems from Stravinsky and Prokofiev, rather than Hindemith. Like Lambert, Berkeley was heavily influenced by French culture, having studied French at Oxford University and then under Nadia Boulanger in France from 1927 to 1933. Here he met Ravel, and became familiar with repertoire by Les Six, especially the piano music of Poulenc. From the French composers Berkeley developed his bitonal harmonic language, and like Lambert and Tippett, the blues also influenced him.

Berkeley's sense of form indicates his classical tendencies. The Sonata is in four movements, consisting of a first movement in sonata form, a scherzo, a slow movement in ternary form and a rondo finale. The allegiance to tradition and use of sonata forms inherited from the classical composers is similar to Prokofiev, whose nine Piano Sonatas are indebted to these well-established forms.

Berkeley's musical maturity occurred quite late and he was in his early forties when this Sonata was written. He is generally less innovative with his rhythms than Tippett, although he uses a limited amount of multimetricism. His second movement is a moto perpetuo, consisting of motoric semiquavers.

Berkeley's harmonies are mainly derived from tonality, but in an individual way. The use of clear, contrapuntal textures associates Berkeley, Tippett and Prokofiev with the prevailing neo-classical aesthetics of the period.

> My attitude to harmony is that it should always be the result of the horizontal movement of parts and not thought of as an alignment of individual chords – this gives point to harmony and enables one to employ chords like the dominant thirteenth (yes, I admit it without shame) which otherwise sound too sugary.[18]

His training in France, which included the study of strict counterpoint, influenced Berkeley's contrapuntal approach to composition. His bitonality results both from the coincidence of melodies and the superimposition of chords. Bitonality provides interest to the harmonies but does not result in a high level of dissonance.

Berkeley's melodies are lyrical, but they are not associated with folk tunes, unlike the melodies of Bax and some of Tippett's. Seemingly

---

[16] See Gillies, 1989, 75.
[17] Ibid.
[18] See Dickinson, *MT*, 1978, 409–11.

conventional melodies are harmonized in an unexpected way, as in Fig. 6.6, taken from the development of the first movement of the Sonata.

Fig. 6.6 Berkeley, Sonata, Chester, First movement, Bars 99–106

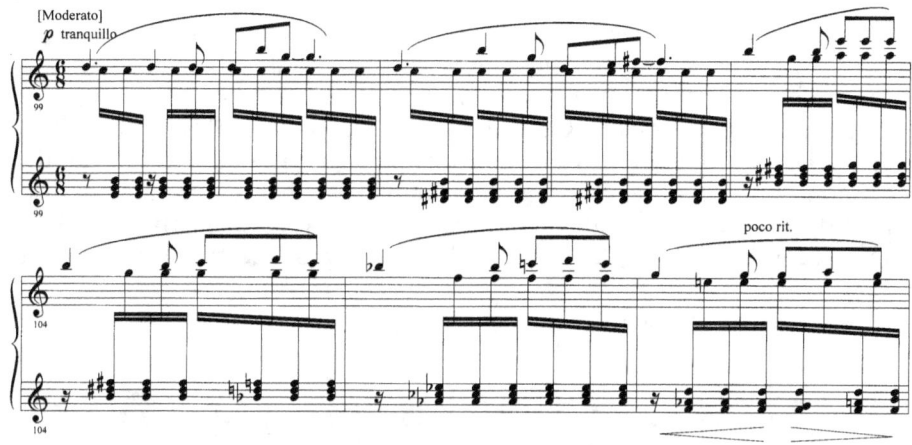

The melody of this passage could be harmonized using primary triads in G major, but Berkeley avoids this, using E minor and B major triads in the first four bars. The note C is repeated in the middle part, as an ostinato. It acts as an added sixth to the E minor triad and as an added second to the B major one. Added seconds and sixths were a characteristic part of Ireland's harmonies, and this passage illustrates Berkeley's affinity with diatonicism. The second half of the phrase introduces an unexpected note in the melody, a B flat, which is the blues third of G. The accompanying chords use a mixture of added minor and major seconds and sixths, and the triads descend chromatically.

The melody contains the interval of the major sixth. This interval acts as a recurring motif throughout the Sonata, appearing in both the first and second subjects of the first movement, and the beginning of the second movement. Berkeley uses methods of thematic transformation, modifying themes on each subsequent repetition. When the first movement's exposition returns for the recapitulation it is shortened considerably and the second subject is modified. In the final movement, the rondo theme is harmonized differently on each occurrence.

Other cross-referencing of material between movements includes the combination of thirds (the inversion of the sixth) and semiquavers in the second section of the third movement (from bar 29). These textures are also used in the rondo theme of the final movement (from bar 26). In the finale, a fragment of the scherzo second movement is recalled (bars 196–201), and the coda of the movement is marked by the return of the introduction (bars 207–15). The ways in which elements of previous movements are recalled in the final one are reminiscent of the principles used by Scott, who advocated the use of principal themes in the finale of a sonata, to provide a sense of unity. This appears to be Berkeley's intention also.

Like Bax, Ireland, Bridge and Bowen, Berkeley wrote prolifically for the piano. His pianistic style is always practicable, and is aimed at the accomplished pianist, not only the professional virtuoso. Despite the appearances of the second movement's toccata, the semiquavers lie comfortably underneath the hands. Berkeley's piano writing demonstrates his familiarity with Austro-German pianism, especially Brahms and Beethoven. There are numerous examples of passages in octaves, and another common texture is that of a melody doubled at the octave, with a filled in third or sixth. This pianistic figuration is derived from Brahms and it can be seen in Fig. 6.7, taken from the opening of the fourth movement.

Fig. 6.7 Berkeley, Sonata, Fourth movement, Bars 1–4

The piano sonatas of the period 1930–1945 demonstrate neo-classical tendencies, influenced by Stravinsky, Prokofiev and Hindemith. The extravagance of late romantic harmonies has been rejected in favour of clarity of texture, and counterpoint has become more important than homophony. Composers are now more preoccupied with the structure of their sonatas, and endeavour to articulate its formal outlines. Of the works discussed in this chapter, Berkeley's is by far the most important. It is a well-constructed work, and its use of traditional pianism and lyricism has endeared it to the public. It has been championed by Colin Horsley, although originally written for and premièred by Clifford Curzon. Raphael Terroni and Christopher Headington have also made recordings. It deserves to stand the test of time and feature in recitals in the twenty-first century.

Conclusions

Germanic influences have been a factor throughout this study. This was not unique to Britain and it is important to remember that the Austro-German language dominated Western music during the nineteenth century. The British lacked a native tradition and needed an existing model to form the basis of their subsequent developments. Tracing other influences has led to consideration of music from France, Russia and America, and suggests that the British composers were not as insular in their approach to composition as was once imagined.

The works of the early 1920s form the climax to the development of the British piano sonata. During the World War I, a sense of national pride and an increased consciousness of British folk music became more important. The piano sonatas of Bax, Ireland, Bridge, Bush and Tippett used folk music or modality to express their national sources. It is significant that during the war itself no piano sonatas were written, but in its immediate aftermath, works by Bax, Ireland, Sorabji and Bridge were completed. The stimulus of war undoubtedly contributed to Bax's Second and Third Sonatas and Bridge's Sonata. Both composers developed a new harmonic language, derived from Scriabin, which attempted to express the atrocities of war. The response to war is the principal factor that links these piano sonatas and makes them identifiably British.

The experience of war provided the incentive to make an emotional statement through the medium of the piano sonata. Thus a type of British expressionism was developed, contemporary with similar developments in Germany. By the 1920s, British composers were able to keep abreast of developments in European music, and were no longer lagging behind. This was in contrast to the British composers of the late nineteenth century, who wrote piano sonatas using classical idioms, which were more than fifty years out of date.

The major British composers, Delius, Elgar, Holst, Vaughan Williams and Britten, had tended to write orchestral works instead of piano works, as they found more expressive potential in an orchestra. This followed a trend exemplified by other major composers such as Tchaikovsky, Wagner, Strauss and Mahler. Debussy, Ravel and Messiaen, who were noted as composers of orchestral music, wrote a considerable number of piano pieces. However, they distanced themselves from the sonata whereas the British did not. In Germany, Schoenberg, Webern and Berg wrote some piano music to articulate their new compositional techniques, but preferred writing for orchestra or voice.

Attention to sonority, and attempts to recreate rich orchestral colours on the piano, were crucial factors in the progress of the British piano sonata. By the early twentieth century, Debussy, Scriabin and Delius were writing impressionistic music that relied on freely flowing ideas as a basis for continuity. Delius proved to be the one British composer whose technique influenced this country's piano sonatas, although he wrote little piano music himself. It was his orchestral music that proved influential. It combines impressionism, the sensuous use of sounds, free flow and African–American elements. These factors have been identified as being significant in British piano sonatas from 1908 to 1936. No other non-Germanic style remained as important over three decades as Delius' music. He prepared the ground for a golden age of piano sonatas.

British piano sonatas demonstrate few innovations in rhythm. In this respect a parallel can be drawn with German music, which is chiefly concerned with melody and harmony. Scott's multimetricism was the first example of irregular rhythms, and Sorabji's complex groupings are a result of the attempt to notate improvising practices, as are Lambert's. It was not until the influence of African–American music, as seen in the Sonatas by Lambert and Tippett, that vitality of rhythm became important. It took nearly two decades for Stravinsky's primitive and irregular rhythms or Messiaen's discoveries in Indian music to influence British music. The British even ruled India until 1947, but no-one was interested in its music. The public preferred lyrical and expressive music to rhythmic styles, and the influence of African–American music proved short-lived.

Scott, Sorabji and Lambert came the closest to breaking away from tradition in their anti-establishment attitudes and the improvisatory style of their music, but it was impossible to reject completely such embedded musical traditions. However, Sorabji's harmonies do not function tonally and his avoidance of sonata form makes his the most radical of the British sonatas.

Although we can now appreciate their significance, none of these piano sonatas made a great impact on the public at the time of their first performance, as we have seen. Sorabji's and Bridge's Sonatas were misunderstood because they were dissonant, and they have been shamefully neglected until recently. They are now being included in recitals and are recorded on compact disc, and it is to be hoped that the public will appreciate them with hindsight. We now seem to be entering an age where all compositions, including unpublished compositions and juvenilia, are available through publication or recording. This is demonstrated by the catalogue and discography in Appendices 2 and 3.

Throughout the seventy-five year period considered here, Germanic influences were constantly present, although they were often subordinate. Initial classical tendencies gave way to late romantic techniques, exemplified

Conclusions

by Wagner and Strauss. The development of this harmonic language to its extreme led to expressionism. By the mid 1920s this style was at the limit of its development. A subsequent reaction to its emotionalism heralded a return to the new classical style, or neo-classicism. It is hardly surprising that composers of the 1950s began to embrace serialism – another Austro-German discovery.

It is ironic that, having tried so hard to break free from the Teutonic stranglehold of classical music in the late nineteenth century, and having demonstrated such passionate anti-German sentiments during World War I, British composers continued to return to German music for inspiration. British composers always brought new dimensions to the Austro-German style, but ultimately they were unable to reject completely the traditions of the previous three hundred years.

Appendix 1: Interview Transcriptions

In 1993, I arranged to meet four composers whose piano sonatas are discussed in the text: Alan Bush, Howard Ferguson, Antony Hopkins and Michael Tippett. Also, I met Geoffrey Bush, the editor of piano music by John Ireland and William Sterndale Bennett, and Alan Frank, who published Constant Lambert's music at Oxford University Press. The following unique conversations were conducted in the relaxed surroundings of the interviewee's own homes, and are reproduced here in order to supplement the information given in the main text.

Alan Bush[1]

You began your composition studies at the Royal Academy of Music in 1918. What do you remember about these lessons?

I was very happy at the Royal Academy of Music, where I studied with Frederick Corder. He was a very good teacher. He taught the facts of music history, which was a very important subject. I wanted to know what had happened in the past, what was important and why it was important. It was a very traditional education. The compositions that I wrote were performed within the four walls of the Royal Academy of Music. I considered it to be very important to get instrumental and orchestral works rehearsed and performed. I played my Op. 2 Piano Sonata there.

Corder had previously taught Benjamin Dale at the Royal Academy of Music and was very impressed with his Piano Sonata. He once referred to your Piano Sonata Op. 2 as "A second Benjamin Dale Sonata".[2] Did you see yourself following in Dale's footsteps?

I do remember Dale, but I cannot recall comparisons being made about our music.

Corder had a passionate interest in Wagner's music.

Yes, that was rather a pity, because Wagner was rather a dangerous composer to be influenced by.

I think that some traces of his influence are discernible in the slow section of your Piano Sonata Op. 2.

No, definitely not. I would avoid being influenced by him. Wagner was a

---

[1] Radlett, 11 March 1993.
[2] Stevenson, 1981, 39.

composer who dominated many people then. I did not want to be one of them.

Did Brahms influence you?

Yes, he did. By studying his works I learnt instrumentation.

To what extent did your piano teachers Benno Moiseiwitsch, Mabel Lander and Artur Schnabel influence your musical taste?

Moiseiwitsch and his assistant Lander taught the Leschetizky method very systematically. Previously I'd been taught by quite a wrong method. I think that it would be true to say that I practised mainly Bach, Beethoven and Brahms. They were the greatest composers of their respective periods. I was encouraged to study seriously and analyse sonatas by Beethoven and Brahms. I would understand the different things that it was possible to do next. You have to decide to do one or the other and that's a very important choice.

As a pianist, you used to perform works by British composers such as Ireland, Bridge and Bax.

Yes, I did. I knew them. I met Britten a number of times. He was a very imperious personality, a very able musician, but he wasn't a person who I'd thought of as a particularly good teacher of composition.

Your piano teacher, Lily West, introduced you to John Ireland, with whom you studied composition from 1921 to 1927. How did Ireland's approach to teaching composition differ from Corder's?

That is a very difficult question to answer. Ireland's lessons were very statutory, and properly organized. I had to play through what I had written. We discussed different passages and he suggested some alterations. Some passages lasted too long, others I needed to make more of. That's how a teacher of composition works. He takes what the pupil has composed and goes through it in detail. That is very important. Then he discusses it with his pupil. Ireland understood what I was trying to do in a particular composition and would criticize to what extent I had succeeded in what I thought I was doing.

Do you remember Ireland helping you with your Piano Sonata?

Yes. He was very careful in what he said but if he thought that something in my piece was not suitable, not sufficient, then he would say so, in a very polite way. Then you'd try to do better!

In 1929 you went to Berlin to study philosophy and musicology. You didn't have lessons with Schoenberg, did you?

No, but I knew his music, though. He taught a strict and intelligent way of composing in many ways, but it was quite severe and tucked away.

Did you consider your compositions to be part of a British tradition?

Yes, I did. I was a pupil of John Ireland and I did think of it from the point of view of a national style. That's a good point you've raised. I practised a national style in principle. There were many German composers, so it was very important to write in a national idiom.

Did you feel part of a group of British composers, or were you an isolated individual?

I felt as if I belonged to a group with Ireland and Bax, not so much with Britten. Britten occupied an individualistic professional position.

You wrote an essay on national style and its importance in music.[3] Did you think that all the music that you composed was national in style?

Yes, that's right. I studied English folk music systematically and tried to derive from it the modes and scales in which it was written. I thought that it was important for setting English literary works to music. English poems set to music ought to be in a national style. At that time there was an organization for the propagating of English folksong.

Can you tell me a little about your methods of composing? Anthony Payne once said that in your compositions the impact of the moment is secondary to the architecture of the piece.[4] You obviously feel that forms and structures are very important, that everything should be organized.

Yes, that's true. In any piece the details should relate to one another within the terms of reference of the particular piece. That is very important. I was the Professor of Composition at the Royal Academy of Music for many years – at least I was described as such! I tried to introduce these ideas in my teaching. I don't know that I can introduce you to many students of mine. I don't have anything to do with them now.

You have a voluminous output of works for the piano, including three completed sonatas, a cycle of Twenty-Four Preludes, smaller pieces and works for piano and orchestra. Do you find that, being a pianist, this is the instrument with which you have the greatest empathy?

Yes, I've written a lot for the piano. It is an instrument that I love. Some of my music is over there, on the piano. I can't play the piano any more – I was a pianist and a conductor. I've even conducted performances on the stage but I haven't done that for some time now. I'm ninety-two years old.

The Op. 2 Piano Sonata is not mentioned in The New Grove, *nor in other recent publications on your music. How important do you consider it to be?*

Well, I am now working on Sonata No. 5, so I have travelled a long way since then! I don't think that I have a copy of it any more. Who publishes it?

Murdoch, Murdoch and Co. It was hard for me to locate, but there is a copy at the British Music Information Centre in Stratford Place. Had you heard Ireland's Piano Sonata or any other British piano sonatas before you wrote your Op. 2?

Not Ireland's, but I knew those by Dale, Bax and Scott.

Can you remember how the audience received your Sonata Op. 2?

No, but when my compositions have been performed, they have been enthusiastically received and successful with the general musical public.

What made you decide to write a sonata for piano?

[3] Bush, 1980, 67 [Original in *Music and Life*, Autumn 1969].
[4] Payne, *MT*, 1964, 263–5.

Appendix 1

Well, I think that if you want to get your works performed, you have to provide the performer with some structure that is to a certain extent imposing. That's why I chose a sonata. What else can you do? I suppose a set of variations – but a sonata gives you some basis by which to proceed from one thing to another.

So do you feel that the use of the word sonata has a certain implication, even in the twentieth century?

Well, it suggests a composition of some magnitude. It is not a short piece.

Your First Piano Sonata was written in 1921 and your Second in 1970. In the meantime you had spent a lot of time composing music for the Worker's Musical Association, inspired by your political beliefs. What made you return to writing piano sonatas?

I wrote four large operas that have political subjects – subjects of social significance, and I also wrote symphonies. The operas have never been staged in this country. I think that it is hard to say how my piano sonatas are influenced by my political beliefs. I have a pianist called Leslie Howard who played my Third Piano Sonata about four years ago [1986] and I am writing another one that I hope that he will play eventually. He's a very fine pianist.

You're now working on a Fourth Sonata?[5]

Yes. I'm very careful not to give anyone a composition until I am completely satisfied with it. I like to take my time, and I revise or modify the work until it pleases me. I want to give this to Leslie Howard when it is completed, as he has played my pieces before. It would be embarrassing for me to send him something that he did not think much of and did not like to say so!

At this point we move into Bush's study where he shows me a pile of manuscript paper that contain versions of his Fifth Piano Sonata. It is dedicated to his late wife, Nancy. This Sonata is in five movements. Numbers are written at the edges of the pages, and 1639 keeps recurring, although Bush cannot remember its significance.

I still compose, you see, with the aid of a magnifying glass. I don't write every day, but I do write more often than not. I don't go for long periods without composing.

I'm glad to hear it. Is this Sonata written using modes, like Op. 113?

Yes, I use traditional modes. I do not invent my own. This is a large work, but I hope that one day it will be completed and performed.

I wish you the best of luck – I'm sure it will!

---

[5] I was unaware of the existence of Sonata No. 4, which had been premièred in 1991. Alan Bush's reply was therefore incorrect also. It seems probable that I actually saw pages from Sonata No. 5.

Geoffrey Bush[6]

Could you tell me how you were first introduced to John Ireland?

I was at Lancing College and when I was about sixteen, there was a new chaplain in the school who came from Chelsea. Ireland was the organist at St Luke's, Chelsea. The chaplain had been the priest at St Cuthbert's, Philbeach Gardens, where Ireland used to go for his own devotions, so they knew each other. This man, Kenneth Thompson, wrote to Ireland, telling him of my hope to become a composer. Ireland replied, and requested to see my compositions. I had been composing since I was ten, so it was a remarkable bundle that was sent off. After a time I received a very pleasant reply. Ireland said that he could see that I wanted to write modern music, but warned that I needed a thorough training first. All great composers such as Bartók and Schoenberg had experienced thorough training in conventional harmony and counterpoint before experimenting. Ireland invited me to come and see him in the school holidays. I went regularly, and we became great friends.

Can you describe how he taught you to compose?

I would bring along my latest masterpiece, and he would put off looking at it for as long as possible, then he would open it at any page at random and find something that was wrong. It sounds like magic, but in fact there's always something wrong on every page but you can't see it yourself. When someone else looks at it, you start to see it in the way that they see it, and mistakes become obvious. It's the same if you have a piece of your music played; you start to listen as the audience does.

You see it from a different perspective.

Yes. Ireland would criticize and make suggestions. He was very critical; it took him a long time to like anything, but when he did, he was very encouraging. There were two pieces of mine that he liked quite early on; one was *Te Deum* (1938) and the other was *Clarinet Rhapsody* (1940). He was very enthusiastic about the latter, and got the BBC to broadcast it. Ireland's motto was "nothing but the best will do". This had been the case in Ireland's own lessons with Stanford and Britten's lessons with Bridge. The teacher set an example of someone who is totally professional. Ireland was very exacting, almost self-critical.

Did Ireland ever discuss his lessons with Stanford?

Stanford's lessons could be quite cruel. Ireland described how for his first orchestral piece, Stanford told him to copy out the parts so that the orchestra could try it out. It sounded awful! That was the lesson, and Ireland learnt from it. What you teach yourself, you remember. You never remember what someone else teaches you. He became quite an expert in his orchestral writing. Even though Stanford could be quite harsh, it did not affect Ireland's attitude to him. Ireland admired Stanford so much that he kept his photograph beside him until the day he died.

---

[6] Golders Green, 19 April 1993.

Appendix 1

When Ireland first went to Stanford, his music was very Brahmsian in style.
Stanford made him write like Palestrina for a year and Ireland was grateful for that later. What cured him of imitating Brahms was finding the music of Debussy, Ravel, early Stravinsky and Tchaikovsky. Not that he copied them, but they influenced him. For instance, *The Island Spell* is very much like Debussy or Ravel in style, and very beautiful it is, too. They helped him to find his own path, and that is the greatest problem for any student composer. Not to find how to be different, but to find how you yourself are.

Do you think that Ireland felt that he was writing English music?
No, he was not a nationalist, but he had a tremendous sense of place. Places like Guernsey, Mai Dun and the Sussex Downs especially. They have connections with the past for which he had a very great feeling – the prehistoric remains served as a reminder that people had once lived there. He greatly admired *The Rite of Spring* and its evocation of the living past.

He was also influenced by literature, especially the Welsh writer Arthur Machen. Was folk music an influence?
Not at all. Vaughan Williams' and Holst's music and ways of thinking were quite alien to him. He didn't like Vaughan Williams' music at all, but he admired his Fifth Symphony, a very quiet and reserved piece. He always admired a person who did something that was not calculated to win public applause. The folksong approach was not for him.

Did he see himself as a conservative or a radical?
I don't know that he ever thought about it. He saw himself as a distinct personality. Someone once asked him, "Do you consider yourself a great composer?" and he replied, "No, but I'm a significant one".

Do you think he felt isolated?
No, he felt sympathetic with a number of other composers: Bax, Scott, Bridge, etc. He was not exactly jealous, but he knew his own worth and thought that others didn't always.

Did the piano writing of these British composers influence him?
No, he had formed his own style by then. There are superficial resemblances between his music and that of Bax, but Bax's is musically overflowing and expansive, generous if you like it, and excessive if you don't! Ireland's music is very economical. Although there are many notes, none of them are unnecessary.

He seemed to prefer writing short, titled piano works in free form, rather than the formality of the sonata.
Yes, impressionistic ones like Debussy or early Ravel, rather than programmatic pieces. He was very conscious of the importance of sonata form. Apart from the Piano Sonata there are violin sonatas, a Cello Sonata, and the Piano Concerto. I remember him saying to me what a complex undertaking a sonata is – everything belongs to everything else and needs to be part of a totally organized whole. He liked doing this, but found it a

great challenge. He wrote a lot for piano because that was his instrument, apart from organ. His first study at the College had been the piano.

Were the titles Ireland's choice, or did publishers pressurize him to use them?

The titles were chosen because they conveyed what the piece was about. *April* encapsulates the feeling of a spring morning in the country. *The Island Spell* also suggests a particular mood.

You have edited Ireland's piano music?

I am the Music Advisor to the John Ireland Trust and I was responsible for having the piano music collected. Pianists Eric Parkin and Alan Rowlands, both of whom worked with Ireland, helped me by pointing out errors. No matter how conscientious a composer is, mistakes creep in. A real edition goes back to the manuscripts and is a major undertaking. I have completed or arranged some works, but my real job was to gather all the material in one place and make it available.

Do you consider his Piano Sonata to be his most important work?

No, it is one of them, but *Sarnia* is just as important. I think that his Sonatina is a very fine piece, one of his most economical. *Chelsea Reach* is a staggering piece. Just because the Sonata is a major form does not mean that it is necessarily more important, but others may think so. It's easier to be perfect on a smaller scale.

How does it fit into a tradition?

Ireland is a late romantic figure, but his sense of form is very classical. He would have learnt that from Stanford. The great classical forms like the sonata are continuously viable, no matter what your idiom may be.

Was the Sonata widely performed here or abroad?

I think that it was fairly widely performed here in his lifetime, but it's quite a difficult piece. Ireland uses big chords in the Sonata – I'd not be able to stretch them. Having said that, Eric Parkin, a leading interpreter, has small hands, so it can be done. Lewis Foreman has been engaged to write a biography of Ireland, so he may know more about the frequency of performance.

Was his piano music popular with audiences? By the end of his life he regretted that his music was considered unfashionable.

Yes, Ireland's piano music was well received. His recurring fear was that he would be considered an old fogey! It is inevitable, and happens to all composers. I don't think he had more cause to regret it than anyone else.

I know that you admire the music of Constant Lambert, and your First Symphony (1954) quotes a passage from Lambert's The Rio Grande. *What drew your attention to it?*

After I'd been at Lancing a couple of terms, there was a revolt amongst the staff, and the music master was sacked. The second music master had not been allowed to do very much before, but he was then appointed as senior music master. He was Jasper Rooper, a pupil of Vaughan Williams. He was passionately interested in all contemporary music. He started a

Appendix 1

conductors' class and a composers' competition and was very encouraging. The chapel choir began singing plainsong and Palestrina motets and he started the Choral Society off with *The Rio Grande*. I fell in love with it. I bought the record, and if I could have had five pounds for every time I'd played it, I'd be a rich man! Once you discover something you like about a composer, it naturally leads you to explore other music of his. The second movement of my First Symphony is a jazz blues, as Lambert would have written himself. The stimulus came when I heard on the radio that Lambert had died.

Did you know Lambert?

No. I'm told he became very trying in his later days, when drink took its effect. I saw him conduct Purcell's *The Fairy Queen* at Covent Garden, shortly after the war, in an edition by Lambert and Michael Ayrton the painter. He tottered into the orchestra pit on sticks, but as soon as the baton was in his hand, he had full control.

How was his music received?

His great grief was that everyone loved *The Rio Grande* and no-one paid any attention to the rest. He got involved in conducting, and that reduced his potential for composing. The work that he thought was his best, *Summer's Last Will and Testament*, which has just been recorded, only had a couple of performances in his lifetime. It's a very depressing work, a very fine piece. The rhythmic aspects of his music and the clear textures he uses are in complete contrast to Ireland.

Were there many performances of Lambert's Piano Sonata?

Not many. It's a very difficult work.

It is interesting that Lambert was the first British composer to use the idiom of jazz in a serious context.

Well, it may be influenced by jazz, but the style has gone a long way from that. I find the Concerto a little easier, but it is a depressing work. The last movement plunges into the depths.

Was he seen as a radical?

Definitely. He was interested in early British music, not just Purcell. The revival of interest in Boyce begins with Lambert, who made a suite out of movements from Boyce's symphonies for the Vic-Wells Ballet, which was very successful. He produced a proper edition. He admired Liszt, Tchaikovsky and Chabrier. British music at the turn of the century was soaked not only in Brahms, but in all German music. That goes back to Beethoven. In 1813 the Philharmonic Society was founded, which had a close connection with him, and later, Mendelssohn. It was generally accepted that the Germans wrote the best music. The idea that French or Russian music could be as good was quite a radical approach. Lambert's opinions on music can be found in *Music Ho!*, but the main impact was felt by the foreign works that he included in his conducting repertory.

Great Britain in the nineteenth century was not as musically barren as we are led to believe. Why do these views still predominate?

People just reproduce the same viewpoint without stopping to question it. Many people can't be bothered with nineteenth-century British music because everyone says it's bad, so one can't find out that it isn't. We rely on the few enthusiasts. More nineteenth-century British music is now being recorded, so we will hope that this might educate some of the public. We are a lazy lot! We have a terrible national inferiority complex and we still see this German worship, which is bad for our morale. Even now, Schoenberg, Webern and Berg are almost idolized. Many people still believe in the Big Bang theory of British music – that there was darkness over the country and then God said, "Let there be Elgar" and instantly, everything was lit up. Elgar couldn't have brought it off if people had not been building up to it. People like Bennett changed the face of British music, although you don't see the fruits of it until later. You have to plough the soil before reaping the harvest.

I first came across the name Sterndale Bennett when I was a choirboy. The church music is the least interesting part of his work. I discovered that he'd written some piano music. Then, there were many serious articles on music in the *Radio Times*, edited by Ralph Hill. I wrote to ask him about Sterndale Bennett's piano music. He replied, telling me not to bother with it as it is terribly old-fashioned. He couldn't have known it.

Would you say that Bennett's piano music demonstrates individualistic traits?

I think that he was English in the same way that Arne was English (whereas Handel never was). Handel was the greater composer, but Arne could do all sorts of fresh, lyrical things in a unique way. Bennett was like that; his piano concertos are better than Mendelssohn's piano concertos, but not as good as his Violin Concerto. Bennett could do a few things that Mendelssohn couldn't.

Bennett's style seems to derive from Mozart. I have studied his Piano Sonata No. 2, The Maid of Orleans, *but that is not the best of his piano works.*

Bennett was only a composer until he was twenty-eight. Then he became a teacher, conductor, organizer and player, but did little composition, except for the beautiful Cello Sonata. In later years he became introverted and the inspiration of his youth had gone. The first movement of *The Maid of Orleans* is very beautiful, but the rest does not quite take off.

Were there any non-Germanic influences on this work?

Well, he comes at the end of the London Piano School. Clementi and Dussek weren't German, but had settled in London. They form the backbone of the style that Bennett adopts – a Mozart-orientated style. Schumann suggested that it may have been Scarlatti-orientated, too, as there was much rapid finger-work, etc.

Bennett edited classical piano sonatas, including one by G. F. Pinto.

Yes, that was part of his teaching work, occurring when he ceased to become a major composer, aged about twenty-eight. Before that he had

Appendix 1

been a pupil at the Academy for about ten years, so he would have studied Mozart, Beethoven, etc.

Did Mozart, Haydn or Beethoven have the most far-reaching effect upon British piano writing?

Probably none of those, but possibly Hummel. The one who has the most influence is not necessarily the most famous or the greatest.

Can we trace a tradition of British piano sonatas through the nineteenth century, which culminates in the two Piano Sonatas by Parry and the (lost) Sonata by Stanford?

I think that is unlikely. Parry more or less began again. I don't think that he would have felt that he was continuing.

He seems to look to a Beethovenian model.

Perhaps, and to other German romantics.

How important do you think that Parry's Sonatas are?

I've never seen the First, but I love the Second. It's rather Schubertian in some respects, and very lyrical. Schubert was a great influence. Mendelssohn admired him and Grove drew attention to him also.

Would Parry's Sonatas have been widely performed?

There were not many public opportunities. The piano recital in England was only launched by Hallé in Manchester in the 1850s, but I don't suppose that Parry's Sonatas were often heard. People would have bought it, but you needed a good technique to play it. Parry wrote largely for himself, didn't he?

Yes, he dedicated the Second Sonata to his friend, Tora. [Here follows a debate whether her name is Tora or Cora, and we study the Victorian lettering on the title page.][7] How did the interest in musicology in the nineteenth century cause the British to re-appraise their musical traditions?

The Purcell Society was founded, and there was a start of British consciousness. It is very important to feel part of a tradition, and musicology helped to investigate this.

Composers looked back to the madrigalists.

They didn't understand them, though. Parry thought that Purcell was a victim of dotted rhythms, and did not realise that it was a natural part of the music. They had no idea of the William Lawes school, either. It was only the beginning, but helped to pave the way. Ernest Walker's *History of Music in England* was pioneering, though one would disagree with much of it now. He investigated things himself; he was a child of his time. One is most hostile to one's grandparents, musically speaking, and he'd just escaped from Mendelssohn.

Influence from non-Germanic countries did not really make itself felt until the twentieth century.

There was some interest before then, certainly in song writing. Maude Valérie White spoke three languages and set poems in each. Arthur Goring

---

[7] Confirmed to be Tora. See Dibble, 1992, 136.

Interview Transcriptions: Geoffrey Bush

Thomas, a pupil of Sullivan, was very interested in French music. When something new appears, there will have been stirrings for some time before.

Can you account for why the great British composers Elgar, Holst, Delius and Vaughan Williams, did not write piano sonatas?

None of them could play the piano. Elgar could, after a fashion, but wasn't a pianist. Nor was Vaughan Williams. Having said that, I think that his Piano Concerto is a brilliant piece. Delius had a great feeling for sensuous sound and I don't think that the piano would have given him what he wanted. He was very hostile to the classical tradition. Fenby tells how his friend played Beethoven's late A flat Sonata and Delius said, "I can't think why you waste your time on such rubbish!"

There was much song writing at the turn of the century, so the piano was used for accompaniment.

Songs had always been going on. You can preserve a tradition much more easily with songs, because they are in your language and this helps to prevent them from being infiltrated from outside.

Do you think that the word sonata has any implication for twentieth-century composers?

No, composers use it to mean what they want. Look at Cage's *Sonatas and Interludes* – there's no relation whatsoever to the classical tradition.

Does it make people take the composition more seriously if the title sonata is used?

Yes, in the early part of the century it would have implied a symphonic undertaking. A sonatina would have been just as serious, but on a smaller scale. The whole concept of sonata form changed during the transition from classical to romantic periods. In the classical sonata, the first and second subjects are thematically the same but it's the key structure that differentiates them. Gradually, the keys become expressed in terms of themes and themes become more important. There is a shift from first and second tonal centres towards first and second tunes, and the key structure is less important. We see this in Beethoven, who widely extends the possible keys. A late nineteenth-century or early twentieth-century composer would have a completely different outlook on sonata form. Whether you could find an early twentieth-century sonata that did not use some sort of sonata form, I would doubt. Does the Dale?

The first movement uses a modified sonata form. The following three movements are quite innovative in that there is a theme and seven variations that are grouped into the slow movement, scherzo and finale. Cyril Scott used the term sonata quite freely. His sonatas show the influence of French impressionism more than Germanic forms, despite his training in Germany.

Certainly by the end of his life, Scott used the term sonata in an entirely individual way.

Have you ever felt the desire to write sonatas yourself?

No, but I've written two Sonatinas. They are not sonatas, as this would

Appendix 1

imply something grandiose, and these, like Ireland's, are very concise (about 8 minutes), though a lot happens in them. I find the piano quite difficult to write for, though I've written more lately. I've just written a Suite for Eric Parkin, which he commissioned, though he actually wanted a sonata. I wrote to him and told him that it's exactly what he wanted, except it isn't a sonata, and it is five years late!

Why did you abandon the idea of a sonata?

I couldn't think of an idea. I often think of things I'd like to write and then can't carry them through. I once began a string quartet, something I'd always wanted to do, but it soon turned into a piece for string orchestra.

Do you find it hard to write something original for piano?

Yes, very, unless you write in Boulez-like sonorities, and even then, Boulez has already done that! Whether you imitate Beethoven or Boulez, there's no difference. They did it first. I think that the Sonata by George Benjamin is a very powerful and individual work. There's an awful lot of work involved in writing for the piano, lots of notes!

Yes, and you need to conceive something that is pianistic.

I think so. As I've got older I've become more interested in opera and song. I do play the piano a little, so I like to have pieces of my own to play. I wouldn't play any solos in public, except my own, maybe. I'll play as an accompanist or as a chamber-music player. I have very small hands.

Howard Ferguson[8]

When you wrote your Piano Sonata, did you see it belonging to a tradition?

It was written in memory of Harold Samuel, a very great friend of mine, a great Bach interpreter. He discovered me in the North of Ireland, at the Belfast Musical Competition, when I was playing there, aged about thirteen. I came from a completely unmusical family. He approached my mother and father and suggested that I should study music more seriously with him, before going to the Royal College of Music. Incredibly, they agreed! They met Samuel once, liked and trusted him. I was very lucky, and I lived with him until he died. That was a very important experience and the Sonata really arose out of it.

Would you say that Harold Samuel had conveyed a love for the great German masters in you? You were brought up on a diet of Bach, Beethoven and Brahms.

Yes, so the writing of a piano sonata was a natural progression to make.

Did Harold Samuel play much twentieth-century music?

No, mainly the great German classics, especially Bach. He did play Ravel's *Ondine*, for instance, but he didn't play *Scarbo*, which is much more violent. He was very fond of Debussy. Harold had been a pupil

[8] Cambridge, 16 April 1993.

of Stanford, and Stanford used to write short piano pieces for him, as Christmas presents. After Harold's death, I discovered a collection of these works, and I sent them to Frederick Hudson at the University of Newcastle. They were mainly preludes and fugues.

Did you feel isolated by not belonging to a group of British composers?

Yes, even when I was at the Royal College. Elizabeth Maconchy was a pupil of Vaughan Williams then and she started a young composers' club for the students. She asked me to join but I never wanted to; I liked working on my own.

Did your contemporaries influence you?

I don't think that one can ever tell about influence in one's own works. They obviously must be there, but one can't identify them. Other people have to do that!

Were you familiar with any other British piano sonatas when you wrote your own?

Well, I knew a great deal of contemporary music of all sorts. Stravinsky, anyone you could name, I knew the music of, but certainly, Stravinsky's music never influenced me at all. Whether others did, your guess is as good as mine!

What was the musical climate at the Royal College at that time? Was Stravinsky popular?

Yes, most of the others were more interested in the progressive trends of modernism than I was. Betty Maconchy was interested in Bartók; she worked in Prague, I think, after she left college, and she was influenced by him in her string quartets.

Was there any French music that appealed to you?

I was very fond of Fauré, Debussy and Ravel. I don't know whether they influenced me – Fauré might have.

Were there any specific Brahms works that may have influenced your Piano Sonata?

No. I used the technique of organic unity that was developed by Brahms. I certainly did not use Brahms' Piano Sonatas as a starting point, because I don't think that they are good Brahms, they are very early works! The F minor is the best of the three. I suppose that the piano writing may be influenced by later Brahms, maybe Intermezzi, Capriccios, etc., or chamber music, but not the Sonatas.

Paul Spicer has drawn comparisons between your Sonata and the Sonata by Frank Bridge.[9] Do you see any connection?

That has always surprised me, as I don't particularly like the Bridge. I knew it from its earliest days, because Frank wanted Harold Samuel to play it. He was an old friend of Harold's as they were at college together. Frank came when the work was still in manuscript and played it to Harold; he was a good pianist himself. I heard this going on, and said to myself that

---

[9] Ferguson, Eightieth Birthday talk, 28 October 1988, BMIC Cassette 584.

Appendix 1

I know Harold will never play that! Sure enough, he wriggled out of it and the first performance was given by Myra Hess, both in England and America. She said that she lost more of her American friends by playing it than anything else!

What was it about the Bridge Sonata that audiences found hard?

Well, for that period, it was rather advanced. Up to that time, Frank's music had been rather easy, like salon music, but his style changed rather suddenly during the war. Oddly enough, I played a piece of Frank's when Harold heard me first, a piece called *Rosemary*. That, and the first movement of Mozart's A minor Sonata. Frank wrote marvellously for all instruments. He was a very good viola player himself. So I'm afraid that a bitter feeling surrounded the Bridge Sonata, and it lasted for some years, until Frank's wife managed to smooth things over.

Did you have fixed opinions on what constitutes a sonata?

No, I don't think that I had a conscious idea about it. The First Violin Sonata was written before the Piano Sonata (1931), and it just came as it came, the Piano Sonata was the same. I suppose the various things that I'd heard would have influenced it. Both works are in sonata form. I think that I just accepted that as the norm.

Do you see your approach to the Sonata as having anything in common with Tippett? Both of you, in some sense, refer to a Beethovenian model.

I wouldn't have thought so, as Tippett was much more experimental than I was. He was influenced from the start by very early music, such as Elizabethan madrigals, which was something that I was not exposed to. He was a very innovative composer. He was at the Royal College at the same time as I was, but he was older. I did know him, but not very well.

Did you ever consider writing a short one-movement work for piano, such as a rhapsody, or did you think that a sonata would be taken more seriously?

I never considered anything like that; it just happened the way it did. Do you know the Five Bagatelles (1944)? I hadn't written anything since the Piano Sonata because of the National Gallery concerts that kept me rather busy. I helped to organize them during the war and they ran for six and a half years, five days a week. When they stopped I said I'll never organize another concert in my life, and I've kept to that! Anyway, large gaps between compositions aren't a very good idea, so I happened to remark to Arnold[10] one day that I was sure that I could write something if someone gave me some notes! First, he gave me the five notes that are shown at the end of the second bagatelle. That was the first one that was written. I thought that it had gone well, and asked him for some more notes. So he gave me notes for the five pieces and I wrote them from that. The concerts went on for a year after the war, and after that I was able to return to writing normally.

How did you set about the composition of your Piano Sonata? Did you begin at the beginning, as this motif permeates the whole work?

---

[10] The South African composer and pianist, Arnold van Wyk.

Interview Transcriptions: Howard Ferguson

Yes, I did. I know that the very end of the work was written before I got there, but I can't remember at what stage. Otherwise it followed logically, but that did not always happen. In the Second Violin Sonata (1946), the second movement was written first, then the last movement, and finally the first.

Did you make a sketch of the work first, so that you knew where you were going, and then return to fill in the details?

No, I started at the beginning of a movement and waited to see what developed. Some composers, for instance Elgar, always had sketches of things all over the place and then put them together, but I did not work like that.

I have seen a copy of the manuscript of your Piano Sonata in the British Library. Is this a final copy?

Yes, one of them. Most of my things are in the Bodleian. The manuscript of the Piano Sonata that is there belonged to Myra.

There are few alterations, except in the last movement.

Once things got to the ink stage, that was it. I worked in notebooks before that. They are not sketches; they are through-composed with alterations. There are twenty bound volumes of my notebooks in the Bodleian Library. When I worked as a student, I found it very helpful to see other people's working method. The only ones that you could see then were Beethoven's sketchbooks. Brahms very carefully destroyed all evidence of his first drafts, although some have survived.

Written onto the manuscript in the British Library are the words "to Mrs. Mac". Who was she?

She was a dear friend from Ireland, whom I knew from playing at the musical competition. She was a widow, and she had been at the Academy as a student. She used to come to London twice a year, on one visit she did theatres and on the other she did opera. She took me to all the operas. I saw several complete *Rings* with her, and all the great singers. She gave me my first copy of the *Ring* for piano. The only Wagner I knew before that was *Tannhauser*. I dedicated the *Diversions* (1939–42) to her.

In the Sonata, the semitone characterizes the work. Was this a conscious decision?

No, it just grew from the initial material, harmonically and melodically.

The work is in F Minor, and you do use tonal centres.

Yes, I consciously use tonality, as opposed to my friend Gerald Finzi. He had no feeling for the structural use of tonality. He could begin a song in one key and end it in another. It's something you're either born with or you're not. It's very important in any large-scale work.

Can you remember how your Piano Sonata was received at its first performance?

It was received very warmly. It was a help to have Myra Hess playing it! She also recorded and broadcast it. Myra played it all over the place, in America and elsewhere, and it was played a number of times at the National Gallery, so I was very fortunate.

Appendix 1

Can composers make progress if they remain writing in a very traditional way?

Change happens gradually rather than suddenly, whether you set out to do it or not. I don't know how pianists play some of today's contemporary music. I was never able to do it. I used to play a lot with the violinist Yfrah Neaman and we were engaged by the BBC to play a work by a Cambridge composer.[11] It was the sort of piece that I did not enjoy playing, but we worked at it very hard. One of my sisters wrote to me after the broadcast and said that she had enjoyed the Brahms A major Sonata, but not the piece that sounded like dropping little pieces of ice into a glass! I must say, I'm with her there!

As a pianist, you played the great classics, but did you play much twentieth-century music?

Well, I really wasn't a solo pianist, you know. I played much chamber music, but the only solo things I ever played were my own works. Part of the reason for that is that I have an appalling musical memory, and that eliminates recital work. I was much more interested in composition than performance. I enjoyed chamber music and I had a fairly wide repertoire. I used to play with the Griller String Quartet, but most of the chamber music I did was with Yfrah Neaman and with the clarinettist Pauline Juler. I played piano duets with Denis Matthews.

Did you perform as a solo pianist whilst at the Royal College?

No, I studied privately with Harold, and did composition and conducting at the College, which was rather curious, as Harold taught there. I wanted to conduct very much, but when I did it I realized that I had not an acute enough ear to be a conductor. I had not got perfect pitch, and you have to be able to pinpoint mistakes very clearly. I realized that it was not for me.

It must have been a hard decision, especially as you'd already given up on the idea of being a piano soloist.

I've always tried to be aware of my limitations; this is why I stopped composing thirty years ago. I'd said all I wanted to. I was lucky enough to go into editing.

At the Royal College, you studied with R. O. Morris. What sort of training did he give you?

He was a marvellous teacher. He had a very clear mind, and he did write music himself, but he had not got a very strong musical personality, so he did not try to impose himself upon his pupils. He was invaluable in spotting where things were going wrong, and in practical matters like orchestration. The strict side happened with the sixteenth-century counterpoint, but then you could compose what you wanted to. My Octet began as a Clarinet Quintet, and quickly gathered extra instruments. When it became a Septet, R. O. said, "Dear Howard, if you're writing for seven instruments, then you might as well write for eight, with the same combi-

---

[11] Possibly Robin Orr's Sonatina (1946) or Sonata (1956)?

Interview Transcriptions: Howard Ferguson

nation as Schubert. It will give you many more performances!" This was perfectly true, as it is nearly always played with the Schubert. A younger composer than myself, who shall be nameless, always writes for outlandish combinations of instruments. One work requires three harps and a choir![12] It's not very practical, and you're not likely to get many performances.

Are your student compositions destroyed now?

Almost all. The slow movement of the Octet began as the slow movement of a Symphony, and I liked it very much. That's the only time I've transferred material from one work to another.

Did you compose much piano music as a student?

Not a great deal. I wrote a Piano and Violin Sonata, which was destroyed. I had a grand conflagration at one stage, when I decided after writing the present First Violin Sonata, that everything before that should be destroyed. The Octet was the only thing to survive. I also studied with Vaughan Williams for a year, when Morris was in America, and I adored him, but he was no good as a teacher. He just seemed rather vague and not very helpful. About half of his pupils found him very stimulating, and the other half didn't. It was marvellous to get to know him as a personality, and he became a great friend. I still often see his widow.

It must be hard to strike a good balance as a composition teacher, not to impose too much upon your pupils, but equally, not to be vague. Ultimately, the pupil needs to find his or her own answers.

It is hard and I speak from experience, having taught at the Academy for fifteen years. One can only really help with technical things like shape and orchestration, and not always then. It depends on the pupil–teacher relationship. In that respect, Morris was marvellous.

You taught composition at the Royal Academy from 1946 to 1961, and your pupils included John Joubert, Richard Rodney Bennett, Cornelius Cardew and Susan Bradshaw. Three of these pupils produced piano sonatas during this period.

I was not aware of this. I had great difficulty in getting Susan to write anything at all. I only remember her producing settings of Hungarian folksongs. We used to play piano duets instead. Cardew was a very curious case. He had an uncle, Phil Cardew, who was a jazz player. He had influenced Cornelius, who wrote nothing but jazz. I tried to get him to write more serious music, but then he came out with things that I could not understand. Oddly enough, he could play Schubert beautifully. I didn't teach counterpoint or harmony, just free composition.

Can you account for Vaughan Williams' lack of interest in writing piano music, or indeed the lack of piano music by other major composers such as Elgar, Holst and Delius? None of them wrote piano sonatas.

Vaughan Williams was a very bad pianist, and I don't think that you can write for the piano unless you can play it. I've tried unsuccessfully

---

[12] Andrzej Panufnik, *Universal Prayer*, 1968–9.

Appendix 1

to write organ music, but I don't play the organ. I did play the violin and the clarinet, so I have an idea about stringed and wind instruments. I can't imagine why Elgar's piano music is so bad. It wasn't his natural medium. In one of his letters he says he doesn't like the instrument. I was asked to edit the keyboard volume of the New Elgar Edition, but I refused because I thought that it was a bad idea to edit music you didn't like.

Did you know Bax?

I met him once, when the BBC had asked Pauline Juler and myself to play his Clarinet Sonata. Neither of us had played it before, so I wrote to Bax to ask him to hear us. We did this, and played it very badly. All he said was "It was lovely", which was not very helpful. I never knew him very well. I knew his Piano Sonatas; they were not often played, except by Harriet Cohen. It was his orchestral music that one heard.

Bax and Stanford consciously retained their Celtic background in their music. How did you look upon your Irish ancestry?

I never wanted to be an Irish composer. I did make a number of settings of Irish folksongs – the *Five Irish Folksongs* (1954) for voice and piano, and the orchestral *Four Diversions* (1939–42). These arose because the BBC in Northern Ireland had a scheme of preserving folksongs, and they invited various people to write music. They bought the rights of a huge collection that had been made by Sam Henry, a customs inspector who travelled round the country to hear people sing. He did not know normal musical notation, so they were written in sol-fa. These appeared in a Londonderry newspaper each week. There were hundreds of them. One of the earliest works of mine to be published was a setting of *Five Irish Folktunes* (1927) for cello and piano. That's a conscious use of folktunes, but I don't think that any of my other music is particularly Irish. I don't know that it's particularly British, but then British music is quite diverse now.

Are you presently working on more editing?

No, I have not done that for quite some time. My latest project has been the writing of a cookery book, which is now complete. No British publishers wanted it, but it has been translated and published in Japanese! Let's hope that one day we'll see it in English!

Alan Frank[13]

When did you first meet Constant Lambert?

I joined the Oxford University Press staff at the age of seventeen, immediately after leaving school. I was a classicist at Dulwich, and the headmaster wanted me to continue in classics, but he quite understood when I told him that I really wanted to work in music. I went in as an office boy and got paid £2.50 each week. There were two young composers, Walton

---

[13] Hampstead, 21 May 1993.

and Lambert, both of whom I later had the honour of handling and got to know very well indeed.

In 1930, you played the clarinet in a production of Oscar Wilde's Salome *at the Gate Theatre, under Lambert's baton.*

Yes, he conducted some performances. Hyam Greenbaum, a close friend, who was married to Sidonie Goossens, conducted others. Greenbaum ("Bumps") was a brilliant conductor, much admired by Constant, Walton and Rawsthorne. He was a very good musician who drank too much and this affected his conducting. I played under Constant a number of times. I'm sure that I played in a suite from his ballet *Pomona*. I got to know Constant quite well, as there was a touring ballet company that he conducted and played the piano for. I remember going with him to Oxford to see the pit that we were to play in. He was very meticulous, he drew up a plan and it was my job to see that the seats and stands were in place. I mention this, as people tend to remember Constant from the end of his life as being a bit of a drunkard, but in his early days he was very precise, especially in his conducting. He needed to be, as much of his music contains syncopation, which needs to be placed exactly. His speaking voice was precise and clipped also.

He narrated Walton's Façade.

Yes, brilliantly and even Walton agreed. No-one could do it as well as him. We used to meet regularly at a pub near Oxford Circus called The George, nicknamed "The Gluepot", because people stayed there drinking far too long. It was very well known and it was a gathering place on Fridays for BBC people, including the orchestral players, if they were rehearsing at Queen's Hall. I used to see Constant there regularly, and his circle included Ralph Hill, the music editor of the *Radio Times*. The *Radio Times* used to carry articles about music every week, unlike now. Both Constant and I wrote for it. They had a page devoted to the symphony concert of the week, which was always of a stereotyped nature – overture, concerto, interval, and symphony. One week, Constant handed his article to Ralph Hill, and apologized that he'd forgotten to make a note of the works that were to be performed, so he asked Ralph to check the article and fill in the titles. He had written the stock article, full of clichés. It was brilliant; it would fit any conventional programme!

Did he show you the music that he was writing then?

Constant and Walton were brought into the firm by my brilliant boss, Hubert Foss, to whom British music owes a great deal. He was also, regretfully, a heavy drinker. It was Peter Warlock who started all this excessive drinking amongst British composers. Foss had a flair for picking up the right composers, he already had Vaughan Williams, of course, and later Rawsthorne joined. Rawsthorne was a close friend of Constant's, as you know from the marital sequence.[14] Due to Foss, OUP collared the best of

---

[14] Lambert's second wife, Isabel, later married Alan Rawsthorne.

Appendix 1

British music. These three were the outstanding figures in British music of the time, apart from Britten in the later period. Britten's *Simple Symphony* was published by OUP, but Boosey and Hawkes collared him. I was told that Britten fell out with Foss because Foss lost Britten's manuscript in a pub.

The piano plays an important role in Lambert's output.

He played the piano for ballets. His playing was extremely rhythmical – he was not a concert pianist, but he played very well. He played with many English companies. Ballet in his youth was just beginning to be created as a British art form, with Camargo and the Vic-Wells. Constant was at the right place at the right time. He played at Dartington (not the summer school), I think, in the early 1930s.

Did he compose at the piano? Much of the orchestral music seems to have been pianistically conceived.

He didn't sit at the piano to compose, but he would have tried out sequences and ideas at the piano. I think that it would be difficult to fault the orchestration of any of his scores.

Lambert had heard The Plantation Orchestra with Florence Mills at the London Pavilion in 1923 and was influenced by the trumpet fanfare that he had heard on that occasion. How did he assimilate the jazz idiom into a personal style?

He borrows certain blues harmonies, for instance in the *Elegiac Blues* (1927), which is dedicated to Florence Mills. He liked Negro jazz and coloured people; hence his first marriage was to a coloured girl, Florence Chuter.

Did he ever go to America?

That's a good question. I don't think so. Nevertheless, he was very familiar with aspects of American music.

So what he knew would have been gleaned from touring artists or from records?

Yes. He would have become attracted to coloured people and their music partly through the theatre. He was interested in Duke Ellington's music. I'm not sure what Negro jazz was available on record. He never spoke to me about records.

It was a very quick assimilation. He said that he was first inspired in 1923 by The Plantation Orchestra. By 1927 he had written The Rio Grande *and in 1928–9 he wrote his Piano Sonata.*

In my opinion, *The Rio Grande* is an absolute masterpiece. Lambert thought that *Summer's Last Will and Testament* was his magnum opus, but it is hardly ever heard today. I think that it is a flawed masterpiece. I like all the ballets in their different ways, especially *Horoscope* (1937). That's one of the few works that does get performed today.

Yes, there's a Suite of five movements. The full score was lost when the ballet company was touring in Holland during the war, and Germany invaded, but the Suite was performed at the Proms in 1938.

Interview Transcriptions: Alan Frank

British music has been dogged by problems with composers losing manuscripts. Alan Rawsthorne lost a lot in a bombing raid in Bristol. His Viola Sonata was lost and a viola player spotted it in a second-hand music dealer's catalogue. He telephoned me and I telephoned Alan. The composer had the ironic distinction of going to the sale and buying his own property! He'd lent it to Ralph Hill, and when Ralph died the manuscript disappeared with his library which was sold. We got it back and it was published!

How was Lambert's Piano Sonata received?

I don't think it had many performances. Angus Morrison played it. He was a close friend, a charming man.[15]

Gordon Bryan gave the first performance.

He was a nice enough chap, but not a particularly distinguished pianist. Bryan did a lot for British music. He was an enthusiast. Apart from the Piano Concerto (1930–1), Sonata and one or two short pieces, that's about all Constant wrote for the piano. He was one of the rare British composers who played the piano, rather well in fact.

The Piano Sonata is dedicated to Thomas W. Earp, the art critic. In later years Louis Kentner played the Piano Sonata also.

I didn't know Earp, but I read his work. Kentner was a friend of Constant's.

The Sonata is a technically demanding piece, and maybe this is why it is so rarely performed.

It needs a crisp touch and extreme rhythmic facility. The Piano Concerto is never heard now, is it?

Not often, although there's a recent compact disc of it, performed by Kathryn Stott and the BBC Concert Orchestra, under Barry Wordsworth.

I don't know whether it's one of his better works.

It's quite different in mood to The Rio Grande. *It's depressing and is a tribute to Peter Warlock, who had committed suicide. The Rio Grande seems to be the work that's withstood the test of time most successfully. I'm trying to trace a tradition of British piano sonatas. Lambert's Sonata particularly interests me in that it is the first time that we see the influence of jazz in this serious form. It's quite different from what Bax and Bridge were doing. Was he seen as a radical?*

Absolutely. Constant and Walton were very keen on John Ireland. Although they were very different in age, he was almost one of the gang, so to speak, and they admired his music.

That is interesting. In Music Ho!, *Lambert says that he deplores the British folksong school, especially Vaughan Williams.*

Personality comes into it, too. They liked John very much. They thought that he was underrated.

---

[15] Both Lambert and Morrison were trained at the Royal College. Later he became Lambert's brother-in-law as his sister, Olga, married Maurice Lambert.

Appendix 1

He doesn't mention Ireland's name in Music Ho! *Did Lambert admire any other British figures?*

Warlock, obviously. Both the quality of composition and the heaviness of the drinking all stem from Warlock and his circle, Cecil Gray and Bernard van Dieren. Drink can be seen either as a good or a bad influence on British music. This circle was a school comparable to Les Six.

Lambert admired them, as they presented music in a light-hearted vein, which other British composers were not so inclined to do.

For a time, Walton and Rawsthorne were all quite scathing about Vaughan Williams. I'm not sure about Constant. Didn't he conduct a lot of Vaughan Williams?

He certainly studied under him at the Royal College. In Music Ho!, *Lambert is not very complimentary about his Pastoral Symphony, seeing its mood dictate the symphonic development. However, he later dedicated* Aubade Héroïque *(1942) to Vaughan Williams.*

I think that Lambert conducted *Job*, and admired it, but that's not a folksong work. Walton was scathing about Vaughan Williams. Late in his life, he asked me to send recordings of Vaughan Williams' symphonies to Ischia. This I did, and he wrote back, asking why I'd hidden all this wonderful music away from him for so long! Walton and Vaughan Williams were in competition with each other and published by the same publisher.

Was there much rivalry between Lambert and Walton?

No, none. There could not have been a warmer regard or mutual admiration between the two. I remember being in Milan with Walton, for a performance of *Troilus and Cressida*, when he remarked to me that there were so many English composers around now that it was hard to compete. In the early days, the only two younger British composers that were any good were Constant and himself. A bit later on came Britten. Constant was very interested in French art in general – painters, poets and the lot. He was bilingual, and drawn to French culture. There is a small influence from Les Six on his music and he was very keen on Debussy.

I'm trying to ascertain how much German music Lambert knew – whether his dislike for it was based on informed opinion or bias towards the French and Russians. He detested Schoenberg.

Well, I don't suppose that he knew much Mahler, but then hardly anyone did. I suppose he knew his Wagner, without being a Wagnerian, although I'm not sure. I think it was unlikely that Constant had made a thorough study of Schoenberg's music before condemning him. I suppose that he'd heard *Pierrot Lunaire*, but there was not much Schoenberg performed in this country. They all liked Berg, and personality came into it. He was a loveable man, whereas Schoenberg was not.

Lambert disliked Stravinsky's music, but admired the Russian nationalists.

I hadn't realized that he disliked Stravinsky. Was it perhaps jealousy? Objectively, one would have expected him to have liked certain periods of Stravinsky.

Interview Transcriptions: Alan Frank

He attacks Stravinsky's neo-classical works, although he is more sympathetic towards Les Noces. *It was Constant's versatility that has led to his comparatively poor reputation today.*

Even before the war he was writing film criticism in French for a French newspaper. That's an achievement for an English musician! He spoke French very well and he loved France. The English don't seem to take to polymaths, and he was the polymath of our time. It did count against him.

One of the problems in being a British composer is that you need to take on other work for income, but then your reputation as a composer will suffer.

Nowadays the difficulties and possibilities in making a living as a composer in this country are similar to those faced in any country in Europe, but it wasn't so in Constant's struggling days. Although there was a Performing Rights Society, there was no Radio 3, which was the most crucial single factor in helping the British composer. Earlier on, of course, it was the enterprise of Sir Henry Wood that had fired enthusiasm.

Yes, some of Lambert's music was performed at the Proms in his lifetime, and he was an associate conductor in 1944–5. When the Third Programme was inaugurated in 1946, Lambert conducted music for it, including programmes of Liszt's music, which was little-known then. Humphrey Searle worked for the BBC and requested Lambert's services. Thus, Lambert helped to educate the British public.

Yes, Humphrey was part of Constant's circle. He was not an outstanding composer but a very nice man. Constant's son, Kit, died at a similar age to his father, didn't he?

Yes, it is quite fascinating to read in Andrew Motion's book, how the three generations (George, Constant and Kit), followed in each other's footsteps.

Constant went to Christ's Hospital School, Horsham. Did he get much musical help there?

He had piano lessons from an Australian, Elsie Hall. At the College he studied under Herbert Fryer and Sargent for conducting.

Yes, that makes sense. Sargent and Constant both had immense precision in their beat.

What type of market did piano music appeal to in the 1930s and 1940s?

We didn't sell much to amateurs. The sales of advanced British piano music were fairly minimal and still probably are, although now there are subsidies from the earnings on recordings and broadcasts.

The only way that people could get to know the sonatas would be to buy the music and try to play them, but you needed to be a competent pianist to attempt this.

All the composers that we've discussed were under contract, so if they wrote a piano piece, we published it.

Did you ever refuse to publish anything? Lambert's final ballet Tiresias *(1950–1) wasn't published.*

This often happened with large-scale, specialized works. They didn't get published in the sense of having a printed score on sale, but it's published

Appendix 1

if the publisher provides the material. It still counts as a publication, but the publisher is not obliged by law to have it on general sale. It doesn't prevent us from collecting performing fees. In the days before the great technology, the parts had to be hand-copied by copyists.

The publisher would have left the composer to write what he wished?

Yes, unless there was a low-level commission. For example, if the publisher was doing a series for school orchestras and he wanted a certain composer to write a piece.

Antony Hopkins[16]

Can you tell me why you decided to write piano sonatas?

I had a very peculiar piano technique, which meant that I could not play the standard repertoire. I'd been very badly taught at school. I squandered my first year at the Royal College doing organ first study, which I hated and had no aptitude for at all. For less than eighteen months I had piano lessons with Cyril Smith, who himself had a wonderful technique, but he seemed to be more interested in hearing me play than teaching me technique. I upbraided him about this some years later, and he said he knew I'd never be a concert pianist anyway, but he enjoyed listening to me. This was an inverted compliment. As I found myself totally unexpectedly in a position of having to play in public, I thought I should write some pieces that I could actually play. What resulted were three piano sonatas that I couldn't play because they were too difficult. That was because the nature of the musical material was such that it demanded to be written that way.

The First Piano Sonata is a large-scale romantic type of piece. Michael Tippett influenced all three sonatas, as he was my idol at the time. I used to sing in a choir at Morley College, which he conducted, and I was involved in the first performances of *A Child of Our Time*. He gave me the stepping stone to a totally new career that I'd never anticipated. My aim had been to become an assistant music master at a public school, which I never did. One day [in 1944] he summoned me to tell me that he'd been asked to write music for Marlowe's play *Doctor Faustus*. He asked if I'd like to do the dirty work, to copy out the parts for a band of a dozen players and go to Liverpool and rehearse it. I was thrilled and said I'd love to. Two weeks before rehearsals were due to begin I went to him and said I needed the music. He said he couldn't be bothered, and I should do it instead! That opened a career writing incidental music for theatre, radio and films, which I did extensively for the next fifteen years or more. I'd always written very easily and fluently, so I wrote pieces that I might include in concerts myself. Some were quite short, like the *Five Studies in the Form of Variations on Three Notes*. I wanted to build the three sonatas as a repertoire group.

[16] Ashridge, 14 May 1993.

Interview Transcriptions: Antony Hopkins

I was touring in France c. 1947, with the singer Sophie Wyss. We did performances of British songs, some Britten and some of my own arrangements. In the middle of the concert I would play a solo group. I normally played my First Piano Sonata, as it is a twenty-minute piece. We did a big tour around France and into Switzerland, and at one stage, in halting schoolboy French, I announced that I'd played my First Piano Sonata at every concert in the last ten days, so tonight for a change, I was going to play my Sonata No. 2. When I came off the platform, Sophie was grinning all over. She said that I'd told the audience that I'd played my First Piano Sonata at every concert for the last ten years! I played the First quite extensively. I thought it was quite a nice piece.

How were the Sonatas received?

If you look in my autobiography, you'll see a fabulous notice from that tour, all in French.[17] They don't write notices like that these days! It did generally have a good reception, both in England and abroad. I had an invitation to play a solo recital at the National Gallery wartime concerts. I had already played with a cellist, a violinist and a singer, playing a solo group of short pieces by other composers. I was thrilled to have the chance to do a whole solo recital. I must emphasize that my piano technique was extremely shoddy, and I was not really equipped to do such a thing, but I practised every day for six or seven hours to produce this programme. During this period there came an overwhelming urge to write the Second Piano Sonata. I tried to put it off, but it wouldn't go away, so the whole sonata was written in two and a half days. On the manuscript it says "July lst–3rd 1945". It was so insistent that I had to write it and then resume my practising. I wasn't writing it for the National Gallery; the programme for that had already been fixed. It's short and concentrated, but I never got it published. It's dedicated to Michael Tippett, and consciously does pay a flattering compliment to his style. He liked it! There's a rhythm in the rondo, which is characteristic of him. The phrases of the main subject of the first movement are very much in his style, but the development of material is my own. It's a tribute to him.

The Third Sonata was a tribute to a wonderful pianist called Noel Mewton-Wood. He was an Australian boy who had studied here with Schnabel, a remarkable pianist, particularly in playing the music of Hindemith. He played things like Hindemith's *Ludus Tonalis* and his Piano Sonatas in such a way that it made you feel that they were the greatest music that had ever been written. I was at the Bryanston Summer School, as it was, before it went to Dartington, and Nadia Boulanger was there. Noel was going to play Stravinsky's Concerto for Two Pianos with her. I listened to them rehearse for the whole afternoon. This young Adonis-like chap came out, bathed in sweat, looking exhausted, followed by this

---

[17] Hopkins, 1982, 130.

indomitable elderly lady with bandages round both her wrists. Noel turned to me and said, "It's no good, I can't hear myself play!"

I admired his playing enormously and I wanted to write a piece for him to play. I thought that a piece that echoed Hindemith would appeal to him most. The Third Sonata does, especially in the first movement. There are chunky chords going out in opposite directions (which also appear in the Second Sonata, but not as a tribute to Hindemith – they were in the air at the time). Unfortunately, he never played it. Tragically he committed suicide shortly after I'd written it and before I'd shown it to him. That was a great sorrow to me. I wrote a second movement that had a very nice compliment paid to it by the Swiss composer Frank Martin, whom I admired very much as well. I thought his *Petite Symphonie Concertante* was one of the wonderful pieces of the twentieth century. He came to dinner one evening, and I played him the Third Sonata. After I'd finished the second movement, he smiled and said, "I would have liked to have written that." I wrote the whole of the Third Piano Sonata in 1946, but then I wrote a different last movement later. I decided to scrap the original one.

Would you say that Hindemith influenced your First Sonata?

No, not really. The First is a romantic piece. There are some influences from Tippett, especially in the phrase in the first movement that's treated canonically. Originally the second movement was in a key that was very similar to the key of the first movement and the scherzo – I forget exactly what. Mátyás Seiber, who was on the staff at Morley College, wrote me a long letter about it. I was extremely flattered that he'd take so much trouble, as he'd never seen a copy, this was all from hearing it. He suggested that I should transpose this movement to give a better tonal contrast. I did this very slackly – I simply stuck flats in front of everything! So it's written in D flat minor, instead of C sharp minor.

You were convinced that this improved the work?

Yes, I was prepared to listen to criticism, although I didn't always accept it. On this occasion, I thought that it was a sound point to make. I do write very quickly. I'm the reverse of someone like Tippett, for instance, who's one of the world's slowest writers, who takes seven years to write an opera. I was trained, through writing incidental music, to write to the clock. I could write the music to a film in one week. For *The Pickwick Papers* (1952) I wrote forty minutes of music in eleven days, which is really pushing on a bit. The radio programmes I could do in a matter of days. I have this fluency in my writing also. You can't change the way you're born. Tippett couldn't make himself compose quickly, and Britten couldn't make himself compose slowly.

Have you ever felt the desire to revise your works?

No, I'm always interested in the next project and forget the last one. I sometimes listen to re-broadcasts of programmes I've written music for years earlier, and I don't remember any of it. As far as the piano repertoire goes, the first piece was *Toccata* (1943), written whilst I was still at college.

Michael said to me, "You may regret having that published." I know what he meant. It was a derivative sort of piece, but it's been played a few times, especially by Frank Wibaut. You need to have something published to tell people that you exist. Then I did the *Five Variations*, which are quite intriguing pieces. When they were printed, I had two reviews, one in the *Musical Times* and one in the *Musical Opinion*. I carried them around for ages because one said that the pieces were written by someone who had no idea how to write for the piano, they were poorly composed and had feeble ideas. The other said that they were brilliantly conceived for the piano and amazingly effective! They contradicted each other almost word for word, so I never take any notice of printed criticism. Then I had *Tango* published. It was from *The Skin of Our Teeth* (1948), a Thornton Wilder play. I was besotted by Vivien Leigh and wrote it for her to make an entrance wearing a red bathing costume and black fishnet tights – it was a seductive piece. There's not really any other published piano music.

What specific Hindemith works did you know?

I'd looked at *Ludus Tonalis*. It was too hard for me to play but I admired Mewton-Wood playing it, and the Piano Sonatas. He gave magnificent performances, of the Third Sonata in particular, and I thought that it was wonderful music. Now it's completely fallen out of fashion and apart from *Mathis der Maler*, people are not interested in his music. I admired Hindemith, but I never took to serial music at all. I don't accept that it is the greatest music of the century. Interestingly, in the last couple of years, serialism has been regarded as unfashionable. Critics are realizing that it is not as good as they first made it out to be. I've always liked tunes, and regard music as a sensuous experience. Hindemith was a complete counter to serialism. I had a long talk with him one day, and he expressed a complete disgust for it. He thought that people should have more talent than to need to fall back on serialism. I felt that Schoenberg was a nineteenth-century romantic composer, who had forced the conceptions of the nineteenth century into a sort of straitjacket. I once said in a lecture that Wagner took music into the bedroom, and Schoenberg gave it a new pair of pyjamas!

Did you read Hindemith's theories of composition?

Yes, but I did not consciously use them. William Glock had given lectures on Hindemith at Bryanston Summer School, and what he said seemed to me to make good sense. Hindemith seemed completely lucid in his approach to the twentieth century. I like lucidity and hate the jargon of the serialists. There are books about twelve-note writing that I cannot comprehend. I've never tried to model my compositions on anything else. The Second Sonata is like a tribute to Tippett. The material has a Tippett flavour, but the way in which I worked it out is entirely my own.

You use some of the flexibility of rhythm that Tippett inherited from the madrigalists, and you also have contrapuntal sections.

Yes, the slow movement of the Second Sonata is virtually a two-part invention. There's only one part where a third voice comes in, and that's a pedal point. It has an extraordinary effect of enriching the texture.

The First Sonata uses much syncopation. Was this influenced by Tippett, or by jazz?

Not consciously. I liked the music of Constant Lambert. I'd heard *The Rio Grande* when I was at school and thought that it was great. No, the opening is a groping theme that comes out of the dark. If anything, it was influenced by my score for *Cupid and Psyche*, or *The Golden Ass* (1944), one of the first radio programmes that I wrote. There's a long sequence where somebody emerges from the underworld, and I had this music that climbs out of the depths of the orchestra. I wanted to put that into a more permanent form. The use of unisons between the hands was something that Tippett did, partly because he was a lousy pianist. He could give a good impression of his music, mainly by singing louder than he was actually playing. I used to spend the occasional weekend at his cottage, and I would take whatever I'd written to him. He'd listen to it and advise me. He'd see where there was a problem, and fetch a score by any composer from Bach to Hindemith and point out a passage where that composer had experienced a similar problem and solved it. I would feel not alone in my problem, and I was able to learn from their solution.

Initially the second movement of the Second Sonata finished simply on a B flat octave. The Rondo begins on an A. I added in an extra two notes, because Tippett showed me a passage in a Beethoven string quartet where the following movement is anticipated by the rhythm at the end of the previous one. Suddenly, my piece flowed onwards and a link was provided. I hadn't consciously looked for it, but it was a definite improvement. It's so short that it's more of a sonatina than a sonata.

It's interesting that you see a difference between a sonata and a sonatina. What implication do you think that the word sonata has?

Hindemith's Piano Sonata No. 2 is a very short piece, about the same length as my Second Sonata. I don't see any reason why you should not have a sonata lasting ten minutes as opposed to fifty, but it depends on the construction. Mine is very clearly a sonata. I even have a double bar at the end of the exposition, although I don't repeat it. It's a textbook first movement, with development and recapitulation, as you would expect. The last movement is a rondo. When I start writing in that sort of circumstance, I don't know how long the piece is going to be, or how long a movement is going to be. I've always written in an unconventional way in that I start at bar one and see what happens – I don't plan. It's the same with my books, I start at page one and write the whole thing in long hand, and I hardly change a word. People can't believe that I don't plan out the contents of each chapter in advance. I wrote a work called *John and the Magic Music Man* (1974) as a younger person's guide to the orchestra, and I began at the beginning and worked through, but I didn't know how the story was going to end. I wrote it in three days, and it works wonderfully with kids. There's a sense of adventure if you start to write a piece and don't know how it's going to finish.

Do you plan how many movements you are going to have in advance?

Yes, but I've never really planned pieces rigidly, so it's unlikely that I'll ever write a concerto or a symphony. As a boy, I used to write pieces in the holidays, including a substantial piece for piano and orchestra when I was about sixteen. It's well over a hundred pages. It's not good music, but I've always had an urge to write, even though I had virtually no encouragement. I wrote a Concertino for Piano and orchestra, which I put out as a two-piano arrangement with orchestration indicated. I produced this at school for a lesson at the beginning of term. I played it to the master, and I had one twenty-minute lesson on it. Halfway through the term, he asked me to bring it again. I was pleased, because he'd been so dismissive before. When I arrived there was another person in the room. My teacher gave me the best lesson he'd ever given me. Only later did I discover that the other person was a HMI [Her Majesty's Inspector].

I had a girlfriend in my teens, who was a very good violinist, and I wrote a couple of violin sonatas for her. I played them at my first harmony lesson at the College, to Dr Darke, and he was quite impressed as no-one else in the class had done anything like it. I never thought of being a composer as a full-time career – I enjoyed it. When it came to writing opera, I couldn't believe that it was happening to me!

What were your experiences of composition teaching at the College?

I never had a composition lesson there. I did one term of orchestration with Gordon Jacob. I'd had his book on orchestral technique as a prize at school, and found it very helpful. I thought that his lessons would be, too, but we would just sit in silence looking at my work and after fifteen minutes of cogitation and pipe smoking, he would say "trumpet there, perhaps?" and that was that. I think that he felt I knew roughly what I was doing. I didn't think it would be of any practical use. I didn't envisage myself writing film scores, etc.

Did you have to do counterpoint exercises?

Someone tried that on me! I found it useless, as I was never going to write anything like it again. I had to do a fugue, which the teacher was impressed with, but I refused to do a second, after having proved that I could do one. I could not see any practical application for it. My highest aim was to be an assistant music master at a public school.

So when you needed to, you found your own compositional style.

Yes, I am very eclectic. Because I was writing much incidental music, I was writing for 1 BC and 21 AD, so I could assume styles. I loved, for example, writing songs in the manner of Arne for Isaak Walton's *Compleat Angler* (1945). I did a large-scale work for the WI [Women's Institute] called *Early One Morning* (1980). The heroine finally meets the right guy, and the chorus sings *Got a Fella* as a send-up of the Hallelujah chorus. It was great fun.

Appendix 1

Did you know any other British piano sonatas when you wrote your own?

No, not Lambert's, Bax's or Bridge's. I would never have been so presumptuous as to think I was doing something in the British tradition, as they were written really just for myself. I could always make up a recital of short pieces – Bach, Mozart and carefully selected Brahms. I could play Brahms' Intermezzi very well. Cyril Smith told me years later that after he'd given me a lesson, he'd go back and try to play the same Intermezzo, because he felt I got to the heart of it in a way that he hadn't. I had no feelings that I had anything of significance to offer as a pianist. I felt that as I couldn't play a work of substance in the middle of the concert, the best thing to do was to play something I'd written myself. That made me a composer-pianist, and people wouldn't know if I went wrong!

English music was not played much then. Phyllis Sellick gave the first performance of Tippett's First Piano Sonata, and she played some of the shorter Bax pieces, but I was amazingly ignorant of such a huge spectrum of music. When I arrived at the College, I'd probably only been to two or three symphony concerts in my life. Music today is so on tap. The only Beethoven symphony I knew at all well was the Second, as someone gave me records of it when I was fifteen. I had only a nodding acquaintance with the others.

Later on, when I was teaching, I had Roger Smalley as a pupil. He had spent two years as assistant librarian in the Henry Watson music library in Manchester and had borrowed scores every night. Adrian Jack was a pupil of mine. He also had an almost encyclopaedic knowledge and it put me to shame. It was the way I was brought up, and the timing. When I was a boy, music was Vaughan Williams' *Toward the Unknown Region*, Parry's *Jerusalem* and *Blest Pair of Sirens*. People just didn't know the music, it wasn't on records and we didn't go to concerts. Apart from a children's concert, I did not go to a London concert until I was seventeen.

Did you come across the music of Stravinsky at the Royal College?

At Morley College we heard performances of *Dumbarton Oaks*. When I was at the College, Dyson was the director and he didn't like modern music, so little was performed. There were no twentieth-century music courses, and I never heard a note of Stravinsky when I was there. Neither did I hear a note of Purcell. It was just mainstream nineteenth-century music. Things have improved enormously now!

If all the training was based on German classics, it is hardly surprising that British composers adopted these models in their music.

Recently there has been a revival of interest in the music of Parry. Orchestral music has become available on record. I could not believe it – pieces that by repute had been written-off as pallid imitations of Wagner, were in fact so good. I prefer Parry's Symphonies in some ways to Elgar's, as they are not quite so diffuse and don't have the same repetition of motives. Recently I conducted the *Elegy on the Death of Brahms* with the National Children's Orchestra and found it a profoundly moving piece. We were brought up to believe that you don't listen to Parry; he's a historic figure, but the music is not of any interest. I'd been involved in performing *Blest Pair of Sirens* and found it very lush, after two minutes you can't take it any more. I am amazed that a Swiss conductor is taking up his music now. Bridge was overshadowed by his pupil, but he's written some remarkably fine music. Recently I conducted Bax's *Tintagel*. It is superbly orchestrated. People turned against the big Irish folktune, but it is a good tune and what's wrong with that?

I am very interested in the psychology of the British composer. Many composers seem to have become disillusioned.

I have written many large-scale works for the young in particular, including a piece called *A Time for Growing* (1967), and *Richman, Poorman, Beggarman, Saint*. In each case, the quality of the work could not really be judged owing to the inadequacy of the performance. The St Francis opera lasts one and a half hours and is scored for large orchestra. There's a big part for the solo tenor, sung brilliantly by Bernard Dickerson. Whenever it's been performed it's been inadequately rehearsed and trained by all except the soloist. If Britten had written it he would have had the ECO [English Chamber Orchestra], Pears, Harper, Tear, etc., three solid weeks of rehearsals, and it would have been very professional. The first performance was a nightmare. The assistant conductor never looked at me once, so the choir and orchestra were not together. In the second performance of *A Time for Growing*, the tenor had not learnt the piece. We had to scrape through.

Your output has now slowed up.

I've always been a prostitute; I do what I'm paid to do. The commissions have died down because the producers for whom I worked in the BBC all retired or died. It had been a great period for the Third Programme. Nowadays, I don't know what they do by way of commissioning. I wrote twelve programmes on insects for the radio. The music is witty and stylish. The music I did for a programme on flies makes people laugh aloud. I would love to do the music for the wildlife programmes that they have on television now.

You've never felt the desire to take up writing for your own pleasure?

No. I had two commissions last year. One was to write a quartet for double basses, which I don't think anyone had ever done before, for a summer school.[18] I remembered that I'd done a piece about beetles before, and one of these was the sisyphus or dung beetle, who gets his name from the fact that he pushes balls of dung up hills and they roll back down. Sisyphus was the legendary figure condemned to the darkest pit of hell, who pushed the stone up the hill. Whenever it got to the top it rolled down, and he went on doing that for ever. I called the piece *Sisyphus*, as the double basses are ideally suited to growling at the bottom of the register and climbing slowly. It begins with a narrator. As soon as I put it into the world

---

[18] Gunther Schuller wrote a Quartet for double basses in 1947.

of a radio programme it came alive. I haven't heard it, but the musicians apparently loved playing it.

How important are your Piano Sonatas?

I would love them to be considered more seriously by pianists. Someone played one at the Wigmore Hall about three years ago. It had a criticism saying that this is an admirably written piece, and I'm sure that it served its purpose in its time, but it's of little interest now. It's unfashionable, but if there's hope for Parry now, maybe there's hope for the Hopkins Sonatas!

You never recorded them?

No, but Lamar Crowson recorded the Third as a last side of a recording of my opera *Three's Company* (1953). He said it was "bloody difficult"! Monique Haas, a French pianist, once sight-read through the first movement of this Sonata up to speed. I was astounded! I wish that I was taken more seriously as a composer, but that is the fatal error of being versatile. Howard Shelley will never be accepted as a conductor because he's such a good pianist. When Ashkenazy started to conduct, his stock as a solo pianist was devalued. It's an extraordinary attitude!

Sir Michael Tippett[19]

My research is concerned with twentieth-century British piano sonatas. I have begun my investigations with the Sonatas by Parry.

I don't know them. I came to London in 1924, and I think by then Parry may have retired from the Royal College. The one who really tottered about as I remember was Stanford.[20]

He too wrote a Piano Sonata, but unfortunately it is lost.

Fortunately or unfortunately?! It may have been interesting – Stanford was no fool.

Did you ever feel that you were continuing a tradition of sonata writing?

No, certainly not a tradition from England.

Maybe in some sense, you were following on from Beethoven.

Yes, sure. I was limited in my knowledge of all of them. Originally my First Sonata was called Fantasy Sonata because I didn't feel it was strictly a sonata. Later I grew to learn more about Beethoven and I realized that it was no problem, so I just let it ride. That was partly the strictness of my own view and a result of my classical training that seemed so real for a while.

Do you think that the word sonata has any particular implications for you?

No, it was a historical thing, although then it did. When I was a student I was a real greenhorn and took it all in like a sponge, as everything was new.

---

[19] Clapham, 19 July 1993.
[20] Parry was at the Royal College from 1883 until his death in 1918. Stanford was there from 1883 until his death in 1924.

The difficulty was that there was no radio or television and if the home didn't have it then you didn't hear it at all. Schools didn't have it in the First World War. It was an extraordinary ignorance. The only compensating thing was that I first heard the Beethoven symphonies in Promenade concerts in 1924. They were memorable to such a degree that I could not nearly recapture. Miniature scores were there, of course. The word sonata, I hadn't taken it in then. I later learnt that it did have a certain amount of meaning. I got that from Vincent d'Indy, from his Suite.[21] I later learnt of the curious keyboard sonatas of Scarlatti, what they were, in binary form. The interest has gone on and on, but sonata form does not make sense any more.

Do we need something to replace it?

That's a difficult question. I can't answer that. It's to do with historiography of some kind. My interest remained in Beethoven's long exploration of the sonata, and its use in his string quartets.

You thought of historical and notional archetypes.

Yes, for a while, that was a sort of upbringing, and I went to it. Slowly I realized it doesn't work quite like that, especially when I had more idea about how Beethoven uses fugue, quite differently to how it was used in Bach's period. They weren't Bach's fugues, they were his own, and very strange they were too. The archetypes landed them in a period. If there were sonatas and symphonies, then by the time it came to Mahler they were different. The semantics of naming a work sonata or symphony are not of great interest to me. We can't define them now.

Composers use the terms in the way they choose.

Yes, it only becomes a problem when you come to write about them. You have to use words that don't have exact meanings, like sonata.

When you composed your sonatas, did you plan out the structure in advance, and then return to fill in the details, or did they evolve?

The former, not the latter. Nothing ever evolved, that wasn't me. As T. S. Eliot once said to me, "The words come last". Here the sound came last. Form is as old as the hills. I don't really understand as a composer what "evolve" would mean. Mind you, in the early days you are derivative and you have to find your own style. In a sense, the First Piano Sonata is the first work that is really free, not totally, but then nothing can be.

Do you have any recollections of the early Piano Sonata in C minor that you wrote c.1928?

No, I know it's there. Bill would know.[22] He's just taken the last of the manuscripts up to London to be given to the Tippett Foundation. It was a work that tried to find my way around. When I went back to study with R. O. Morris I was about twenty-five or twenty-six, and all these early works were put aside. Nothing remained as I began again.

---

[21] Op. 91 for flute, string trio and harp.
[22] Meirion Bowen.

Appendix 1

Did your piano repertoire give you ideas for your own compositions?

I wasn't a pianist in any real sense. I didn't practise properly, so I never had a proper technique. The very nice man who taught me, Aubin Raymar, could see that I was an interested as well as interesting young figure. I was lively and active, and he had to realize that he hadn't got a pianist on his hands at all. He tried to help a great deal, by finding some things for me to play of more up-to-date style than simply the classical piano sonatas. One of these was Ravel's *Sonatine*. I can now only remember the sarabande-like movement. It seemed to me to be a sarabande, but I don't think Ravel called it such.[23] Much later, I heard it performed in the old Queen's Hall, possibly during the 1930s, and Ravel himself was there. Individual composers were invited. I remember Stravinsky and Ravel coming. We, as students, went to see what they were up to. I remember seeing Ravel stand up and conduct something for a small ensemble, I think. He seemed to be a very tall and straight figure. He had what appeared to be a pencil and conducted with very small gestures, which was not common at the time. People usually used big gestures and long sticks. A young Parisian played the *Sonatine* in a very dry style, obviously how the master wanted, very neoclassical. It was so memorable, I can almost hear it now. That didn't mean that I knew anything about how you write for the piano, though.

I knew later what Stravinsky was, as he was trying to make his music more widely understood, in Europe at least, and he was a very fine pianist. Willy Strecker, who later became my publisher, suggested that Stravinsky should give up composition for a month or so each year, and make arrangements for piano and one or two other instruments of all his music that was up-to-date, and tour with it. He had Samuel Dushkin the violinist, a clarinettist, a double bass player and someone on drums, I think, and he played the piano. He played *Petrushka* with a startling sound and vigour. The other one he played was the incidental music to *Histoire du Soldat*. These things fascinated me as a composer, and of course his piano playing, but I could not do that myself.

When did you first become aware of jazz?

It was not in the Royal College at all and I didn't know enough not to get it very muddled. A figure who seemed to be moving away towards a new standard in European music was a man my own age, Constant Lambert. In *The Rio Grande* it isn't jazz of course, it is more Latin American music. It has a long piano recitative which I thought I should like to find out how it was done. In that sense it did matter what I heard.

Did you know Lambert's Piano Sonata?

No. I'm not exactly sure when *The Rio Grande* came out but it was at a Promenade concert.[24] No, the influence from jazz goes back before that.

---

[23] Ravel called the second movement *Mouvement de Menuet*.
[24] Composed 1927, broadcast 1928. First public performances: 12 and 13 December 1929 (Manchester and Queen's Hall) by Lambert, Sir Hamilton Harty, Hallé Orchestra.

About 1910–11, two girls came into the village and they sang the latest ragtime songs – *Alexander's Ragtime Band* and *Everybody's Doing It*. These went right into my head to my sound world, and I thought they were marvellous. I'd absolutely no idea what they were about or where they came from, even where America was! They again, were not jazz.

What did you think of the jazz-influenced compositions of Les Six, Walton, Stravinsky, etc.?

I can't remember. It came later, on records, the 78s. There weren't many of them. The main ones were things like Django Reinhardt and the Hot Club de Paris, and I got them all muddled.[25] I suppose this is what Stravinsky heard. There are some small piano pieces of his that I liked, but I never studied them properly. The real memory that caused a lot of comment in the Royal College was the arrival of *Rhapsody in Blue*, not long after New York.[26] There was a great deal of argumentation between critics about it, whether it belonged in music, and what was it? I can remember it and was fascinated by it, but I couldn't analyse it. Nor do I remember in what form it came, whether it was in the original orchestration or not. *Rhapsody in Blue* knocked me out. I thought that it was marvellous, but I still could not take part properly in the argumentation about it. I didn't see what it was until many years later. I think that it was in 1949 that an all black cast from America brought over a Gershwin opera.

There was one chap at the Royal College who seemed to know a lot about it, called Jeffrey Mark. He was just old enough to have been caught in the First World War, which deeply hurt him and he never really got over it. Those who had been conscripted in the last part of the war and had not completed their education were allowed to return to continue their studies free. The Royal College was not what it is now. There was no examination to get in, as I remember. There were no grants. My Dad had not much money but he found enough to pay for me. Jeffrey Mark was an important figure. He was trying to heal himself. He was about nineteen or twenty years old. He went to America and he had experienced jazz. I remember asking him what it was and he said it was really a piano technique. The main thing was an anticipation of the beat, which was unlike the straight classical style. By 1938, a book came out, called *Jazz: Hot and Hybrid*, which tried to analyse what the blues was, the blues note, etc. It was an extraordinary book, written by Winthrop Sargeant, whom I later met. These were all part of my explorations to find out what it was and what it meant.

This would have interested you from an intellectual point of view?

Well, more from a sound point of view. I supposed it helped me to

---

[25] Django Reinhardt and Stephane Grappelli formed the Quintette du Hot Club de France in 1934.

[26] Composed 1924 for jazz band and piano. Gershwin performed it at Queen's Hall in 1924. Paul Whiteman played it at the Royal Albert Hall, 11 April 1926. Gershwin was there and did not approve of his interpretation.

Appendix 1

understand what Stravinsky had been interested in, but he never went into the world very far, whereas Gershwin did.

It was not until the 1960s that you first went to America to experience it first-hand.

No, but I'd heard plenty of records before that. I just took what I wanted from jazz. There's not that much in the First Piano Sonata. It's there in the last movement to a vague degree, but not really. The blues, if there is such a thing in the strict sense, I had to learn about and that came through opera.

It's more of a vocal medium.

Yes, I felt it was. It was recordings of Bessie Smith and Louis Armstrong that affected me most deeply. Sargeant analysed it very well, how limited the vocal range was, but only later did I realize how Louis Armstrong's playing shadowed Bessie's singing. He virtually copied the vocal line on the trumpet. It was a vocal technique, and it didn't finally flower until the Third Symphony (1970–2). It got mixed up with other things. Purcell did similar things. His setting of "wondrous machine" has the vocal line imitated by the oboe in the same rhythm.

Like Purcell, you have been eclectic, especially in the First Piano Sonata, which is very international in its approach. You imitate Elizabethan virginal music and gamelan music for example.

Yes, that's why I thought it was a Fantasy Sonata, as I realized it was not of a classic model. Later I realized that Beethoven was more flexible in his approach, as the Ninth Symphony was to show. The gamelan music came entirely from records. I'd never heard one till much later, when I was in Australia. Big collections of music came onto record and reached Europe in this way. It opened my ears and gave me all sorts of ideas. Jeff Mark had a preoccupation with Northumbrian bagpipe music, and he said if you really want to hear highly decorated music, then go and hear pibroch. I looked into those things and took what I wanted, you're quite right.

Did you hear pibroch on record, or live?

I realized that pibroch was too special and so I gave up on the bagpipes. Jeff Mark was a different one. He believed, as was common at the time (1930s), that folksong had some reality in the music of any particular place. Vaughan Williams felt this very strongly, and that so much of the music we played in concert halls was derivative of German folksong. He thought that you could begin again and produce another music but I knew perfectly well you couldn't. The variations were originally planned as a complete entity. It was essentially a variety rather than as in classical variations or Brahms, where the theme would remain in the same key throughout. I knew a lot of Beethoven's variations.

I have been looking at the manuscript of your Second Piano Sonata (1962) that is held in the British Library, and I noticed that you originally called the work Arrest and Movement.

Did I? The idea of Arrest and Movement was eventually used in the Third Symphony. It came out of a book on dancing, on the difference between old

Egyptian and old Cretan dance.[27] The Cretan dance was lively and vigorous, with movement. There were pictures and argumentation. The Egyptian art was powerful, but it was static. This seemed to me to be an intellectual idea that could be translated into sound, and a form could arise out of that. I had forgotten that I used this idea in the Piano Sonata. I must have felt that I was trying it out.

Maybe it can be seen in the contrast between static harmonic sections and the rapid-moving quaver sections.

Yes. I knew that it was quite different. It was not a classic sonata. It was more like a mosaic where sections are placed next to each other but are not linked by developments. It was a wholeness made by bits. I suppose I did once consider calling it *Mosaics*, but I can't really remember. I was already moving out of any relation with the classical sonata. Titles and names of works were really secondary to the actual music. By that time, I knew a lot more music and realized that these titles are purely historical things – they shift both archetypally and in practice.

In 1965 at the Edinburgh Festival, you'd heard works of Boulez that reawakened this idea of Arrest and Movement.[28]

Yes, the music seemed to me entirely "arrest" and I felt that it needed some other element. This was a negative thing that took place before the creative impulse began to work. I had this notion that you could eventually put these things together in a sort of jam session. You couldn't on the piano, so it was a trick in the Second Piano Sonata. I used this idea on a larger scale in the Concerto for Orchestra that immediately followed it.

Did you ever consider writing a Sonata for two pianos, to superimpose the themes?

Yes, I would have liked to in some ways, but I don't know that I could ever have done it. I thought highly of Stravinsky's Sonata for Two Pianos. I don't think that I could have ever thought it out – it's bad enough thinking about one piano, let alone two! It's fascinating thinking about the possibilities of the hands.

According to the manuscript, you once considered having the pianist strike the wood of the piano with their hands, but you have never written extended techniques into your Sonatas.

Did I? I think that the piano is a lovely instrument. I would only consider striking the piano to extend it into a rhythmical instrument, to create a percussive effect. There's a similar passage in *The Blue Guitar* (1982–3), but it doesn't really work, in my opinion. They are really drum techniques. I love the sound of the piano and want to explore its colours, but I've always been aware that things I write may be difficult for the pianist, as I had never

---

[27] H. A. Groenewegen-Frankfort, *Arrest and Movement*, London, 1951, whose title is borrowed from Eliot's *Burnt Norton*, II.

[28] According to Meirion Bowen, the work in question was *Pli selon Pli*. Ian Kemp cites Boulez's Second Piano Sonata.

done them myself. When I first showed my Piano Sonata to Cyril Smith, who had just married Phyllis Sellick, he said that he couldn't play it as it involved learning a new set of fingering for the return of the theme in a new key. The black and white notes came in different positions. I realized that I would have to wait until I found the right person. That operated early on. It was the same with Clifford Curzon, who was the best of all the British pianists of my age. He took one look at the Piano Concerto and said it was unplayable.[29] Paul Crossley tells me that the Fourth Sonata is the most pianistic of them all. He has given me help on certain things, such as the pedal techniques that were used at the end of the nineteenth century; the changes that came with the Spanish composers and Liszt, through to Debussy. This was helpful, because he knew things that I didn't.

In the Third Sonata (1972–3), you use palindrome, as you do in several other works. Is this to create a circular form?

Yes, it's a technique that's been evolved for a composer to take if he wants. Oddly enough, the palindrome at the end of the Third Sonata was never intended to work as it did. I realized that it was not enough for it to go forwards then back, it would have to go forwards again. I can't tell you why – it was a judgement I made. I wanted to vary it but Crossley pointed out that it couldn't work. There would have been too many trills at once and it would make it physically impossible.

With the Third Sonata, I can't remember how it came about, but the central thing was the big imaginative adventure of the variations, which were elaborate. I had to decide how many variations there should be, and what they do. The other sections served as a preludial movement and a scherzo-finale to end. Those sections contrasted with the huge slow movement. The variations themselves move. In the first movement there is the very pianistic idea of having the hands far apart. The "two handedness" I felt belonged to the technique of playing the piano. The first section is short, and this is the main idea. It begins miles apart and explores this symmetry. The slow movement is a very extended affair, and very difficult. The pianist has to hold it. It's difficult to play from memory. It's difficult to hear the variations on the seventeen chords. The last movement was a throwaway – a great piece of virtuosity. It came straight out of Beethoven for that matter.

The Fourth Sonata (1984) was originally conceived as a set of five bagatelles.

Yes, this is what happens! I thought that I did not want to go back to sonata form, but lo and behold, yes I did. It is very intricately made, notes come back again, and I knew what I was up to by then. On the television, I saw someone trying to play some Bach on a double keyboard. I realized how amusing it would be if the hands could cross over so that the left hand went up the keyboard whilst the right came down. These ideas went into my imagination, and an elaborate thing arose. At the end was the thing I'd

---

[29] The intended soloist was Julius Katchen, and he declared the Concerto unplayable.

longed to write for many years, a set of variations similar to Beethoven's in his Op. 109 Piano Sonata. His are in E major, and at the end, the theme comes back exactly as it was at first. It has this curious effect of being an end, though it had been a beginning. That's what I wanted to achieve. You get a sense of an ending, forever.

In this work you use quotation, from the Fourth Symphony, the Triple Concerto and The Mask of Time.

Yes, there's not many of them, but they're there. Although in a sense all the pieces have their own parameters, they're no bigger than what they are. Bach, all of them used their own material again to some degree. You can't help that because you are one person.

Do you hope that the listener will connect the quotation with its source?

No, not at all, how can he?

Does this also apply in the Second Piano Sonata, where you use quotations from the War Act of King Priam*?*

Yes, heaps of people have heard the Piano Sonata but not *King Priam*. Maybe I'm just lazy, but the themes are different in new contexts.

Have you ever heard the Piano Sonata by Maxwell Davies? That, also, looks back to Beethoven.

Well, we all do. Someone once asked me why my First Piano Sonata was like Hindemith and we discovered we'd both looked back to Scarlatti. That's probably the case here. I'm lazy – I never listen to anybody.

Are there any plans for a Fifth Piano Sonata?

No, absolutely none. I retired about eight weeks ago. At the end of his life, Brahms got very lonely and used to play things on the piano. They are lovely pieces, but he was a pianist and could amuse himself in that way. I can't do that because I can't play the piano.

Any more orchestral works?

No, nothing at all. Sixty years of composition is quite enough I think!

Appendix 2:
Catalogue of Piano Sonatas 1870–1945

The catalogue includes details of all piano sonatas written by a composer whose first sonata was completed prior to 1945.
Information is given in the following form:

Surname, Christian name (Dates)
Title of sonata – Year of composition
Location of Manuscript (if known). Publisher Year of Publication.
Duration Dedication
Notes concerning commissions and first performances

All manuscripts, with the exception of Sorabji's, are held in Great Britain, and standard library sigla are used to indicate their location.

Alwyn, William (1905–85)
Sonata alla toccata – 1942

Arnold, Malcolm (1921–2006)
Sonata – 1942
MS with publishers. Roberton 1992
Dur: 9' Dedication: To Mother
f.p. R. Deering, BMIC, 15 May 1984

Ashton, Algernon (1859–1937)
Sonata Op. 101 (E flat minor)
C. Hofbauer, Leipzig 1882 or 1888?
Dedication: Fraulein Gisella Grosz

Sonata No. 2 Op. 150 (G major)
Ries & Erler, Berlin 1925
Dur: 20' Dedication: Thomas Dunhill

Sonata No. 3 Op. 161 (B flat major)
Ries & Erler, Berlin 1925
Dedication: Isador Epstein

Sonata No. 4 Op. 164 (D minor)
Ries & Erler, Berlin 1925
Dedication: Willy Rehberg

Sonata No. 5 Op. 168 (F sharp major)
Rob. Forberg, Leipzig 1925
Dedication: Sir Herbert Thompson, Bart.

Sonata No. 6 Op. 170 (A minor)
Murdoch Murdoch & Co. 1925
Dedication: Cecil Goodall

Sonata No. 7 Op. 172 (C sharp minor)
Rob. Forberg, Leipzig 1925
Dedication: George Woodhouse

Sonata No. 8 Op. 174 (F major)
Goodwin & Tabb 1926
Dedication: Rita Neve

Austin, Ernest (1874–1947)
Sonata Op. 1 (D major) – 1897
Sonata No. 2 Op. 31 (B flat minor)
Novello 1907

Baines, William (1899–1922)
Sonata (D minor) – 1914
Lbm Add MS 50212. Unpublished

Catalogue of Piano Sonatas 1870–1945

Sonata No. 1 Op. 3 (D minor) – 1916
Lbm Add MS 50214. Unpublished
Dedication: Mr A. Jowett, Mus. Bac. Oxon.

Sonata No. 2 Op. 13 (A minor) – 1917
Lbm Add MS 50218. Unpublished
Dedication: "To all those whose aims and ideals are high"

Sonata Op. 4 (F sharp minor) – 1918, rev. 1919 and 1921
Lbm Add MSS 50219 and 50221.
Unpublished

Banister, Henry Charles (1831–97)

Sonata (F minor)
performed 1874

Sonata (F sharp minor)
performed 1875

Barnett, John Francis (1837–1916)

Sonata Op. 45 (E minor) – 1886
Augener 1895

Sonata romantique No. 2 (A minor)
Hutchings & Romer 1917

Bax, Arnold (1883–1953)

Sonata (D minor) *No. 5* **– 1897–8**
Lbm Add MS 54768. Unpublished

Sonata Op. 1 – 1898
MS Eire C. Unpublished

Sonata in D minor – 1900
Lam. MS 319. Unpublished
Dur: 6'

Romantic Tone Poem **– 1910 (version of First Piano Sonata)**
Unpublished
f.p. M. Hess, Bechstein Hall, 25 April 1911

Symphonic Phantasy **– 1917 (version of First Piano Sonata)**
Unpublished
f.p. M. Hess, Wigmore Hall, 9 Oct. 1919

Sonata No. 1 (F sharp minor) – 1910, rev. 1917–21
MS lost. Murdoch Murdoch & Co. 1920, Chappell 1949
Dur: 20'
f.p. H. Cohen, Wigmore Hall, 15 June 1920 and 12 April 1921

Sonata in D minor – 1911
MS lost
f.p. M. Hess, Aeolian Hall, 2 June 1911

Sonata in F major (No. 2 Scherzo) – 1913
Lbm Add MS 54767. Unpublished
Dur: 9'
Orchestrated 1917 and issued on pianola roll

Sonata No. 2 (G) – 1919, rev. 1920
Lbm Add MS 54767. Murdoch Murdoch & Co. 1921, Chappell 1943
Dur: 25'   Dedication: Harriet Cohen
f.p. A. Alexander, Aeolian Hall, 24 Nov. 1919; H. Cohen, Queen's Hall, 15 June 1920

Sonata (E flat) – 1922
Lbm Add MS 54724. Unpublished
Dur: 34'
Original version of First Symphony

Sonata No. 3 (G sharp minor) – 1926
Lbm Add MS 54767. Murdoch Murdoch & Co. 1929, Chappell 1945
Dur: 25'   Dedication: Harriet Cohen
f.p. H. Cohen, British Music Society, Liverpool, 18 Nov. 1927

Sonata No. 4 (G major) – 1932
Murdoch Murdoch & Co. 1934, Chappell 1945
Dur: 16'   Dedication: Charles Lynch
f.p. H Cohen, New York, 1 Feb. 1934 and Wigmore Hall, 18 May 1934

Bennett, William Sterndale (1816–75)

Sonata No. 1 Op. 13 (F minor) – 1837
Edwin Ashdown 1841
Dedication: Mendelssohn

Sonata No. 2 Op. 46 (A flat major) *The Maid of Orleans* **– 1869–73**
Lamborn Cock 1873, Kistner 1876
Dedication: Arabella Goddard
f.p. Miss Channell, 1873

Berkeley, Lennox (1903–90)

Sonata Op. 20 (A major) – 1942–5
Chester
Dur: 22'   Dedication: Clifford Curzon
f.p. C. Curzon, Wigmore Hall

Appendix 2

Bowen (Edwin) York (1884–1961)

Sonata No. 1 Op. 3 (E minor) – late 1890s
MS Lam. Unpublished

Sonata (E major) – late 1890s
MS Lam. Unpublished

Sonata (E minor) – late 1890s
MS Lam. Unpublished

Sonata No. 1 Op. 6 (B minor) – 1900
MS Lam. Privately printed. Dinham, Blyth 1902
Dedication: Claude V. Gascoigne
f.p.? Y. Bowen, St James' Hall, 21 Feb. 1901

Sonata No. 2 (F minor) – 1901
MS Lam. Unpublished

Sonata No. 2 Op. 91 (C sharp minor) – 1901
MS Lam. Unpublished
f.p.? Y. Bowen, Aeolian Hall, 8 Oct. 1912

Sonata No. 3 Op. 12/1 (D minor) – 1912
MS Lam. Unpublished

Short Sonata Op. 35/1 (C sharp minor) – pre-1908
Swan/Arcadia 1922
Dur: 15'   Dedication: To my wife and son

Sonata No. 4 Op. 35/3 *Sonatina*
Williams

Sonata No. 5 Op. 72 (F minor) – 1923
Swan/Arcadia 1923, Josef Weinberger
Dedication: W. Bowker Andrews
f.p. Y. Bowen, Jan. 1924

Sonata No. 6 Op. 160 (B flat major) – 1961
MS Lam. Josef Weinberger

Bridge, Frank (1879–1941)

Sonata – 1921–4
Lcm MS H 160 and Lbm Add MS 54366.
Augener 1925, Stainer & Bell 1979
Dur: 32' Dedication: Ernest Bristowe Farrar
f.p. M. Hess, Wigmore Hall, 15 Oct. 1925

Britten, Benjamin (1913–76)

Sonata No. 1 (A flat major) – 1923
MS Aldeburgh, Britten–Pears Library.
Unpublished

Sonata No. 2 (E minor) *Sonata fantasti* – 1923
MS Aldeburgh, Britten–Pears Library.
Unpublished

Sonata No. 3 (G minor) – 1922–3
MS Aldeburgh, Britten–Pears Library.
Unpublished

Sonata No. 4 (E flat major) – 1924
MS Aldeburgh, Britten–Pears Library.
Unpublished
Dedication: Edith Rhoda Britten
Renumbered No. 1

Sonata No. 5 (C major) – 1924
MS Aldeburgh, Britten–Pears Library.
Unpublished
Renumbered No. 2

Sonata No. 6 (B flat major) *Grande Sonata* – 1925
MS Aldeburgh, Britten–Pears Library.
Unpublished
Renumbered No. 3

Sonata No. 7 (F minor) *Grand Sonata* – 1925
MS Aldeburgh, Britten–Pears Library.
Unpublished
Renumbered No. 4

Sonata No. 8 (C minor) *Grand* – 1926
MS Aldeburgh, Britten–Pears Library.
Unpublished
Dedication: Edith Rhoda Britten

Sonata No. 9 (C sharp minor) – 1926
MS Aldeburgh, Britten–Pears Library.
Unpublished
Dedication: Ethel Astle

Sonata No. 10 (B flat major) – 1927
MS Aldeburgh, Britten–Pears Library.
Unpublished

Sonata No. 11 (B minor) – 1927–8
MS Aldeburgh, Britten–Pears Library.
Unpublished

Sonata No. 12 (B minor) *Sonatina* – 1928
MS Aldeburgh, Britten–Pears Library.
Unpublished

Burrows, Benjamin (1891–1966)

Sonata – 1934
F W Smith & Lewis 1941 Dedication:
Maud Randle

Catalogue of Piano Sonatas 1870–1945

Bush, Alan (1900–95)

Sonata No. 1 Op. 2 (B minor) – 1921
Murdoch Murdoch & Co. 1923
Dur: 22′   Dedication: Philip Agnew
*f.p. private, A. Bush, Lyceum Club, London,
10 May 1921*
f.p. public, A. Bush, RAM, 6 July 1921

Sonata No. 2 Op. 71 (A flat major) – 1970
Lbm MS Mus. 356, ff. 90–122. Alan Bush Trust, 2010
Dur: 20′   Dedication: Ronald Stevenson
f.p. R. Stevenson, Bath Festival, 28 May 1972

Sonata No. 3 Op. 113 (G major) – 1986
Lbm MS Mus. 364, ff. 1–34. Alan Bush Trust, 2010
Dur: 16′
f.p. L. Howard, BMIC, 28 Oct. 1986

Sonata No. 4 Op. 119 – 1987
Alan Bush Trust, 2010
f.p. P. Jacobs, BMIC, 1991

Sonata No. 5 in five movements – year unknown – *Incomplete*
Lbm MS Mus. 365, ff. 1–7 (start of 1st mvt and end of 5th mvt)
Dedication: To the memory of my dearly beloved wife, Nancy.

Chisholm, Erik (1904–65)

Sonata in A *An Riobain Dearg* (*The Red Ribbon*) – 1939 (abridged, 2004)
Erik Chisholm Trust
f.p. W. Henderson, Glasgow, Nov. 1939

Coke, Roger Sacheverell (1912–75)

Sonata No. 1 Op. 12 (D minor) – 1935
Unpublished Dur: 14'

Sonata No. 2 Op. 26 (G) – 1936
Chappell 1936
Dur: 18′   Dedication: Charles Lynch

Sonata No. 3 Op. 28 (A minor) – 1937
Unpublished Dur: 18′

Collingwood, Lawrance (1887–1982)

Sonata No. 1
P Jurgenson (Moscow) *c.* 1915

Sonata No. 2
P Jurgenson (Moscow) 1913

Cooke, Arnold (1906–2005)

Sonata No. 1 (A) – 1938
MS c/o Anglo-American publishers.
Unpublished
Dur: 16′
f.p. Manchester, 1939

Sonata No. 2 (B flat major) – 1965
MS c/o Anglo-American publishers.
Anglo-American
Dur: 17′
f.p. R Wright, Cheltenham Festival, 6 July 1966

Cyriax, Rudolf

Sonata (E minor) – pre-1908

Dale, Benjamin (1885–1943)

Sonata (D minor) – 1902–5
Lam MS 5057 and Lbm Add MS 50490 (1st mvt). Avison 1906, Cary & Co., Novello
Dedication: York Bowen
f.p. (1st mvt) Y. Bowen, Queen's Hall, 22 Feb. 1905 and complete, 14 Nov. 1905

Davis, J. D.

Sonata (G minor) – pre-1908

Edmonstoune, Duncan (1886–1920)

Sonata Op. 100 (D minor)
Vincent Music Co., 1906

Edwards, Julian (1855–1910)

Sonata (D major)
pub. 1876

Farjeon, Harry (1878–1948)

Sonata Op. 12 (B flat) *Miniature*
Augener 1906

Sonata Op. 43 (E)
Ashdown 1920
Dedication: Willie B. Manson

Ferguson, Howard (1908–99)

Sonata Op. 8 (F minor) – 1938–40
Lbm Add MS 57955 and Ob c.339, 353–55. Boosey 1940
Dur: 22′   Dedication: Harold Samuel
f.p. M. Hess, National Gallery Concerts, April 1940

Appendix 2

Gardner, Charles (1836–?)
Sonata (A major)
pub. 1871?

Gardner, John (1917–2011)
Sonata No. 2 – 1934
Sonata No. 3 Op. 183 (B flat major) – 1988

German, Edward (1862–1936)
Sonata – 1884
MS with David Russell Hulme. Banks 1987
f.p. S. Webbe, RAM, 1884

Greenwood, John (1889–1975)
Sonata No. 3
Unpublished

Sonata – mid 1930s

Hadow, William Henry (1859–1937)
Sonata (G minor)
pub. 1886?

Hall, Richard (1903–82)
Sonata Op. 20 (F major) – 1931, rev. 1935 as No. 15

Sonata No. 1 Op. 42 (C major) *The Mountains Under the Sea* – 1934

Sonata No. 2 Op. 45 (B flat minor) *Caerleon* – 1935

Sonata No. 3 Op. 46 (E flat minor) *Wantage* – 1935

Sonata No. 4 Op. 47 (D minor) – 1935

Sonata No. 5 Op. 48 (A minor) *Sherwood* – 1935

Sonata No. 6 Op. 49 (F major) – 1935

Sonata No. 7 Op. 50 (B flat major) *Dunkirk* – 1935

Sonata No. 8 Op. 51 (B minor) *Ashbourne* – 1935

Sonata No. 9 Op. 52 (C minor) *Studland* – 1935

Sonata No. 10 Op. 53 (E minor) *Carlton* – 1935

Sonata No. 11 Op. 54 (G major) *Victoria* – 1935

Sonata No. 12 Op. 55 (D) – 1935
Sonata No. 13 Op. 56 (F sharp minor) – 1935
Sonata No. 14 Op. 57 (A major) – 1935
Sonata No. 15 Op. 20 (F major) – 1931/5
Sonata No. 16 Op. 59 (D major) – 1935
Sonata No. 17 Op. 61 (E minor) – 1935
Sonata No. 18 Op. 63 (F sharp minor) – 1935
Sonata No. 19 Op. 69 (B minor) – 1936
Sonata Op. 97 (C minor) – 1939
Sonata Op. 102 (A minor) – 1940
Sonata Op. 105 (C major) – 1941–5
Sonata Op. 108 – 1941
Sonata Op. 111 (F major) – 1941
Sonata – 1955

Heward, Leslie (1897–1943)
Sonata – 1910

Hickin, Welton (1876–1968)
Sonata (E flat) – pre-1908

Holbrooke, Joseph (1878–1958)
Sonata No. 1 Op. 124 (C major) – 1936
Modern Music Library 1954
BBC broadcast, 3 Oct. 1936

Sonata No. 2 Op. 128 (B minor) – 1938
Modern Music Library 1943
Dedication: Lydia Stace
f.p. L. Stace, Broadcast 16 March 1938

Holland, Theodore (1878–1947)
Sonata (E)

Hopkins, Antony (1921–)
Sonata No. 1 (D minor) – 1944
Chester 1947
Dur: 20'   Dedication: Edward Sackville-West

Sonata No. 2 (F sharp minor) – 1945
MS with composer. Unpublished
Dedication: Michael Tippett

218

Catalogue of Piano Sonatas 1870–1945

Sonata No. 3 (C sharp minor) – 1946, rev. 1948 (new last mvt)
Chester 1949
Dur: 14'   Dedication: Noel Mewton-Wood

Howell, Dorothy (1898–1982)
Sonata – 1916
MS Bewdley. Unpublished
2 movements

Sonata (E) – 1955
MS Bewdley. Unpublished

Hurlstone, William Yeates (1876–1906)
Sonata (F minor) – 1894
Lcm MS 4817. Unpublished

Ireland, John (1879–1962)
Sonata (E minor) – 1918–20, rev. 1951
Lbm Add MS 52889. Augener 1920 and 1951, Stainer & Bell
Dur: 25'
f.p. F. Lamond, London, 12 June 1920

Jervis-Read, H. V. (1883–1945)
Sonata
Murdoch 1925 Dedication: N. W.

Lambert, Constant (1905–51)
Sonata – 1928–9
OUP 1930
Dedication: Thomas W. Earp
f.p. G. Bryan, Aeolian Hall, 30 Oct. 1929

Livens, Evangeline
Sonata – 1915
f.p. E. Livens, Duke's Hall, RAM, 4 Nov. 1915

Livens, Leo (?1896–c.1961)
Sonata
Anglo-French 1914

Lutyens, Elizabeth (1906–83)
Sonata
Lbm Add MS 64597 (Lutyens Collection). Unpublished

Macfarren, George Alexander (1813–87)
Sonata No. 1 (E flat major) – 1842?, rev. 1887
pub. 1842

Sonata No. 2 (A major) *Ma Cousine*
pub. 1845

Sonata No. 3 (G minor)
Novello 1880
Dedication: Agnes Zimmermann

Matthay, Tobias (1858–1945)
Sonata (B minor) – pre-1908

McEwen, John (1868–1948)
Sonata (E minor) – 1903
Novello 1904

Morgan, R. O.
Prize Sonata – pre-1908
Ashdown

Oakeley, Herbert (Stanley) (1830–1903)
Sonata (A major)
pub. *c.*1873

Parry, Charles Hubert Hastings (1848–1918)
Sonata No. 1 (F major) – 1876
MS Ob (incomplete). Lamborn Cock 1877
Dedication: George Grove

Sonata No. 2 (A major) – 1876
MS Ob (incomplete). Stanley Lucas 1878, Augener 1903
Dedication: Tora

Reizenstein, Franz (1911–68)
Sonata No. 1 Op. 19 (B) – 1944
Lengnick 1948
Dur: 25'   Dedication: William Walton
f.p. Wigmore Hall, 1945

Sonata No. 2 Op. 40 (A flat) – 1964
Galliard 1966, Lengnick
Dur: 26'   Dedication: slow mvt in memory of C. Hassall
f.p. June 1965

Appendix 2

Roberts, Mervyn (1906–90)

Sonata (E flat minor) – 1934, rev. 1949
Novello 1951
Dur: 8'   Dedication: J. H. C. and H. R. C.
f.p. H. Perkin, March 1950, LCMC concert. Won Edwin Evans Prize, 1950

Rowley, Alec (1892–1958)

Sonata No. 1
Durand 1939

Sonata No. 2 (D major)
Chester 1949 Dur: 11'

Scott, Cyril (1879–1970)

Sonata Op. 17 – c.1901
MS Grainger Museum, Melbourne.
Unpublished
Dedication: P. Grainger
f.p. E. Suart, 1903. Revised as Handelian Rhapsody, *1909*

Sonata No. 1 Op. 66 – 1908, rev. 1910 and 1935
Elkin 1909; Schott 1910 and c.1935 (new edition), Edwin Kalmus
Dedication: Alfred Hoehn
f.p. C. Scott, Bechstein Hall, 17 May 1909

Sonata No. 2 – 1935
Universal Music Agencies 1935; Elkin (year not known)
Dedication: Walter Gieseking

Sonata No. 3 – 1955
Elkin 1956; reissued 1983
Dur: 15'
f.p. E. Fisher, broadcast 25 Sept. 1958

Shepherd, Charles Henry (1847–86)

Sonata
Augener 1871

Smyth, Ethel (1858–1944)

Sonata No. 1 (C major) – 1877
Lbm Add MS 46857. Unpublished
Dedication: To "la madre"

Sonata No. 2 (C sharp minor) *Geistinger* **– 1877**
Lbm Add MS 46857. Unpublished

Sonata No. 3 (D major) – 1877
Lbm Add MS 46857. Unpublished

Sorabji, Kaikhosru Shapurji (1892–1988)

Sonata (unnumbered) Op. VII – 1917
MS Sorabji Archive, Bath. Unpublished.
Not performed

Sonata No. 1 – 1919
MS US-Wc. London & Continental 1921
Dur: 22'   Dedication: Busoni (on MS but not published score)
f.p. K. Sorabji, Mortimer Hall, London, 2 Nov. 1920

Sonata No. 2 – 1920
MS US-Wc. F & B Goodwin 1923
Dur: 40'   Dedication: Busoni
f.p. K. Sorabji, Musikverein, Kammersaal, Vienna, 13 Jan. 1922

Sonata No. 3 – 1922
MS US-Wc. Curwen 1925
Dur: 73'
f.p.? Y. Solomon, London, 16 June 1977

Sonata No. 4 – 1928–9
MS Sorabji Archive, Bath. Unpublished.
Dur: 90'   Dedication: F. G. Scott
f.p. K. Sorabji, Stevenson Hall, Glasgow, 1 April 1930

Sonata No. 5 *Opus Archimagicum* **– 1934–5**
MS Sorabji Archive, Bath. Unpublished.
Dedication: Clinton Gray-Fisk
Not performed

Speer, Charlton T. (1859–1921)

Sonata (G major)
Novello 1875

Speer, William Henry (1863–1937)

Sonata Op. 2 (D major)
Breitkopf & Härtel 1893

Stanford, Charles Villiers (1852–1924)

Sonata (D flat major) Op. 20 – c.1884
MS Lost. Unpublished
f.p. A. Zimmermann, Saturday Popular Concerts, St James' Hall, 4 Feb. 1884

Tippett, Michael (1905–98)

Sonata No. 1 (originally titled Fantasy Sonata) – 1936–8, rev. 1942

MS Lost. Schott 1942 and 1954
Dur: 21'   Dedication: Francesca Allinson
f.p. P. Sellick, Queen Mary Hall, London, 11 Nov. 1938

Sonata No. 2 – 1962
Lbm Add MSS 61784 and 61785. Schott 1962
Dur: 14'   Dedication: Margaret Kitchin
f.p. M. Kitchin, Freemason's Hall, Edinburgh Festival, 3 Sept. 1962

Sonata No. 3 – 1972–3
Lbm Add MSS 61799 and 61800. Schott 1975
Dur: 22'   Dedication: Anna Kallin
commissioned by and f.p. P. Crossley, Assembly Rooms, Bath Festival, 26 May 1973

Sonata No. 4 – 1984
Lbm Add MS 63840. Schott 1986
Dur: 36'   Dedication: Michael Vyner
commissioned by Los Angeles Philharmonic Association, f.p. P. Crossley, LA, 14 Jan. 1985

Truscott, Harold (1914–92)

Sonata (A major) – 1941
f.p. London, 1947

Sonata (B flat major) – 1941–2

Sonata (F major) – 1942

Sonata No. 1 (D flat major) – 1945
Dur: 28'
f.p. H. Truscott, Guildhall School of Music, 1947

Sonata No. 2 (C major) – 1945–7
Dur: 52'
f.p. H. Truscott, St Martin's School of Art, London, Mar. 1948

Sonata No. 3 (G sharp minor) – 1947–8
Lynwood Music
Dur: 21'
f.p. P. Jacobs (rec), St John's, Clerkenwell, London, Sept. 1981

Sonata No. 4 (E flat major) – 1948–9
Dur: 26'
f.p. D. Amato, BMIC, 24 Oct. 1989

Sonata No. 5 (B minor) – 1951–5
Dur: 25'   Dedication: Nicolas Medtner

f.p. P. Jacobs (rec), St John's, Clerkenwell, London, Sept. 1981

Sonata No. 6 (E major) – 1955–6
Dur: 41'
f.p. P. Jacobs (rec), St John's, Clerkenwell, London, Sept. 1984

Sonata No. 7 (C major) – 1956
Dur: 10'   Dedication: Havergal Brian
J. Ogdon, BBC broadcast, 30 Aug. 1969, f.p. P. Jacobs, RCM, Sept. 1981

Sonata No. 8 (E minor) – 1958–60
Dur: 35'
f.p. D. Amato, London, 24 Oct. 1989

Sonata No. 9 (E minor) – 1960
Dur: 22'
f.p. P. Jacobs (rec), St John's, Clerkenwell, London, Sept. 1983

Sonata No. 10 (E minor) – 1962
Dur: 14'
J. Ogdon, BBC broadcast, 30 Aug. 1969

Sonata No. 11 (A minor) – 1950–64
Dur: 10'
f.p. P. Jacobs, RCM, London, Sept. 1981

Sonata No. 12 (C major) – 1967
Dur: 11'
f.p. P. Jacobs (rec), St John's, Clerkenwell, London, Sept. 1982

Sonata No. 13 (A minor/C sharp minor/E major) – 1967
Dur: 10'
f.p. P. Jacobs (rec), St John's, Clerkenwell, London, Sept. 1983

Sonata No. 14 (G major) – 1967
Dur: 18'

Sonata No. 15 (B minor) – 1976–81
Dur: 11'
f.p. P. Jacobs (rec), St John's, Clerkenwell, London, Sept. 1983, f.p. Jacobs, BMIC, 9 Oct. 1989

Sonata No. 16 (E flat major) – 1981–
Unfinished

Sonata No. 17 (G minor) – 1982
Dur: 5'
f.p. P. Jacobs (rec), St John's, Clerkenwell, London, Sept. 1984, f.p. Jacobs, BMIC, 9 Oct. 1989

Sonata No. 18 (A flat major) – 1982–
Incomplete

Appendix 2

Wolstenholme, W. (1865–1931)
Sonata (E flat minor) – pre-1908

Wood, Christopher
Sonata No. 3 (D major)
OUP 1943

Wordsworth, William (1908–88)
Sonata Op. 13 (D minor) – 1939
Lengnick
Dur: 22'

Appendix 3: Discography

The discography attempts to document the recording history of the piano sonatas mentioned in the text. Please note that not all of the recordings are currently available.

Section 1: Recordings of Piano Sonatas

William Alwyn

Sonata alla Toccata
 David Willison, Lyrita LP 61 (1959); SRCD 293 (2008)

Malcolm Arnold

Sonata
 Benjamin Frith, Koch 3–7162–2HI (1994); Decca 472900 & ArkivMusik (2009)
 Mark Bebbington, SOMMCD 062 (2006) (c/w Lambert Sonata)

Algernon Ashton

Piano Sonata No. 4 in D minor Op. 164 and No. 8 in F major Op. 174
 Daniel Grimwood, Toccata Classics TOCC0063 (2010)
 Leslie De'Ath, Dutton Vocalion CDLX7248 (2010)
Complete Piano Sonatas
 Leslie De'Ath, Dutton Vocalion CDLX7248 (2010)

Arnold Bax

Sonata No. 1
 Iris Loveridge, Lyrita LP RCS 10 (1959); Musical Heritage Society LP MHS 7011; REAM 3113 (3 CDs) (2008)
 Frank Merrick, Frank Merrick Society LP FMS 7 (1963)
 Joyce Hatto, Revolution LP RCF 010 (1970), reissued on Concert Artists/ Fidelio FED TC 011; Concert Artist CACD 9011–2
 Eric Parkin, Chandos LP: ABRD 1206 (1987); TC: ABTD 1206; CD: CHAN 8496 (1985); CHAN 10132 (2003) (4 CDs) (Bax: Complete Piano Sonatas)
 Noemy Belinkaya, B'nai Brith BB104 (1989)
 Marie-Catherine Girod, Opes 3D 8008; 3D Classics 122184 (1992) (Bax: Complete Piano Sonatas)
 Ashley Wass, Naxos 8557439 (2004) (Bax: Piano Sonatas 1 and 2)
 Michael Endres, Oehms OC 565 (2006) (Bax: Complete Piano Sonatas)

Appendix 3

Malcolm Binns, BMS 434–435 (2 CDs) (2008) (Bax: Complete Piano Sonatas, c/w Ireland and Bridge Sonatas)

Sonata in F (No. 2 Scherzo)
Malcolm Binns, Pearl SHE 565 (1981)

Sonata No. 2
Iris Loveridge, Lyrita LP RCS 11 (1960); Musical Heritage Society LP MHS 7012; REAM 3113 (3 CDs) (2008)
Frank Merrick, Frank Merrick Society LP FMS 6 (1963)
Peter Cooper, Pye LP GGC 4085; GSGC 14085 (1967) (c/w Tippett Piano Sonata No. 2); GSGC 2061; TC ZGGC 2061
Malcolm Binns, Pearl LP SHE 565 (1981); BMS 434–435 (2 CDs) (2008) (Bax: Complete Piano Sonatas, c/w Ireland and Bridge Sonatas)
Eric Parkin, Chandos LP: ABRD 1206 (1987); TC: ABTD 1206; CD: CHAN 8496 (1985); CHAN 10132 (2003) (4 CDs) (Bax: Complete Piano Sonatas)
John McCabe, Continuum CCD 1045 (1992)
Marie-Catherine Girod, Opes 3D 8008; 3D Classics 122184 (1992) (Bax: Complete Piano Sonatas)
Ashley Wass, Naxos 8557439 (2004) (Bax: Piano Sonatas 1 and 2)
Michael Endres, Oehms OC 565 (2006) (Bax: Complete Piano Sonatas)

Sonata for Piano in E flat (original version of Symphony No. 1)
Noemy Belinkaya, Ensemble EMS 136
John Simons, Ensemble Triad 001 (*Lento con molto espressione* only)
John McCabe, Continuum CCD 1045 (1992)

Sonata No. 3
Frank Merrick, Frank Merrick Society LP 7 (1963)
Iris Loveridge, Lyrita LP RCS 12 (1964); Musical Heritage Society LP MHS 7013; REAM 3113 (3 CDs) (2008)
Eric Parkin, Chandos LP: ABRD 1207 (1988); TC: ABTD 1207; CD: CHAN 8497 (1988); CHAN 10132 (2003) (4 CDs) (Bax: Complete Piano Sonatas)
Marie-Catherine Girod, Opes 3D 8008; 3D Classics 122184 (1992) (Bax: Complete Piano Sonatas)
Ashley Wass, Naxos 8557592 (2004) (Bax: Piano Sonatas 3 and 4)
Michael Endres, Oehms OC 565 (2006) (Bax: Complete Piano Sonatas)
Malcolm Binns, BMS 434–435 (2 CDs) (2008) (Bax: Complete Piano Sonatas, c/w Ireland and Bridge Sonatas)

Sonata No. 4
Iris Loveridge, Lyrita LP RCS 26 (1965); Musical Heritage Society LP MHS 7014; REAM 3113 (3 CDs) (2008)
Frank Merrick, Frank Merrick Society LP 8 (1964) (c/w Ireland Sonata)
Joyce Hatto, Revolution LP RCF 010 (1970), reissued on Concert Artists/Fidelio FED TC 011; Concert Artist CACD 9011–2
John McCabe, Decca LP SDD 444 (1974) (slow movement only)
Eric Parkin, Chandos LP: ABRD 1207 (1988); TC: ABTD 1207; CD: CHAN 8497 (1988); CHAN 10132 (2003) (4 CDs) (Bax: Complete Piano Sonatas)
Marie-Catherine Girod, Opes 3D 8008; 3D Classics 122184 (1992) (Bax: Complete Piano Sonatas)

Discography

Ashley Wass, Naxos 8557592 (2004) (Bax: Piano Sonatas 3 and 4)
Michael Endres, Oehms OC 565 (2006) (Bax: Complete Piano Sonatas)
Malcolm Binns, BMS 434–435 (2 CDs) (2008) (Bax: Complete Piano Sonatas, c/w Ireland and Bridge Sonatas)

William Sterndale Bennett

Sonata No. 1 in F minor Op. 13
    Ilona Prunyi, Marco Polo 8223526 (1992)
    Alexander Kelly, British Music Society 413 (1992) (Sonatas No. 1 and 2)
    Simon Callaghan, De Rode Pomp (2009)

Sonata No. 2, *The Maid of Orleans*, Op. 46
    Ian Hobson, Arabesque ABQC6596 (Cass.); Arabesque Z6596 (CD) (1989)
    Ilona Prunyi, Marco Polo 8223512 (1992)
    Alexander Kelly, British Music Society 413 (1992) (Sonatas No. 1 and 2)

Lennox Berkeley

Sonata
    Colin Horsley, Lyrita RCS 9 (1959); REAM 2109 (2008)
    Raphael Terroni, Pearl SHE 576 (1985); British Music Society 416 (1993)
    Christopher Headington, Kingdom CKCL2012 (Cass.) & KCLCD2012 (CD) (1989)
    Margaret Fingerhut, CHAN 10247 (2004)

York Bowen

Piano Sonatas Nos. 1–3, 5 and 6 and Short Sonata Op. 35/1
    Danny Driver, Hyperion CDA67751/2 (2009)

Sonata No. 5 in Fm Op. 72
    Stephen Hough, Hyperion CDA66838 (1995)
    Joop Celis, CHAN 10410 (2006)

Sonata No. 6 Op. 160
    Joop Celis, CHAN 10277 (2005)

Short Sonata Op. 35/1
    Joop Celis, CHAN 10506 (2009)

Frank Bridge

Sonata
    Peter Wallfisch, Pearl SHE 513, 514 (1974)
    Eric Parkin, Unicorn RHS 359 (1979)
    Meral Güneyman, Finnador LP SR 9031 (1981)
    Peter Jacobs, Continuum CCD 1019 [Complete Piano Works on CCD 1016, 1018 & 1019]; Continuum CCD 1040 (1990) (c/w Lambert Piano Sonata played by John McCabe)
    Kathryn Stott, Conifer CDCF 186, MCFC 186 (1991)
    Mark Bebbington, SOMMCD 056 (2006)
    Ashley Wass, Naxos 8557921 (2007)

Malcolm Binns, BMS 434–435 (2 CDs) (2008) (c/w Bax Sonatas 1–4 and Bridge Sonata)

Alan Bush

Sonata in B minor Op. 2
  Mark Bebbington, SOMMCD 069 (2007)

Erik Chisholm

Sonata in A, *An Riobain Dearg* (*The Red Ribbon*)
  Murray McLachlan, Dunelm Records DRD 0222 (2004), Divine Art DDV 24131 (2008)

Arnold Cooke

Piano Sonatas 1 and 2
  Raphael Terroni, Dutton Vocalion CDLX7247 (2008)

Benjamin Dale

Sonata
  Peter Jacobs, Continuum CCD1044 (1992)
  Mark Bebbington, SOMMCD 097 (2010) (c/w Hurlstone Sonata)
  Danny Driver, Hyperion 67827 (2011)

Howard Ferguson

Sonata
  Myra Hess, HMV C 3335–7 (1942), reissued on Biddulph Mono LHW025 (1996)
  Clive Lythgoe, Concert Artist LPA1075 (1954)
  Howard Shelley, Hyperion CDA66130 (1984)
  Mark Bebbington, SOMMCD 038 (2004)
  Raphael Terroni, Naxos 8572289 (2010)

Antony Hopkins

Sonata No. 2 (Rondo only)
  Michael Hampton, Divine Art dda 21217 (2012)

Sonata No. 3
  Lamar Crowson, Argo RG51–RG52 (LP) (1955)
  Philip Fowke, Divine Art dda 21217 (2012)

Dorothy Howell

Sonata
  Sophia Rahman, Dutton Vocalion CDLX7144 (2003)

William Yeates Hurlstone

Sonata
  Mark Bebbington SOMMCD 097 (2010) (c/w Dale Sonata)

Discography

John Ireland

Sonata
    Eric Parkin, Argo ARS 1004 RG4 (1953); Lyrita SRCS88 (1977) SRCD 2277 (2007); Chandos 9056 (1992)
    Frank Merrick, Frank Merrick Society 8 (1964) (c/w Bax Sonata No. 4)
    Alan Rowlands, Lyrita RCS24 (1964); REAM 3112 (2008)
    Malcolm Binns, BMS 434–435 (2 CDs) (2008) (c/w Bax Sonatas 1–4 and Bridge Sonata)
    John Lenehan, Naxos 8570461 (2008)
    Mark Bebbington, SOMMCD 074 (2008)

Constant Lambert

Sonata
    Rhondda Gillespie, Argo ZRG 786 (1974)
    David Brain, British Music Society ENV 017 (1991)
    John McCabe, Continuum CCD 1040 (1991) (c/w Bridge Sonata played by Peter Jacobs)
    Anthony Goldstone, CHAN 9382 (1995)
    Ian Brown, Hyperion CDA66754 (1995)
    Mark Bebbington, SOMMCD 062 (2006) (c/w Arnold Sonata)

John McEwen

Sonata
    Geoffrey Tozer, Chandos 9933 (2001)

Charles Hubert Hastings Parry

Sonatas 1 & 2
    Anthony Goldstone, Albany Troy 132–2 (1994)

Franz Reizenstein

Sonata No. 1
    Franz Reizenstein, Lyrita LP RCS 19 (1958); REAM 2105 (2008)

Cyril Scott

Sonata Op. 17
    Leslie De'ath, Dutton Vocalion, CDLX7155 (2005)

Sonata No. 1 (original version)
    Marthanne Verbit, Genesis GS 1049, USA (1974); Albany Troy 070–2 (1995)
    Dennis Hennig, Etcetera KTC 1132; ABC Classics 5317941 (2002)
    Leslie De'ath, Dutton Vocalion, CDLX7155 (2005)
    Michael Schäfer, Genuin GEN85049 (2006)

Sonata No. 2
    Leslie De'ath, Dutton Vocalion, CDLX7155 (2005)
    Michael Schäfer, Genuin GEN85049 (2006)

Appendix 3

Sonata No. 3
    Evelinde Trenkner, Lorion ORS 76236, USA
    Raphael Terroni, British Music Society 401 (1981)
    Eric Parkin, Chandos DBRD 2006 (1983)
    Leslie De'ath, Dutton Vocalion, CDLX7155 (2005)
    Michael Schäfer, Genuin GEN85049 (2006)

Ethel Smyth

Sonatas 1, 2 & 3
    Liana Serbescu, Classic Production Osnabruck, Germany 999327–2 (2 CDs) (1992–3)

Kaikhosru Shapurji Sorabji

Sonata No. 1
    Marc-André Hamelin, Altarus AIR CD 9050 (1990)

Sonata No. 2
    Tellef Johnson, Altarus AIR CD 9049 (1999)

Sonata No. 4
    Jonathan Powell, Altarus AIR CD 9069 (2004)

Michael Tippett

Fantasy Sonata (original version of Sonata No. 1)
    Phyllis Sellick, (Decca), Rimington, van Wyck Ltd., CP920/61 [sic], 922/3, 924 (1941) [12″, 78 rpm], also issued as RVW 108–110, NMCD103 (2005), SOMM 079 (2008)

Sonata No. 1
    Margaret Kitchin, Lyrita RCS 5 (1960); Musical Heritage Society 7022 (1975); REAM 2106 (2008)
    John Ogdon, EMI CMS 7 63522–2 (1966); HMV ASD2321/2 (1967); EMI EX290228 (1984); EMI CMS 7 63522 2 (1991, 1993), EMI Classics 0724358658620 (2005)
    Paul Crossley, Argo RG528 & ZRG 528; BBCTR134288; Philips 6580 093 & 6500534 (1974) & Philips 6598950 (1978) (fourth movement only), CRD LP11301 (1985); CRDC 4130/1 (2 Cass.) (1985); CRD 34301 (1998); Decca 000529702 (2005)
    Stephen Savage, Queensland Conservatorium Musicon TAM 0639 & YPRX 2139 (1984)
    Murray Perahia, Sony SX4K63380 (4CD) (1986, 1997)
    Ananda Sukurlan, Erasmus Muziek Producties WVH 139 (1993)
    Nicholas Unwin, CHAN 9468 (1995)
    Peter Donohoe, Naxos 8557611 (2005)
    Steven Osborne, Hyperion CDA 67461/2 (2007)

Sonata No. 2
    John Ogdon, EMI CMS 7 63522–2 (1963); HMV ALP 2073 (mono); ASD

621 (stereo) (1965); EMI EX290228 (1984); EMI CMS 7 63522 2 (1991, 1993), EMI Classics 0724358658620 (2005)

Peter Cooper, Pye GGC 4085 (mono); GSGC 14085 (stereo) (1967) (c/w Bax Piano Sonata No. 2); PRT GSGC 2061 (stereo) (1982); ZCGC 2061 (Cass.) (1982)

Paul Crossley, BBCTR 134289; Philips 6580 093 & 6500534 (1974); CRD LP11301 (1985); CRDC 4130/1 (2 Cass.) (1985); CRD 34301 (1998); Decca 000529702 (2005)

Margaret Kitchin, BBCTR 109633 & BIRS M197W; REAM 2106 (c/w Hamilton Piano Sonata Op. 13 and Wordsworth Sonata Op. 13) (2008)

Thalia Myers, Phoenix DGS 1013 (1982) (c/w Hoddinott Sonata No. 6)

Stephen Savage, Queensland Conservatorium Musicon TAM 0639 & YPRX 2139 (1984)

Steven Neugarten, Métier MSV CD 92008 (1994)

Nicholas Unwin, CHAN 9468 (1995)

Peter Donohoe, Naxos 8557611 (2005)

Steven Osborne, Hyperion CDA 67461/2 (2007)

Richard Uttley, UHRecordings 20011009 (2007)

Sonata No. 3

Paul Crossley, BBCTR 134290; Philips 6580 093 & 6500534 (1974); CRD LP11301 (1985); CRDC 4130/1 (2 Cass.) (1985); CRD 34301 (1998); Decca 000529702 (2005)

Stephen Savage, Queensland Conservatorium Musicon TAM 0639 & YPRX 2139 (1984)

Graham Caskie, Métier Sound and Vision MSV CD92004 (1993)

Nicholas Unwin, CHAN 9468 (1995)

Peter Donohoe, Naxos 8557611 (2005)

Steven Osborne, Hyperion CDA 67461/2 (2007)

Sonata No. 4

Paul Crossley, CRD LP11301 (1985); CRDC 4130/1 (2 Cass.) (1985); CRD 34301 (1998)

Nicholas Unwin, Métier MSV CD 92009 (1994) (2003 – c/w Saxton Sonata)

Steven Osborne, Hyperion CDA 67461/2 (2007)

Harold Truscott

Sonatas 3, 7 & 11
Peter Jacobs, Altarus AIR 2 9008

Sonatas 5 & 12
Peter Jacobs, Altarus AIR 2 9002 (1985)

Sonatas 6 & 17
Peter Jacobs, BMS 410

Sonatas 9, 13 & 15
Peter Jacobs, Altarus AIR 2 9003 (1985)

Appendix 3

William Wordsworth

Sonata in D Minor Op. 13
 Margaret Kitchin, Lyrita RCS 5 (1960); REAM 2106 (2008)

Section 2: Other recordings referred to in the text

William Baines

Piano Music – *Silverpoints*, *Coloured Leaves*, *Twilight Pieces*, *Tides*, Seven Preludes
 Eric Parkin, Lyrita SRCS 60 (1972) (LP); SRCD266 (2007); Priory PRCD550 (1995)

Arnold Bax

Complete Symphonies
 Bryden Thomson, London Philharmonic Orchestra, CHAN 8906/10 (1990)
 Vernon Handley, BBC Philharmonic, CHAN 10122 (2003)

York Bowen

Selected Piano Works
 Marie-Catherine Girod, Opès 3D 8012 (1994)

Benjamin Britten

Music for Piano (Solo and Duet)
 Stephen Hough & Ronan O'Hora, Virgin Classics VC791203–2; EMI Classics (2001)

Edward Elgar

Piano Works
 Peter Pettinger, Chandos 8438 (1986)

Gustav Holst

Complete Piano Works
 Anthony Goldstone & Caroline Clemmow, Chandos 9382 (1995), (c/w Lambert Sonata)

Herbert Howells

Piano Works
 Margaret Fingerhut, Chandos 9273 (1993)

Constant Lambert

The Rio Grande
 Sally Burgess, Jack Gibbons, Opera North Chorus, English Northern Philharmonia, David Lloyd-Jones, Hyperion CDA 66565 (1992)

Discography

Piano Concerto
    Kathryn Stott, BBC Concert Orchestra, Barry Wordsworth, Argo 436118–2 (1992)
    Ian Brown, Nash Ensemble, Lionel Friend, Hyperion CDA 66754 (1995) (c/w Lambert Piano Sonata)

Summer's Last Will and Testament
    William Shimell, Leeds Festival Chorus, English Northern Philharmonic, David Lloyd-Jones, Hyperion CDA 66565 (1992)

Charles Hubert Hastings Parry

Complete Symphonies
    Matthias Bamert, London Philharmonic Orchestra, Chandos 9120/2 (3 CD) (1990–92)

Bibliography

Abraham, G. E. H.: "Six British Piano Sonatas, III: The Two Bax Sonatas", *Music Teacher*, July 1926, 418
Allis, Michael John: "The Creative Process of C. Hubert H. Parry" (2 vols.), PhD, King's College London, 1994
Ambrose, Anna (dir.): *Alan Bush – A Life*, Arts Council, VHS Video, 1983
Anderson, Robert: *Elgar*, London, Dent, 1993
Anderton, H. Orsmond: "Cameo Portraits No. 20: an Unassuming Artist – Mr. B. J. Dale", *Musical Opinion* xlv, 1922, 603–5
Anon.: "Brief Summary of Country News", *Musical Times* xvi, 1874, 367
—— "The Maid of Orleans. Sonata for the Pianoforte by Sir William Sterndale Bennett", *Musical Times* xvi, 1874, 391
—— "The Gloucester Music Festival", *Musical Times* xxi, 1880, 498–9
—— "Monday and Saturday Popular Concerts" [Review of Stanford's Piano Sonata], *Musical Times* xxv, 1884, 147
—— "Review" [Ashton's Violin Sonata], *Musical Times* xxx, 1889, 616
—— "Review" [Ashton's Cello Sonata No. 2], *Musical Times* xxxiv, 1893, 613
—— "Charles Villiers Stanford", *Musical Times* xxxix, 1898, 785–93
—— "Edward German: A Biographical Sketch", *Musical Times* xlv, 1904, 20–4
—— "Sonata in E minor for the Pianoforte. Composed by John B. McEwen", *Musical Times* xlvi, 1905, 31–2
—— *The Society of British Composers Yearbook 1907–8,* London, 1908
—— *The Society of British Composers Yearbook 1912,* London, 1912
—— "Music and Musicians" [Review of Bax's *Romantic Tone Poem*], *The Queen*, 6 May 1911, 781
—— "Ireland", *The Monthly Musical Record* xlv, 1915, 192
—— "Music and Musicians" [Review of Bax's *Symphonic Phantasy*], *The Times*, 10 October 1919
—— *Miniature Essays: Arnold Bax*, London, Chester, 1921
—— *Miniature Essays: John Ireland*, London, Chester, 1923
—— "Ad Libitum", *Musical Times* lxiv, 1923, 613
—— "London Concerts. Miss Myra Hess. Mr. Bridge's New Sonata", *Daily Telegraph*, 16 October 1925, 15
—— "Miss Myra Hess and New Pianoforte Sonata" [Bridge], *The Times*, 16 October 1925, 12
—— "New Sonata by Mr. Frank Bridge", *Morning Post*, 16 October 1925
—— "Reviews" [Piano Sonatas by Jervis-Read, Ashton (Op. 170), Bridge], *Musical Times* lxvii, 1926, 331–2
—— "Occasional Notes" [German], *Musical Times* lxviii, 1927, 135
Anon.: "Two English Piano Sonatas" [Ireland and Bridge], *Manchester Guardian*, 2 December 1927, 17

—— "New Bax Sonata" [No. 3], *Musical Times* lxix, 1928, 67
—— "Three Young English Composers" [Review of Lambert's Piano Sonata], *The Times*, 1 November 1929
—— "Phyllis Sellick. Fantasy Sonata for Piano [Tippett]", *Gramophone* xix, 1941, 64
—— "Review" [Scott's Third Piano Sonata], *Music and Letters* xxxvii, 1956, 312
—— "York Bowen – Obituary", *Royal Academy of Music Magazine* clxxxi, 1962, 13
Armstrong, Thomas: "The Frankfort Group", *Proceedings of the Royal Musical Association* lxxxv, 1958, 1–16
Arnell, Richard: "Arnold Cooke: A Birthday Conversation", *Composer* xxiv, 1967, 18–20
Austin, Ernest: "Myself and Others", *Musical Opinion* vi, 1939, 786–8
Bacharach, A. L. (ed.): *British Music of Our Time*, Harmondsworth, Pelican, 1946
—— *The Music Masters. Volume 3: The Victorian Age*, London, Cassell, 1952
—— *The Music Masters. Volume 4: The Twentieth Century*, London, Cassell, 1954
Banfield, Stephen: *Sensibility and English Song* (2 vols.), Cambridge, Cambridge University Press, 1985
—— "'Too much of Albion?' Mrs. Coolidge and her British Connections", *American Music* iv, Spring 1986, 59–88
—— (ed.) *The Twentieth Century*, The Blackwell History of Music in Britain Vol. 6, general editor Ian Spink, Oxford, Blackwell, 1995
Banister, Henry C: *George Alexander Macfarren: his Life, Works and Influence*, London, 1891
Bax, Arnold: "A Native British Art", *Musical Standard*, 11 April 1914, 342
—— "Bax Defines his Music", *Musical America*, 7 July 1928, 9
—— "Frederick Corder", *The Times*, 27 August 1932, 12
—— "Arnold Schoenberg", *Music and Letters* xxxii, 1951, 307
—— "New Light on a Genius" [Review of Letters of Richard Wagner], *National and English Review*, March 1952, 172–4
—— and Lewis Foreman (eds.): *Farewell, My Youth*, Aldershot, Scolar Press, 1992 (first edition Longmans, Green & Co., 1943)
Bennett, Barry Sterndale: "Sir William Sterndale Bennett", *British Music Society Journal* i, 1979, 41–6
Bennett, James Robert Sterndale: *The Life of William Sterndale Bennett*, Cambridge, Cambridge University Press, 1907
Bird, John: *Percy Grainger*, London, Faber, 1982 (first edition Elek, 1976)
Blom, Eric: *Music in England*, London, Pelican, 1947 (first edition 1942)
—— "Arnold Bax's Piano Sonatas", *The Listener*, 12 October 1944, 417
—— (ed.), *Grove's Dictionary of Music and Musicians* (9 vols.), London, Macmillan, fifth edition, 1954
Blume, Friedrich (ed.): *Die Musik in Geschichte und Gegenwart* (13 vols.), Kassel, Bärenreiter-Verlag, 1949–86
Boughton, Rutland: "A Musical Impressionist", *Musical Times* lxvii, 1926, 212–14
Bowen, Meirion: *Michael Tippett*, The Contemporary Composers Series, ed. N. Snowman, London, Robson, 1985 (first edition 1982)

Bibliography

Bray, Trevor: "Frank Bridge and Mrs. Coolidge", *Music and Musicians* xxvi, October 1977, 28–30
—— "Frank Bridge's First Visit to America", *British Music Society Journal* viii, 1986, 12–25
Brook, Donald: *Composers' Gallery,* London, Rockliff, 1946
Brooks, Edward: *The Bessie Smith Companion*, Oxford, Bayou Press, 1989 (first edition 1982)
Brown, James: "Edward German", *British Music Society Journal* vii, 1985, 11–16
Brown, James D. and Stephen S. Stratton: *British Musical Biography*, New York, Da Capo, 1971 (reprint of London, 1897)
Browne, Arthur G.: "The Music of Kaikhosru Sorabji", *Music and Letters* xi, 1930, 6–16
Burn, Andrew: "The Music of Howard Ferguson", *Musical Times* cxxiv, 1983, 480–2
Burton-Page, Piers: *Philharmonic Concerto – the Life and Music of Sir Malcolm Arnold*, London, Methuen, 1994
Bush, Alan: "What is Modern Music?", *Proceedings of the Royal Musical Association* lxiii, 1936, 21–37
—— "The Crisis of Modern Music", *Keynote* i/4, 1946, 4–7
—— *In my Eighth Decade and Other Essays*, London, Kahn & Averill, 1980
Bush, Geoffrey: "Sterndale Bennett – the Solo Piano Works", *Proceedings of the Royal Musical Association* xci, 1964–5, 85–97
—— "Sterndale Bennett – a note on his Chamber and Piano Music", *Musical Times* cxiii, 1972, 554–6
—— *Left, Right and Centre – Reflections on Composers and Composing*, London, Thames, 1983
—— *An Unsentimental Education*, London, Thames, 1990
Caldwell, John: *The Oxford History of English Music, Vol. 2 (c. 1715 to the Present Day)*, Oxford, Oxford University Press, 1999
Carpenter, Humphrey: *Benjamin Britten – A Biography*, London, Faber, 1992
Carpenter, Roger: "Baines and Britten: Some Affinities", *Musical Times* xcvii, 1956, 185–7
—— *Goodnight to Flamboro' – The Life and Music of William Baines*, Bristol, Triad Press, 1977
Chaffer, John: "An Introduction to the Piano Music of John Ireland", *The Chesterian* xxxvi, 1961, 22–5
Child, William: "New Music" [Ireland's Sonata], *Musical Times* lxi, 1920, 556
Chisholm, Erik: *Kaikhosru Shapurji Sorabji*, London, Oxford University Press, c.1938 (reprinted privately, c.1964)
Clane, E. (ed.): *A Tribute to Alan Bush on his Fiftieth Birthday*, London, Workers Musical Association, 1950
Cobbe, Hugh: "Howard Ferguson at 80", *Musical Times* cxxix, 1988, 507–10
Cobbett, Walter Willson: *Cyclopedic Survey of Chamber Music* (3 vols.), London, Oxford University Press, second edition, 1963 (first edition 1929)
Cohen, Harriet: *A Bundle of Time*, London, Faber & Faber, 1969
Cole, Hugo: *Malcolm Arnold – An Introduction to his Music*, London, Faber, 1989
Colles, H. C. (ed.): *Grove's Dictionary of Music and Musicians* (5 vols.), London, Macmillan, third edition, 1927–8

Bibliography

—— *The Royal College of Music. A Jubilee Record, 1883–1933*, London, Macmillan, 1933

—— (ed.) *Grove's Dictionary of Music and Musicians* (6 vols.), London, Macmillan, fourth edition, 1940

Collis, Louise: *Impetuous Heart – The Story of Ethel Smyth*, London, William Kimber, 1984

Colls, Robert and Philip Dodd (eds.): *Englishness: Politics and Culture 1880–1920*, London, Croom Helm, 1986

Cooke, Deryck: "Another Look at Music Ho!", *The Listener*, 29 November 1962, 910–12

Cooke, Margaret Winnifred: "John Ireland – A Biographical and Critical Study with Special Reference to the Works involving Pianoforte", MA, University of Wales, 1972

Corder, Frederick: "Sterndale Bennett and his Music", *Musical Times* lvii, 1916, 233–4

—— "Benjamin Dale's Piano Sonata", *Musical Times* lix, 1918, 164–7

—— *A History of the Royal Academy of Music, 1822–1922*, London, Corder, 1922

Craggs, Stewart: *John Ireland: A Catalogue, Discography and Bibliography*, Oxford, Clarendon Press, 1993

—— (ed.) *Alan Bush: A Source Book*, Aldershot, Ashgate, 2007

Crichton, Ronald (ed.): *The Memoirs of Ethel Smyth*, Harmondsworth, Penguin, 1987

Croft, Gordon Simon: "The Pianoforte Works of John Ireland – Contexts for Study", MPhil, University of Birmingham, 1995

Dale, Kathleen: "Dame Ethel Smyth", *Music and Letters* xxv, 1944, 191–4

—— "Ethel Smyth's Prentice Work", *Music and Letters* xxx, 1949, 329–36

—— *Nineteenth Century Piano Music: a Handbook for Pianists*, London, Oxford University Press, 1954

Darson, Thomas Henry: "The Solo Piano Works of Cyril Scott", PhD, City University of New York, 1979

Daubney, Brian Blyth: "Benjamin Burrows 1891–1966: The Life and Music of the Leicester Composer", MPhil, University of Leicester, 1979

Dawney, Michael: "Arnold Cooke", *Composer* xlv, Autumn 1972, 5–9

Dawson, Frederick: "On the Interpretation of William Baines' Music", *Musical Opinion* xlvi, 1922, 245

Demuth, Norman: *Vincent d'Indy*, London, Rockliff, 1951

—— *Musical Trends in the Twentieth Century*, London, Rockliff, 1952

Dibble, Jeremy: "Structure and Tonality in Parry's Chamber Music", *British Music Society Journal* iii, 1981, 13–23

—— "Hubert Parry and English Diatonic Dissonance", *British Music Society Journal* v, 1983, 58–71

—— "The Music of Hubert Parry: a Critical and Analytical Study", PhD, University of Southampton, 1986

—— *C. Hubert H. Parry – His Life and Music*, Oxford, Clarendon Press, 1992

Dickinson, Peter: "Berkeley on the Keyboard", *Music & Musicians* xi, April 1963, 10

—— (ed.) *Twenty British Composers,* The Feeney Trust Commissions, London, Chester, 1975

Bibliography

—— "Lennox Berkeley – Interview on his 75th Birthday", *Musical Times* cxix, 1978, 409–11
—— "The Achievement of Ragtime – An Introductory Study", *Proceedings of the Royal Musical Association* cv, 1979, 63–76
—— "Lord Berners 1883–1950", *Musical Times* cxxiv, 1983, 669–72
—— "Lord Berners (1883–1950): Composer, Author, Painter and Eccentric", *Royal Society of Arts Journal,* 1984, 313–24
—— "Reviews" [*Tippett* by I. Kemp], *Music and Letters* lxvi, 1985, 245–7
—— *The Music of Lennox Berkeley,* 2nd enlarged edition, Woodbridge, Boydell & Brewer, 2003
—— (ed.) *Lennox Berkeley and Friends: Writings, Letters and Interviews,* Woodbridge, Boydell & Brewer, 2012
Dunhill, Thomas F.: "Edward German: 1862–1936", *Musical Times* lxxvii, 1936, 1073–77
Dyson, George: *The New Music,* London, Humphrey Milford, 1924
Eggar, Katharine E.: "The Piano Pieces of Arnold Bax", *The Music Student* xiv, November 1921, 65–7
—— "The Piano Music of John Ireland", *Music Teacher* xiv, June 1922, 465–7
—— "The Music of William Baines", *Music Teacher* iv, December 1925, 735
Ehrlich, Cyril: *The Piano – A History,* Oxford, Clarendon Press, 1990 (first edition Dent, 1976)
—— *Harmonious Alliance – A History of the Performing Right Society,* Oxford, Oxford University Press, 1989
Eliot, T. S.: *Selected Essays,* Glasgow, The University Press, third edition, 1951
Evans, Edwin: "Modern British Composers: Arnold Bax", *Musical Times* lx, 1919, 103–5 and 154–6
—— "Modern British Composers: Frank Bridge", *Musical Times* lx, 1919, 55–61
—— "Modern British Composers: Benjamin Dale", *Musical Times* lx, 1919, 201–5
—— "Modern British Composers: John Ireland", *Musical Times* lx, 1919, 394–6 and 457–62
—— "Wigmore Hall. Myra Hess' Recital" [Bax's *Symphonic Phantasy*], *Pall Mall Gazette,* 10 October 1919, 8
—— "The Arnold Bax Concert", *Musical Times* lxiii, 1922, 874
—— "Walton and Lambert", *Modern Music,* April–May 1930, 26–31
—— "Frank Bridge", *The Listener,* 6 March 1941, 353
Evans, John, Philip Reed and Paul Wilson: *A Britten Source Book,* Aldeburgh, Britten Estate, 1987
Evans, Peter: "Sonata Structures in Early Britten", *Tempo* lxxxii, 1967, 2–13
—— *The Music of Benjamin Britten,* London, Dent, 1989 (first edition 1979)
Fisher, Esther: "Cyril Scott", *Recorded Sound* lxi, January 1976, 502–10
Finzi, Gerald: "Hubert Parry – A Revaluation", *Music Maker* v, Summer 1949, 4–8
Flothuis, Marius: *Modern British Composers,* London, Sidgwick & Jackson, 1949
Foreman, Christopher: "The Music of B. J. Dale (1885–1943)", *Royal Academy of Music Magazine* ccxxxviii, Summer 1985, 2
Foreman, R. L. E. [Lewis]: "Bibliography of Writings on Arnold Bax", *Current Musicology* x, 1970, 124–40

—— "The Musical Development of Arnold Bax", *Music and Letters* lii, 1971, 59–68
—— "A Catalogue of Autograph Manuscript Sources of Music by Sir Arnold Bax", *RMA Research Chronicle* xii, 1974, 91–105 Foreman, Lewis: *British Music Now*, London, Paul Elek, 1975
—— (ed.) *The Percy Grainger Companion*, London, Thames, 1981
—— "Arnold Bax at the RAM", *Royal Academy of Music Magazine* ccxxxiii, Autumn 1983
—— *Bax – A Composer and his Times*, London, Scolar Press, 1988 (first edition 1983)
—— *From Parry to Britten – British Music in Letters 1900–45*, London, Batsford, 1987
—— *Music in England 1885–1920, as recounted in Hazell's Annual*, London, Thames, 1994
—— (ed.) *The John Ireland Companion*, Woodbridge, Boydell & Brewer, 2011
Foss, Hubert: "Constant Lambert", *Musical Times* xcii, 1951, 449–51
—— "The Music of Constant Lambert", *The Listener*, 24 January 1952, 158
Frank, Alan: "The Music of Constant Lambert", *Musical Times* lxxviii, 1937, 941–5
—— *Modern British Composers*, London, Dennis Dobson, 1953
Frank, Jonathan: "York Bowen – An Appreciation", *Musical Opinion* lxxx, 1957, 591
Fuller-Maitland, John A.: *English Music in the XIXth Century*, Portland, Maine, Longwood Press, 1976 (first edition 1902)
—— (ed.), *Grove's Dictionary of Music and Musicians* (5 vols.), London, Macmillan, second edition, 1910
—— *The Music of Parry and Stanford*, Cambridge, Heffer and Sons, 1934
Galant, Jed Adie: *The Solo Piano Works of Frank Bridge*, DMA, Peabody Institute of the John Hopkins University, 1987
Garratt, Percival: "English Composers and the Pianoforte", *The Sackbut* viii, 1928, 353–5
Gilbert, Richard: "The Rio Grande", *Disques* i, August 1930, 201–2
Gillies, Malcolm: *Bartók in Britain*, Oxford, Clarendon Press, 1989
Godbolt, Jim: *A History of Jazz in Britain 1919–50,* London, Quartet Books, 1984
Goddard, Scott: "Frank Bridge", *The Monthly Musical Record* lxxi, March–April 1941, 59–63
Goehr, Alexander: "Richard Hall: a Memoir and a Tribute", *Musical Times* cxxiv, 1983, 677–8
Grace, Harvey: "Review" [Publication of Sorabji's Sonata No. 1], *Musical Times* lxii, 1921, 781
—— "Review" [Publication of Sorabji's Sonata No. 2], *Musical Times* lxv, 1924, 520
Grainger, Percy: "The Music of Cyril Scott", *The Music Student* v, October 1912, 31–3
Gray, Cecil: *A Survey of Contemporary Music*, London, Oxford University Press, second edition, 1927 (first edition 1924)
—— *Musical Chairs*, London, Hogarth Press, 1985 (first edition Home & Van Thal, 1948)

Gray-Fisk, Clinton: "Reviews" [Bowen Piano Sonata in F minor], *Musical Opinion* lxxx, 1956, 71
—— "Pen Portrait: York Bowen", *Musical Times* xcviii, 1957, 664–5
—— "Kaikhosru Shapurji Sorabji", *Musical Times* ci, 1960, 230–2
Greenall, Matthew: "Sounds Around" [Review of Berkeley's Piano Sonata], *British Music Society News* lx, 1993, 265
Greene, Harry Plunket: *Charles Villiers Stanford*, London, Edward Arnold and Co., 1935
Grew, Sidney: *Our Favourite Musicians from Stanford to Holbrooke*, London, Peter Davies Ltd, 1922
Grove, George (ed.): *The Grove Dictionary of Music and Musicians* (4 vols.), first edition, London, Macmillan, 1878
Guregian, Elaine: "Paul Crossley. Tippett Piano Sonatas 1–4", *Clavier* xxv, December 1986, 26
Hallé, C. E. and M.: *The Life and Letters of Sir Charles Hallé*, London, Smith Elder, 1896
Harries, Meirion and Susie: *A Pilgrim Soul – The Life and Work of Elisabeth Lutyens*, London, Michael Joseph, 1989
Harrison, Max: "Baines' Piano Works", *Gramophone* xlix, 1972, 1908
—— "Ireland's Piano Works", *Gramophone* liv, 1977, 1573–4
Hepokoski, James: "Masculine–Feminine", *Musical Times* cxxxv, 1994, 494–9
Hill, Peter: "Tippett's Piano Sonatas 1–3", *Tempo* cxiv, 1975, 43–4
Hill, Ralph (ed.): *Penguin Music Magazine* ii, Middlesex, 1947
Hindemith, Paul: *The Craft of Musical Composition*, London, Schott & Co., 1937 (trans. by A. Mendel, 1942), rev. 1945
Hindmarsh, Paul: *Frank Bridge – A Thematic Catalogue 1900–41*, London, Faber, 1983
—— "Frank Bridge: Seeds of Discontent", *Musical Times* cxxxii, 1991, 695–7
Hitchcock, H. Wiley and Stanley Sadie: *The New Grove Dictionary of American Music* (3 vols.), London, Macmillan, 1986
Holbrooke, Joseph: *Contemporary British Composers*, London, Cecil Palmer, 1925
Holmes, William Henry: *Musical Times* vii, 1856, 177
Hopkins, Antony: *Beating Time*, London, Michael Joseph, 1982
Howells, Herbert: "Frank Bridge", *Music and Letters* xxii, 1941, 208–15
Howes, Frank: *The English Musical Renaissance*, London, Seeker & Warburg, 1966
Hughes, Eric and Timothy Day: "Discographies of British Composers: Sir Michael Tippett", *Recorded Sound* lxxviii, July 1980, 73–89
Hull, A. Eaglefield: "The Neo-British School", *The Monthly Musical Record* li, 1921, 52, 76, 100, 124
Hull, A. Eaglefield: *Cyril Scott: Composer, Poet and Philosopher*, London, Kegan Paul, 1926 (first edition 1918)
Hull, R.: "The Music of Lennox Berkeley", *The Listener*, 16 March 1944, 309
Hurd, Michael: "New BMS Releases" [Sterndale Bennett's Piano Music], *British Music Society News* lvi, 1992, 159–60
Hurlstone, Katherine (ed.): *William Hurlstone, Musician: Memories and Records by his Friends*, London, Cary and Co., 1947

Bibliography

Inglis, Brian: "The Life and Music of Kaikhosru Shapurji Sorabji", MA, City University, London, 1993

Kalish, Alfred: "London Concerts" [Ireland and Bax Sonatas], *Musical Times* lxi, 1920, 462–3

Keir, Patricia: "John Ireland: A Practical Guide to Selected Works for Pianoforte", MMus, Royal College of Music, London, 1989–90

Kemp, Ian (ed.): *Michael Tippett: A Symposium on his Sixtieth Birthday*, London, Faber, 1965

—— *Hindemith*, Oxford Studies of Composers, London, Oxford University Press, 1970

—— *Tippett: The Composer and his Music*, Oxford, Oxford University Press, 1987 (first edition Eulenburg, 1984)

Kemp, Ian and I. Rayment: "The Composer [Tippett] Speaks", *Audio and Record Review*, February 1963, 27–8

Kennedy, Michael: *Portrait of Walton*, Oxford, Oxford University Press, 1990 (first edition 1989)

—— *Britten*, Dent Master Musicians Series, ed. S. Sadie, London, 1993 (first edition 1981)

Kennett, Christian: "The Harmonic Species of Frank Bridge: An Experimental Assessment of the Applicability of Pitch-Class Generic Theory to the Analysis of a Corpus of Works by a Transitional Composer", PhD, University of Reading, 1995

Kernfeld, Barry (ed.): *The New Grove Dictionary of Jazz* (2 vols.), London, Macmillan, 1988

Klein, H.: *Thirty Years of Musical Life in London, 1870–1900*, London, Heinemann, 1903

Lambert, Constant: "Jazz", *Life and Letters* i, July 1928, 124–31

—— *The Star*, 14 December 1929

—— *Music Ho! A Study of Music in Decline*, Plymouth, Latimer Trend & Co., second edition 1945 (first edition Faber, 1934)

Lamond, Frederick: "Some Remarks on John Ireland's New Sonata", *The Monthly Musical Record* 1, August 1920, 170–2

Lassimonne, Denise and Howard Ferguson (eds.): *Myra Hess by her Friends*, London, Hamish Hamilton, 1966

Latham, Morton: *The Renaissance of Music*, Stott, 1890

Lee, E. Markham: "The Student Interpreter – Bax's Fourth Piano Sonata", *Musical Opinion*, December 1935 and January 1936, 219 and 312

Leitzmann, A.: "Benjamin Dale", *Die Musik* vi/4, 1906–7, 306

Lewis, Geraint (ed.): *Michael Tippett O.M.: A Celebration*, Tunbridge Wells, The Baton Press, 1985

Little, Karen: *Frank Bridge – A Bio-Bibliography*, New York, Greenwood Press, 1991

Lockspeiser, E.: "The Music of Lennox Berkeley", *The Listener*, 10 July 1947, 76

Longmire, John: *John Ireland: Portrait of a Friend*, London, John Baker, 1969

Lowe, George: "Cyril Scott's Piano Works", *Musical Standard* xxxi, 29 May 1909, 341–2

MacDiarmid, Hugh: *The Company I've Kept*, London, Hutchinson, 1966

Macdonald, Malcolm: "Ireland" [Piano Sonata], *Gramophone* xlii, 1964, 201

Bibliography

Macfarren, George: "The National Music of our Native Land", *Musical Times* xiv, 1870, 519–22 and 551–5
—— *On the Structure of a Sonata*, London, 1871
Mackenzie, John M. (ed.): *Imperialism and Popular Culture*, Manchester, Manchester University Press, 1986
Mackerness, Eric D.: *A Social History of English Music*, London, Routledge and Kegan Paul, 1964
Mason, Colin: "Arnold Cooke", *Musical Times* cviii, 1967, 228–30
Matthews, David: *Michael Tippett: An Introductory Study*, London, Faber, 1980
McBurney, Gerard: "Howard Ferguson in 1983", *Tempo* cxlvii, 1983, 2–6
McCarthy, Albert: *The Dance Band Era*, London, November Books, 1971
McEwen, John: *The Foundation of Musical Aesthetics*, London, Kegan Paul, 1917
—— *An Introduction to the Unpublished Edition of the Piano Sonatas of Beethoven*, London, 1932
McGrady, Richard: "The Music of Constant Lambert", *Music and Letters* li, 1970, 242–58
McNaught, W.: "Dame Ethel Smyth", *Musical Times* lxxxv, 1944, 207–12
Mellers, Wilfred: "Tippettan Discovery", *Scrutiny* x, January 1942, 309–12
Mike, Celia: "Dorothy Howell 1898–1982", *British Music Society Journal* xiv, 1992, 48–58
Misc.: "Arnold Bax: 1883–1953", *Music and Letters* xxxv, 1954, 1–14
Mitchell, Donald: *Cradles of the New – Writings on Music 1951–91*, selected by Christopher Palmer and edited by Mervyn Cooke, London, Faber, 1995
Mitchell, Donald and Philip Reed (eds.): *Letters from a Life – Selected Letters and Diaries of Benjamin Britten 1913–76*, Vols. 1 and 2, London, Faber, 1991
Morrison, Angus: "Obituary: Constant Lambert", *Royal College of Music Magazine*, November 1951, 107–10
Morton, Brian and Pamela Collins: *Contemporary Composers*, Chicago and London, St James' Press, 1992
Motion, Andrew: *The Lamberts – George, Constant and Kit*, London, The Hogarth Press, 1987 (first edition 1986)
Musgrave, Michael: *The Musical Life of the Crystal Palace*, Cambridge, Cambridge University Press, 1995
Nelson, Stanley, *All About Jazz*, London, Heath Cranton, 1934
Newell, H. G.: *William Yeates Hurlstone, Musician and Man*, London, Chester, 1936
Newman, William S.: *The Sonata since Beethoven*, Chapel Hill, University of North Carolina Press, 1969
Oliver, Michael: "Tippett Piano Sonatas 1–4", *Gramophone* lxiii, 1985, 529
Orga, Ates: "Alan Bush, Musician and Marxist", *Music and Musicians* xvii, August 1969, 20–2
—— "Tippett Piano Sonatas 1–3", *Records and Recording* xviii, 1974, 1984–5
Ottaway, D. Hugh: "Cyril Scott", *Musical Opinion* lxxiii, 1949, 143–5
—— "The Piano Music of John Ireland", *The Monthly Musical Record* lxxxiv, 1954, 258–66
—— "Ireland's Shorter Piano Pieces", *Tempo* lii, 1959, 3
Palmer, Christopher: "Constant Lambert – A Postscript", *Music and Letters* lii, 1971, 173–6

―― "Record Reviews – William Baines' Piano Music", *Musical Times* cxiii, 1972, 873
―― *Impressionism in Music*, London, Hutchinson, 1973
―― "Cyril Scott – Centenary Reflections", *Musical Times* cxx, 1979, 738–41
―― *George Dyson – Man and Music*, London, Thames, 1996
Parkin, Eric: "John Ireland and the Piano", *Music Teacher* liii, June, July, August and September 1974, 11, 15, 12, 13
Parlett, Graham: *Arnold Bax: A Catalogue of his Music*, London, Triad Press, 1972
―― "The Music of Arnold Bax: Documentation and Analysis", PhD, University of London, 1994
Parrott, Ian: *Cyril Scott and his Piano Music*, London, Thames, 1991
Parry, Charles Hubert Hastings: "Sonata", in *Grove's Dictionary of Music and Musicians,* i, 1878, 554–83
―― *The Art of Music*, London, Kegan Paul, 1893 (revised as *The Evolution of the Art of Music*, 1896)
―― *Johann Sebastian Bach*, Putnam, 1946 (first edition, 1909)
―― *Style in Musical Art*, London, Macmillan and Co., 1911
Payne, Anthony: "Alan Bush", *Musical Times* cv, 1964, 263–5
―― "Frank Bridge: The Early Years", *Tempo* cvi, 1973, 18–25
―― "Frank Bridge: The Last Years", *Tempo* cvii, 1973, 11–18
―― *Frank Bridge – Radical and Conservative*, London, Thames, 1984 (revised 1999)
Payne, Anthony, Foreman, Lewis and Bishop, John: *The Music of Frank Bridge*, London, Thames, 1976
Pears, Peter: "Frank Bridge", *Recorded Sound* lxvi and lxvii, April–July 1977, 666
Pettitt, Maxwell W.: "Sir George Alexander Macfarren, the Compleat Victorian", *British Music Society Journal* viii, 1986, 26–35
Pirie, Peter: "Frank Bridge", *Musical Opinion* lxxxviii, 1965, 531
―― *Frank Bridge*, London, Triad Press, 1971
―― "The Lost Generation", *Music and Musicians* xx, May 1972, 36–40
―― "William Baines", *Music and Musicians* xxi, November 1972, 36–40
―― "Frank Bridge's Piano Sonata", *Music and Musicians* xxiv, January 1976, 28–32
―― *The English Musical Renaissance*, London, Gollancz, 1979
―― "The Search for Sorabji", *Music and Musicians* xxviii, November 1979, 16–20
Ponsonby, D.: "Pages from the notebooks of Hubert Parry", *Music and Letters* i, 1920, 318–29
Porte, John F.: *Sir Charles Villiers Stanford*, London, Kegan Paul, 1921
Porter, Andrew: "Tippett Piano Sonatas 1–3", *Gramophone* lii, 1974, 925
Posner, Bruce: "Sorabji", BSc, New York, 1975
Poulton, Alan: *The Music of Malcolm Arnold: A Catalogue*, London, Faber, 1986
Rankin, W. Donald: *The Solo Piano Music of John Ireland*, DMA, Boston University, 1970
Rapoport, Paul: "Sorabji Returns?", *Musical Times* cxvii, 1976, 995
―― *Opus Est: Six Composers from Northern Europe*, London, Kahn and Averill, 1978

―――― (ed.), *Sorabji: A Critical Celebration*, Aldershot, Scolar Press, 1992
Reizenstein, Franz: "Hindemith: Some Aspersions Answered", *Composer* xv, April 1965, 7–9
Ridout, Alan (ed.): *The Music of Howard Ferguson*, London, Thames, 1989
Roberts, Peter Deane: *Modernism in Russian Piano Music – Skryabin, Prokofiev and their Russian Contemporaries*, Bloomington, Indiana University Press, 1993
Robertson, A.: "Bax and Ireland" [Piano Sonatas], *Gramophone* xli, 1964, 523
Rosen, Charles: *Sonata Forms*, London, Norton, 1988 (first edition 1980)
Routh, Francis: *Contemporary British Music*, London, Macdonald, 1972
Rubbra, Edmund Duncan: "Constant Lambert's Sonata", *The Monthly Musical Record* lx, December 1930, 356
―――― "The Younger English Composers: Howard Ferguson", *The Monthly Musical Record* lxviii, May 1938, 100–3
Russell, Dave: *Popular Music in England 1840–1941: A Social History*, Manchester, Manchester University Press, 1987
Russell, John: "Howard Ferguson: A 'Lonely' Composer", *The Listener*, 16 October 1958, 624
Rust, Brian: *Jazz Records 1897–1942* (2 vols.), Chigwell, Essex, Storyville, fifth edition, 1982
Sackville-West, Edward: "Reviews" [Tippett Piano Sonata], *The New Statesman and Nation* xxii, 1 November 1941, 397–8
Sadie, Julie Ann and Rhian Samuel: *The New Grove Dictionary of Women Composers*, London, Macmillan, 1994
Sadie, Stanley (ed.): *The New Grove Dictionary of Music and Musicians* (20 vols.), London, Macmillan, sixth edition, 1980
St. John, Christopher: *Ethel Smyth*, London, Longmans, 1959
Salter, Lionel: "Ireland", *Gramophone* xxxi, 1953, 17
Sargeant, Winthrop: *Jazz: Hot and Hybrid*, New York, Da Capo, third edition, 1975 (first edition 1938)
Schafer, R. Murray: *British Composers in Interview*, London, Faber, 1963
Scholes, Percy: *The Mirror of Music 1844–1944. A Century of Musical Life in Britain as Reflected in the Pages of the Musical Times*, London, 1947
Schonberg, Harold C: *The Great Pianists*, London, Gollancz, 1964
Schott: *Michael Tippett: A Man of Our Time*, Exhibition Catalogue, London, Schott, 1977
Scott, Cyril: *The Philosophy of Modernism and its Connection with Music*, London, Kegan Paul, Trench, Trubner & Co., 1917
Scott, Cyril: "Suggestions for a More Logical Sonata Form", *The Monthly Musical Record* xlvii, May 1917, 104
―――― *My Years of Indiscretion*, London, Mills and Boon, 1924
―――― *Music, its Secret Influence through the Ages*, London, Rider and Co., 1950 (first edition 1933)
―――― *Bone of Contention*, London, The Aquarian Press, 1969
Scott, W. H.: *Edward German – An Intimate Biography*, London, Chappell, 1932
Scott-Sutherland, Colin: "Some Unpublished Works of Arnold Bax", *Music Review* xxiv, 1963, 322–6
―――― *Arnold Bax*, London, Dent, 1973
―――― *John Ireland*, Rickmansworth, Triad Press, 1980

Bibliography

—— "British Piano Music of the Georgian Era 1910–36, an Anthology", *Journal of the British Music Society* iv, 1982, 19–56
Searle, Humphrey and Robert Layton: *Twentieth Century Composers Vol. 3 – Britain, Scandinavia and the Netherlands*, London, Weidenfeld and Nicolson, 1972
Searle, Muriel V.: *John Ireland – The Man and his Music*, Tunbridge Wells, Midas Books, 1979
Segnitz, Eugen: "Algernon Ashton" [Piano Sonata in E minor], *Musikalisches Wochenblatt* xxxii, 1901, 165
Serbescu, Liana: "Ethel Smyth's Piano Music", *European Piano Teachers' Association Journal* xvi, 1995, 11–15
Shaw, George Bernard: *Music In London 1890–94,* Vols. 1–3, London, Constable and Co., 1932
Shead, Richard: *Constant Lambert*, London, Thames, second edition, 1986 (first edition, 1973)
Shedlock, John S.: *The Pianoforte Sonata: Its Origin and Development*, New York, Da Capo, reprinted 1964 (first edition London, Methuen, 1895)
Sorabji, Kaikhosru S.: "Modern Piano Technique", *The Sackbut*, July 1920, 116–23
—— "The Modern British Piano Sonata", *Musical News and Herald*, 2 January 1926, 4–7
—— [Fourth Piano Sonata], *The New Age*, 17 April 1930, 284
—— *Around Music*, London, Unicorn Press, 1932 (Reprinted Westport, Hyperion Press, 1979)
—— [Scriabin], *The New Age*, 19 July 1934, 141–2
—— *Mi Contra Fa: The Immoralisings of a Machiavellian Musician*, London, Porcupine Press, 1947 (Reprinted New York, Da Capo Press, 1986)
Spicer, Paul: "Howard Ferguson", *Classical Music*, 16 November 1991, 14–15
Spink, Gerald W.: "Schumann and Sterndale Bennett", *Musical Times* cv, 1964, 419–21
Stanford, Charles Villiers: *Musical Composition – A Short Treatise for Students*, London, Macmillan & Co. and Stainer & Bell Ltd, 1911
—— *Interludes, Records and Reflections*, London, John Murray, 1922
Statham, H. H.: "Sterndale Bennett's Piano Music", *Musical Times* xix, 1878, 130–4
Stevenson, Ronald: "Alan Bush, Committed Composer", *Music Review* xxv, 1964, 323–42
—— *Western Music – An Introduction*, London, Kahn and Averill, 1971
—— (ed.), *Alan Bush: Time Remembered: An Eightieth Birthday Symposium*, Kidderminster, Bravura, 1981
Stradling, Robert and Meirion Hughes: *The English Musical Renaissance 1860–1940, Construction and Deconstruction*, London and New York, Routledge, 1993
Suckling, Norman: "John Ireland and the Pianoforte", *The Listener*, 24 December 1953, 1101
—— "Bax and his Piano Sonatas", *The Listener*, 17 June 1954, 1069
Sutton, Wadham: "Contemporary British Piano Sonatas: Antony Hopkins Sonata No. 3 in C sharp minor", *Music Teacher and Piano Student*, October 1965, 401

Bibliography

—— "Contemporary British Piano Sonatas: Constant Lambert", *Music Teacher and Piano Student*, November 1965, 443
—— "Contemporary British Piano Sonatas: Lennox Berkeley", *Music Teacher and Piano Student,* December 1965, 488
Temperley, Nicholas (ed.): *The Romantic Age 1800–1914*, The Athlone History of Music in Britain Vol. 5, general editor Ian Spink, London, Athlone Press, 1981
Theil, Gordon: *Michael Tippett, a Bio-Bibliography*, Westport, Greenwood Press, 1989
Thomas, William Henry: "Are we on the Eve of a Great Musical Triumph?", *Daily Mail*, 5 August 1904, 7
Tippett, Michael: "Music and Life – 1938", *The Monthly Musical Record* lxviii, July–August 1938, 176–7
—— *Moving into Aquarius*, London, Routledge & Kegan Paul, 1959
—— *Music of the Angels*, London, Eulenburg, 1980
—— *Those Twentieth Century Blues: An Autobiography*, London, Hutchinson, 1991
—— and M. Bowen (eds.): *Tippett on Music*, Oxford, Clarendon Press, 1995
Tomason, Geoffrey: "Richard Hall (1903–02)", *British Music Society Jounal* vi, 1984, 47–59
Townshend, Nigel: "The Achievement of John Ireland", *Music and Letters* xxiv, 1943, 65–74
Trend, Michael: *The Music Makers – The English Musical Renaissance from Elgar to Britten*, London, Weidenfeld and Nicholson, 1985
Truscott, Harold: "Algernon Ashton: 1859–1937", *The Monthly Musical Record* lxxxix, July–August 1959, 142–8
Van der Merwe, Peter: *Origins of the Popular Style*, Oxford, Clarendon Press, 1989
van Dieren, Bernard: *Down Among the Dead Men*, London, Oxford University Press, 1935
Vaughan Williams, Ralph: *Heirs and Rebels*, Letters written to each other by Vaughan Williams and Gustav Holst edited by Ursula Vaughan Williams and Imogen Holst, London, Oxford University Press, 1959
Walker, Ernest: *A History of Music in England*, Oxford, Clarendon Press, 1966 (first edition 1907)
Warrack, John: "A Note on Frank Bridge", *Tempo* lxvi and lxvii, 1963, 27–32
Watson, Monica: *York Bowen – A Centenary Tribute*, London, Thames, 1984
Webb, Patrick: "Algernon Ashton 1859–1937", *British Music Society Journal* xiv, 1992, 26–34
Westerby, Herbert: *The History of Pianoforte Music*, London, Kegan Paul, 1924
Whitcomb, Ian: *Irving Berlin and Ragtime America*, London, Century, 1987
Whittall, Arnold: "The Isolationists", *Music Review* xxvii, 1966, 122–9
—— "Sorabjiana", *Musical Times* cvii, 1966, 216–17
—— *The Music of Britten and Tippett*, Cambridge, Cambridge University Press, second edition, 1990 (first edition, 1982)
—— "Thirty (More) Years On", *Musical Times* cxxxv, 1994, 143–7
Willetts, P.: "Autograph Music MSS of Arnold Bax", *British Museum Quarterly* xxiii, 1961, 43–5
Williams, Christopher à Becket: "The Music of Kaikhosru Sorabji", *The Sackbut* iv, June 1924, 315–19

Bibliography

Wolf, Henry Samuel: "The Twentieth Century Piano Sonata", PhD, University of Boston, 1957
Wood, Hugh: "Frank Bridge and a Land without Music", *Tempo* cxxi, 1977, 7–11
Woolgar, Alan: "A Tippett Discography", *Records and Recording,* xxiii/5, 1979–80, 26
Young, Percy M.: *The Concert Tradition, from the Middle Ages to the Twentieth Century*, London, Routledge & Kegan Paul, 1965
—— *A History of British Music*, London, Benn, 1967
Zoete, Beryl de: "The Younger English Composers: Constant Lambert", *The Monthly Musical Record* lix, 1 April 1929, 97–9

Index

African–American music 127–9, 130, 138, 140, 141, 142, 151, 156, 157, 166, 172, 194
Alexander, Arthur 73, 74, 215
Alkan, (Charles-) Valentin 111
Allen, Hugh 124, 160
Alwyn, William 214, 223
America 61, 113, 124, 126, 141, 143, 171, 187, 189, 209, 210
Armstrong, Louis 128, 141, 163, 210
Arne, Thomas 183, 203
Arnold, Malcolm 159, 163, 164, 166, 214
   Piano Sonata 163, 214, 223
Ashkenazy, Vladimir 206
Ashton, Algernon 33–5, 39, 53, 65, 214
   Sonata No. 3 34, 214, 223
Athenaeum School *see* Royal Scottish Academy of Music and Drama
Austin, Ernest 214

Bach, Johann Sebastian 5, 9, 16, 54, 56, 57, 110, 161, 186, 202, 204, 207, 212–13
   Mass in B minor 102
Bache, Walter 15
Baines, William 69, 91–3, 215, 227, 230
   Paradise Gardens 93
   Piano Concerto 91
   Piano Sonata in D minor (unpublished) 92, 215
   Piano Sonata No. 1 in D minor 91–2, 215
   Piano Sonata No. 2 in A minor 92, 215
   Piano Sonata in F sharp minor 92–3, 215
   Prelude No. 4 92
   Symphony 91
Balakirev, Mily Alexeyevich 73
Banister, Henry Charles 215
Bantock, Granville 65
Barnett, John Francis 215
Bartlett, Ethel & Robertson, Rae 96

Bartók, Béla 66, 79, 106, 113, 123, 160, 167, 179, 187
   Four Orchestral Pieces 167
   Piano Sonata 167–8
   Violin Sonatas 167
Bax, Arnold 5, 36, 42, 48, 49, 52, 53, 65, 69, 69–84, 84, 88, 90, 91, 92, 93, 94, 95, 99, 103, 120, 123, 125, 139, 146, 159, 168, 170, 171, 176, 177, 180, 192, 195, 204, 215, 223–5, 230
   Clarinet Sonata 192
   Ideala 74
   Legend 79
   Mediterranean 79, 83
   Mountain Mood 74
   Paean 79
   Piano Concerto for left hand 83
   Piano Sonata in D minor 70, 215
   Piano Sonata in F (No. 2 Scherzo) 73, 215, 224
   Piano Sonata in E flat (original version of First Symphony) 78–9, 215, 224
   Piano Sonata No. 1 71–3, 83, 101, 125, 215, 223, 224
   Piano Sonata No. 2 74–8, 79, 83, 101, 125, 171, 215, 223, 224
   Piano Sonata No. 3 79–82, 83, 86, 94, 101, 125, 146, 148, 171, 215, 224
   Piano Sonata No. 4 79, 82, 83, 86, 125, 158, 215, 224–5
   Romantic Tone Poem 71, 215
   Symphonic Phantasy 71, 215
   Symphonic Variations 74, 79
   Symphony No. 4 159
   Symphony No. 5 159
   Symphony No. 6 159
   Symphony No. 7 159
   Tintagel 83, 205
   Winter Waters 74
Bayreuth 7, 15
BBC *see* British Broadcasting Corporation
Beethoven, Ludwig van 2, 3, 4, 5, 8, 12, 14, 17, 20, 25, 28, 36, 39, 46, 53, 69,

Index

Beethoven, Ludwig van *(cont.)*
   70, 94, 96, 130, 142, 143, 150, 153, 156, 161, 165, 170, 176, 182, 184, 185, 186, 188, 189, 202, 204, 206–7, 210, 213
   Hammerklavier Sonata Op. 106 102, 122
   Piano Concerto No. 4 51
   Piano Sonata Op. 31/1 2
   Piano Sonata Op. 109 213
   Piano Sonata Op. 110 19, 185
   Piano Sonata Op. 111 3, 108, 145
   Sonata Pathètique Op. 13 20
   Symphony No. 9 15, 115, 210
Benjamin, George
   Piano Sonata 186
Bennett, Richard Rodney 191
Bennett, William Sterndale 1, 2, 7, 9–11, 12, 14, 23, 28, 32, 35, 95, 175, 183, 215, 225
   Piano Sonata No. 1 9, 225
   Piano Sonata No. 2, *The Maid of Orleans* 3, 4, 9–11, 23, 183, 225
   Suite de Pièces 9
Berg, Alban 120, 122, 123, 124, 160, 171, 183, 196
   Piano Sonata 4
Berlin, Irving 141
Berlioz, Hector 15, 25, 35
Berkeley, Lennox 50, 157, 168–70, 216
   Piano Sonata 169–70, 216, 225
Birtwistle, Harrison 167
Bliss, Arthur 79, 119
   Bliss– A One Step 129
   Rout 129
   Rout Trot 129
Blues 127–8, 132, 133, 134, 135, 139, 141, 145, 152, 156, 168, 169, 210
Borodin, Alexander 73
   Second Symphony 36
Boughton, Rutland 95
Boulanger, Nadia 82, 168, 199–200
Boulez, Pierre 186, 211
Boyce, William 140, 182
Bowen, (Edwin) York 1, 42, 47, 48, 48–51, 53, 65, 70, 84, 109, 159, 170, 216, 217, 225, 230
   Piano Sonata No. 1 in B minor 49, 50, 216, 225
   Piano Sonata No. 3 in D minor 49, 216, 225
   Piano Sonata No. 5 in F minor 48, 50–1, 216, 225

   Piano Sonata No. 6 in B flat minor 49, 50, 51, 216, 225
   Twenty-Four Preludes and Fugues Op. 102 49, 51
Bradshaw, Susan 191
Brahms, Johannes 2, 3, 5, 14, 15, 20, 23, 26, 28, 32, 34, 35, 36, 39, 46, 85, 94, 96, 113, 130, 144, 156, 161, 162, 170, 176, 182, 186, 187, 189, 190, 204, 210, 213
   Liebeslieder waltzes 25
   Piano sonatas 4, 15
   Piano Quintet 15
   Rhapsody in B minor Op. 79/1 40
Brian, Havergal
   Symphony No. 2 159
   Symphony No. 3 159
   Symphony No. 4 159
   Symphony No. 5 159
Bridge, Frank 39, 49, 68, 69, 83, 84, 88, 90, 93, 95, 98, 100, 113–26, 132, 158, 159, 160, 161, 163, 170, 171, 176, 179, 180, 195, 204, 216, 225–6
   Bridge chord 116, 117, 118, 119, 121, 122, 123, 124, 161
   Cello Sonata 113
   The Christmas Rose 113
   Dainty Rogue 122
   Dramatic Fantasia for piano 114
   Ecstasy 119, 122
   Fragrance 122
   Gargoyle 124
   Lament for strings 113
   Phantasy Quartets 114
   Phantasy Trio 114
   Piano Sonata 77, 91, 95, 101, 113–25, 133, 139, 158, 161, 171, 172, 187–8, 216, 225–6
   Retrospect 119, 122
   Rosemary 161, 188
   Solitude 119, 121–2
   Sunset 122
   Speak to me, my love, from Four Songs 115, 116
   String Quartet No. 3 124
   Summer 115, 116
   Three Improvisations for left hand
British Broadcasting Corporation (BBC) 47, 79, 83, 95, 113, 128, 167, 179, 190, 192, 193, 197, 205
Britten, Benjamin 96–100, 124, 125, 157, 159, 160, 166, 171, 176, 177, 179, 194, 196, 199, 200, 205, 216, 230

Index

Holiday Diary 96
Night Piece (Notturno) 96
Piano Concerto 96, 122
Piano Sonata No. 1 in A flat 96, 216
Piano Sonata No. 2, *Sonata Fantasti* 96, 216
Piano Sonata No. 6 in B flat 96–7, 216
Piano Sonata No. 9 in C sharp minor 97–8, 216
Piano Sonata No. 10 in B flat 98, 216
Simple Symphony 96–7, 193–4
War Requiem 120
Broadwood, Walter 14
Bruckner, Anton 15, 70, 125
Bryan, Gordon 137–8, 195
Bülow, Hans von 3
Burrows, Benjamin 217
Bush, Alan 52, 53, 69, 91, 93–5, 124, 148, 159, 171, 175–8, 217, 226
  Dialectic 95
  Piano Sonata Op. 2 93–5, 175–8, 217, 226
  Piano Sonata No. 2 95, 217
  Piano Sonata No. 3 95, 178, 217
  Piano Sonata No. 4 95, 177–8, 217
  Prelude and Fugue Op. 9 148
  Suite for two pianos 93
Bush, Geoffrey 11, 140, 175, 179–86
  Clarinet Rhapsody 179
  Sonatinas 185
  Suite 186
  Symphony No. 1 140, 181–2
  Te Deum 179
Busoni, Ferrucio 4, 109, 110, 220
  Fantasia Contrappuntistica 110

Cage, John
  Sonatas and Interludes 185
Cakewalk 127, 151–3
Cambridge 7, 9, 12, 23, 24, 35, 166
Cardew, Cornelius 191
Chabrier, Emmanuel 182
Chausson, Ernest 109
Chisholm, Erik 217, 226
Chopin, Frederick 1, 2, 3, 5, 40, 49, 52, 70, 72, 83, 92, 93, 99, 106, 107, 109, 121
  Piano Sonata No. 2 Op. 35 37, 85, 150
Christie, Winifred 91
Clarke, Edward 167
Clementi, Muzio 1, 2, 9, 183
Cobbett, Walter Wilson 41, 74
Cohen, Harriet 1, 48, 71, 74, 78, 79, 82, 83, 192, 215

Coke, Roger Sacheverell 217
Coleridge-Taylor, Samuel 39
Collingwood, Lawrance 217
Composer-pianist 1, 50, 52, 110
Confrey, Zez 132
Cooke, Arnold 159, 166–7, 217
  Piano Sonata No. 1 158, 167, 217, 226
Coolidge, Elizabeth Sprague 113, 114
Copland, Aaron 158
Corder, Frederick 36, 42, 43, 45, 47, 48, 49, 52, 93, 159, 175, 176
Cramer, John Baptist 1, 2
Craxton, Harold 48
Crossley, Paul 212, 221, 228–9
Crotch, William 35
Crowson, Lamar 206, 226
Cui, César 15
Curzon, Clifford 170, 212, 216
Cyriax, Rudolf 217

Dale, Benjamin 5, 33, 39, 42–8, 49, 51, 53, 57, 65, 70, 71, 73, 84, 93, 140, 159, 175, 177, 217, 226
  Horatius 42
  Piano Sonata 4, 23, 42–8, 52, 79, 103, 175, 185, 217, 226
Dance music 127–8, 139, 141, 154
Dannreuther, Edward 15, 39
Davies, Peter Maxwell 167, 213
Davis, J. D. 217
Davison, J. W. 3
Debussy, Claude 36, 49, 56, 59, 72, 85, 87, 92, 99, 106, 160, 171, 172, 180, 186, 187, 196, 212
  General Lavine 87
  Golliwog's Cake-walk 128
  Reflets dans l'eau 59
  Prélude à l'après midi d'un faune 58
Delius, Frederick 33, 58–9, 65, 68, 83, 93, 95, 99, 108, 109, 132, 135, 139, 152, 171, 172, 185, 191
  Appalachia 58, 135–6
  Brigg Fair 58
  Piano Concerto 58, 139
  The Walk to the Paradise Garden 135
Diaghilev 73, 129
Dublin, Trinity College, 7
Dunhill, Thomas 39, 214
Durham 7
Dussek, Jan Ladislav 1, 2, 183
Dvořák, Antonin 36
Dyson, George 160, 204

Index

Edinburgh 7, 14
Edmonstoune, Duncan 217
Edwards, Julian 217
Elgar, Edward 21, 23, 30, 31, 33, 65, 83, 99, 171, 183, 185, 189, 192, 204, 230
    Organ Sonata No. 1 31
    Pomp and Circumstance Marches 21
    Sonatina 31
    Symphony No. 2 88
Ellington, Duke 128, 130, 132, 133, 140, 194
    Black and Tan Fantasy 130
    Creole Rhapsody 130
    Hot and Bothered 130
    Mood Indigo 130, 133
    Swampy River 130
English Musical Renaissance 2, 6, 7, 9, 11, 70, 99, 160
Expressionism 122, 171, 173

Farjeon, Harry 217
Farrar, Ernest Bristowe 113, 216
Fauré, Gabriel 59, 84, 187
Ferguson, Howard 123, 159, 160, 164, 175, 186–92, 218, 226
    Diversions 189
    Five Bagatelles 188
    Five Irish Folksongs 192
    Octet 190–1
    Piano Sonata 160–3, 186, 187–9, 217, 226
    Violin Sonata No. 1 188, 191
    Violin Sonata No. 2 189
Ferneyhough, Brian 107
Field, John 1, 2, 72
Finnissy, Michael 107
Finzi, Gerald 189
Folk music 68, 70, 77, 81, 82, 83, 84, 90, 94, 115, 125, 127, 139, 143, 146–7, 158, 163, 168, 171, 177, 180, 192, 196, 210
Foss, Hubert 193–4
Foulds, John 109
Fox, Douglas 113
France 126, 129, 168, 171, 197
Franck, César 54
Frank, Alan 138, 139, 140, 175, 192–8
Frankfurt Group (*also known as* Frankfurt Gang) 33, 53, 65, 67
Frith, Benjamin 163, 223

Gamelan 145, 150, 210
Gardiner, Balfour 53, 54, 83
Gardner, Charles 218
Gardner, John 159, 218
George, Stefan 53
German, Edward 29–32, 218
    First Impromptu 30
    Piano Sonata 4, 29–32, 52, 218
    Piano Trio in D 29
Germany 7, 9, 14, 23, 25, 33, 34, 35, 47, 53, 65, 95, 124, 171
Gershwin, George 141, 153, 210
    Porgy and Bess 153
    Rhapsody in Blue 128–9, 141, 209
Gieseking, Walter 66, 220
Gilbert and Sullivan 5
Glazunov, Alexander 53, 73
    Piano Sonata No. 1 43
Goddard, Arabella 10, 215
Goehr, Alexander 167
Goossens, Eugene 95
Goossens, Sidonie 193
Grainger, Percy 53–4, 58–60, 65, 68, 220
    Bush Music 58
    Hill Songs 58
    Train Music 58
Gray, Cecil 129, 167, 196
Greenbaum, Hyam 193
Greenwood, John 218
Grieg, Edvard 5, 15, 49, 54
    Piano Sonata 37, 85
Grove, George 16, 35, 184, 219
Guildhall School of Music 6

Habermann, Michael 112
Hadow, William Henry 218
Hall, Richard 167, 218
Hallé, Charles 2, 3, 184
Hambourg, Mark 47
Handel, George Frederick 7, 57, 183
Handley, Vernon 83, 230
Hartvigson, Fritz 15
Haydn, Joseph 8, 9, 13, 32, 70, 184
Head, Michael 95
Headington, Christopher 170, 225
Herzogenberg, Heinrich von 25
Heseltine, Philip (Peter Warlock) 83, 105, 110, 129, 130, 167, 193, 195, 196
Hess, Myra 1, 48, 71, 73–4, 124, 160, 188, 189, 215, 216, 218, 226
Heward, Leslie 218
Hickin, Welton 218
Hiller, Ferdinand 36
Hindemith, Paul 66, 82, 113, 123, 128,

Index

150, 158, 163, 165–6, 167, 168, 170, 199–200, 201, 202, 213
Ludus Tonalis 165, 199, 201
Mathis der Maler 201
Piano Sonatas 165, 199, 201, 202
String Quartet No. 3 113
Holbrooke, Joseph [Josef] 48, 159, 218
Holland, Theodore 218
Holst, Gustav 68, 83, 95, 98, 99, 146, 171, 180, 185, 191, 230
Beni Mora 109
Hymn of Jesus 143
Planets 120
Hopkins, Antony 159, 160, 164–6, 175, 198–206, 219, 226
Cupid and Psyche, or *The Golden Ass* 202
Early One Morning 203
Five Studies in the Form of Variations on Three Notes 198
John and the Magic Music Man 202
Piano Sonata No. 1 164, 166, 198, 199, 202, 218
Piano Sonata No. 2 165, 166, 199, 200, 201, 202, 219, 226
Piano Sonata No. 3 165–6, 199–200, 206, 219, 225, 226
The Pickwick Papers 200
Richman, Poorman, Beggarman, Saint 205
Tango 201
Three's Company 206
A Time for Growing 205
Toccata 200
Horsley, Colin 170, 225
Howard, Leslie 95, 178, 217
Howard-Jones, Evlyn 91
Howell, Dorothy 52, 219, 226
Lamia 52
Piano Sonata 52, 219, 226
Howells, Herbert 228, 230
Hummel, Johann Nepomuk 4, 9, 184
Humperdinck, Engelbert 53
Hurlstone, William Yeates 39–42, 49, 219, 226
Capriccio in B minor 40
Five Easy Waltzes 39
Four Characteristic Pieces 42
Phantasy String Quartet 41
Piano Concerto in D 41
Piano Sonata 4, 39–41, 219, 226
Piano Trio Op. 2 39

Impressionism 56, 59, 68, 69, 72, 79, 84, 85, 87, 91, 92, 93, 99, 102, 106, 109, 122, 124, 125, 172, 180
Improvisation 57–8, 60, 61, 106, 107, 108, 109, 130, 131, 138, 139, 145, 166, 172
D'Indy, Vincent 15, 150, 152–3, 207
Suite 207
Ireland 70
Ireland, John 5, 39, 49, 69, 77, 79, 83, 84–91, 91, 93, 95, 101, 119, 120, 123, 125, 147, 159, 169, 170, 171, 175, 176, 177, 179–81, 186, 196, 219, 227
April 181
Cello Sonata 180
Chelsea Reach 181
Decorations 85
I have Twelve Oxen 88
The Island Spell 180–1
London Pieces 85, 87
Piano Concerto 84, 180
Piano Sonata 85–91, 92, 95, 125, 139, 181, 219, 227
Sarnia 181
The Scarlet Ceremonies 87
Soliloquy 90
Sonatina 91, 181
Violin Sonata No. 2 85, 180
Ives, Charles
Concord Sonata 61, 108
Piano Sonata No. 1 61

Jack, Adrian 204
Jacob, Gordon 203
Jacobs, Peter 48, 217, 221, 225, 225, 226, 229
Jadassohn, Salomon 25
Janácek, Leos 79
Jazz 127–9, 130, 138, 139, 141, 145, 150, 151, 157, 158, 163, 166, 182, 191, 194, 195, 202, 208, 209, 210
Jervis-Read, H. V. 219
Joachim, Joseph 14, 25
Johnson, Stephen 155
Camptown Races 155
Joplin, Scott 152
Joubert, John 191

Kalisz, Effie 48
Kelly, Frederick 113
Kentner, Louis 138, 195
Kiel, Friedrich 23
Klindworth, Karl 15
Knorr, Iwan 33, 53
Kodály, Zoltan 79

Index

Koninsky, Sadie 151
   Eli Green's Cake Walk – Characteristic March 151
Kuhlau, Friedrich 5

Lambert, Constant 50, 58, 110, 127, 129–40, 141, 142, 143, 145, 157, 158, 159, 160, 163, 166, 168, 172, 175, 181–2, 192–8, 202, 204, 208, 219, 227, 230–1
   Aubade Héroïque 196
   Concerto for nine players 130
   Eight Poems of Li Po 130
   Elegiac Blues 129, 130, 194
   Horoscope 194
   Piano Concerto 130, 137, 195, 231
   Piano Sonata 129–40, 150, 157, 158, 164, 172, 182, 194–5, 208, 219, 227
   Pomona 193
   The Rio Grande 130, 134, 135–6, 138–9, 140, 141, 164, 181–2, 194, 195, 202, 208, 230
   Romeo and Juliet 129
   Summer's Last Will and Testament 135, 140, 182, 194, 231
   Tiresias 197
   Trois Pièces Nègres pour les Touches Blanches 130
Lamond, Frederick 91, 219
Lander, Mabel 175
Langrish, Vivian 48
Latin American music 132, 208
Lawes, William 184
Lawton, Ralph 91
Leigh, Walter 167
Liapunov, Sergei 50
   Etudes d'exécution Transcendante Op. 11 Nos. 3 and 8 71
Liszt, Franz 1, 2, 3, 4, 5, 15, 29, 31, 35, 36, 39, 40, 43, 49, 50, 61, 69, 71, 74, 84, 91, 94, 101, 110, 116, 121, 182, 197, 212
   Piano Sonata in B minor 30, 42, 46, 49, 57, 91, 93, 101
Livens, Evangeline 52, 219
   Piano Sonata 52, 219
Livens, Leo 48, 52, 53, 219
   Piano Sonata 52, 219
Liverpool 3, 65, 82
London 2, 6, 7, 15, 24, 33, 35, 65, 69, 110, 129, 183, 206
London Piano School 1, 183
Lucas, Charles 35
Lutyens, Elizabeth 159, 219

Lympany, Moura 48
Lynch, Charles 82, 215, 217

MacDowell, Edward 61
   Piano Sonata, *Eroica* 81
Macfarren, George Alexander 1, 3, 7, 9, 11–14, 16, 23, 32, 35, 219
   Sonata No. 1 11, 219
   Sonata No. 2, *Ma Cousine* 11–12, 219
   Sonata No. 3 11–14, 24, 219
Machen, Arthur 85
Mackenzie, Alexander 35–6, 49
Maconchy, Elizabeth 160, 187
Madrigals 142
Maeterlinck, Maurice 53
Mahler, Gustav 70, 109, 125, 171, 196, 207
Manchester 2, 7, 167, 184, 204
Mark, Jeffrey 141, 145, 146, 209, 210
Martin, Frank
   Petite Symphonie Concertante 200
Matthay, Tobias 36, 47, 48, 52, 53, 93, 219
Mayerl, Billy 128, 132
McEwen, John 36–9, 47, 49, 52, 219
   Piano Sonata in E minor 37–9, 219, 227
   Sonatina in G minor 39
Medtner, Nicolai 50, 73
   Piano Sonata No. 2 109
Mendelssohn, Felix 1, 5, 9, 14, 16, 21, 23, 32, 35, 182, 183, 184, 215
Merrick, Frank 48, 223–4, 227
Messiaen, Olivier 106, 171, 172
Mewton-Wood, Noel 165, 199–200, 201, 219
Milhaud, Darius 117, 132
   Le Bœuf sur le toit 128
   La Création du Monde 128
Mills, Florence 129, 194
Mitchell, Edward 91
Moeran, Ernest John 95
Moiseiwitsch, Benno 48, 93, 175
Morgan, R. O. 219
Morris, R. O. 143, 160, 190, 191, 207
   Canzoni Ricertati 143–4
Morris, Thomas 113
Morris, William 53
Morrison, Angus 138, 159, 195
Moscheles, Ignaz 2, 9
Moszkowski, Moritz 4
Mozart, Wolfgang Amadeus 8, 9, 12, 26, 28, 32, 184, 188, 204
Musical League 65

Index

Multimetricism 58, 61, 65, 68, 92, 165, 168, 172
Mussorgsky, Modest 73
Mystic chord 66, 103, 106, 117, 123

National Training School for Music 35
Nationalism 7, 68, 84, 90, 94, 125, 176, 177, 180
Negro Spirituals 127, 142, 153–6
  Deep River 154
  Do Don't Touch-a my Garment, Good Lord, I'm Gwine Home 154–6
  Hallelujah! 153–5
  John saw the Holy Number 154–5
  Peter, Go Ring Dem Bells 153–4
  Somebody's Knocking at your Door 153–4
  Steal Away 153
Neo-classicism 82, 86, 127, 158, 168, 173, 197

Oakeley, Herbert (Stanley) 219
Ogdon, John 167, 221, 228
O'Neill, Norman 53, 83
Owen, Wilfred 114
Oxford 7, 14, 16, 35, 168

Pachmann, Vladimir de 4
Paderewski, Ignacy Jan 4, 41
Palestrina, Giovanni Pierluigi da 85, 180, 182
Parkin, Eric 83, 91, 93, 181, 186, 223, 224, 225, 227, 230
Parratt, Walter 35
Parry, Charles Hubert Hastings 7, 11, 14–23, 23, 24, 25, 26, 33, 35, 65, 84, 147, 160, 166, 184, 204, 206, 219–20, 227, 231
  Blest Pair of Sirens 204, 205
  Characterbilder – Seven Ages of Mind – Studies for the Pianoforte 16
  Großes Duo 16
  Jerusalem 204
  Piano Sonatas 3
  Piano Sonata No. 1 15, 16, 17, 18, 19, 20–22, 23, 30, 184, 219, 225, 227
  Piano Sonata No. 2 15, 16, 17, 18–19, 20, 22–23, 184, 220, 227
  Prometheus Unbound 6
  Sonata for piano duet 15
  Variations on a theme by Bach 14
Pauer, Ernst 41
Philharmonic Society 9, 36, 182
Pianola roll 48

Pibroch 145, 210
Pierson, Henry Hugo 14, 33
  Hurrah for Merry England 14
  Jerusalem 14
Piggott, Patrick 79
Pinto, George Frederick 1, 183
Poulenc, Francis 168
Powell, John
  Sonata Teutonica 102
Powell, Lloyd 91
Potter, Cipriani 1, 12, 35
Pre-Raphaelite art 53–4, 65, 67
Programme music 10, 11, 27, 28, 180
Prokofiev, Sergei 163, 167, 168, 170
  Chout 160
Prout, Ebenezer 36
Purcell, Henry 7, 142, 160, 184, 204, 210
  The Fairy Queen 182

Quilter, Roger 53

Rachmaninov, Sergei 4, 50, 73, 109
Raff, (Joseph) Joachim 32, 33, 61
Ragtime 127, 129, 131, 132, 134, 137, 141, 142, 151–2, 156, 158
RAM *see* Royal Academy of Music
Ravel, Maurice 49, 59, 82, 85, 87, 99, 106, 156, 158, 168, 171, 180, 186, 187, 208
  Oiseaux tristes 58
  Sonatine 208
  La Vallée des cloches 58
  Violin Sonata 128
Rawsthorne, Alan 193, 195, 196
  Viola Sonata 195
Raymar, Aubin 208
RCM *see* Royal College of Music
Reger, Max 32, 43, 110
Reicha, Antoine
  Thirty-six Fugues 58
Reinecke, Carl Heinrich 5, 23, 25, 33
Reinhardt, Django 209
Reizenstein, Franz 167, 220, 227
Rheinberger, Joseph 32
Richter, Hans 96, 167
Rimsky-Korsakov, Nicolai 73
Roberts, Mervyn 159, 220
Robertson, Rae (*see* Ethel Barlett)
Rowlands, Alan 181, 227
Rowley, Alec 220
Royal Academy of Music (RAM) 1, 5, 9, 12, 13, 29, 31, 35–6, 36, 39, 42, 47, 48, 49, 50, 52–3, 69, 70, 93, 159, 175, 177, 184, 189, 191

253

Index

Royal College of Music (RCM) 6, 24, 33, 35–6, 39, 52–3, 85, 113, 121, 124, 125, 140, 141, 143, 156, 159, 160, 163, 164, 181, 186, 187, 188, 190, 197, 198, 203, 204, 206, 208, 209
Royal Manchester College of Music 167
Royal Scottish Academy of Music and Drama 36
Rubbra, Edmund Duncan 67, 138, 160
Rubinstein, Anton 3, 4, 15, 61
Rubinstein, Nicolai 15
Russia 53, 71, 95, 171
Russian nationalists 49, 68, 69, 73

Saint-Saëns, Camille 15, 49
Samuel, Harold 123, 159, 161, 186, 187–8, 218
Satie, Eric
  Parade 128
  Le Picadilly 128
Scarlatti, Domenico 156, 183, 207, 213
Scharrer, Irene 48
Schnabel, Artur 93, 176, 199
Schoenberg, Arnold 84, 95, 113, 123, 148, 150, 160, 171, 176, 179, 183, 196, 201
  Three Piano Pieces Op. 11 84
  Pierrot Lunaire 196
  String Quartets 114
Schubert, Franz 2, 5, 22, 29, 39, 99, 184, 191
  Wanderer Fantasia 57
Schumann, Clara 3, 14, 53
Schumann, Robert 2, 3, 4, 5, 9, 14, 20, 32, 34, 45, 61, 99, 144, 183
  Carnaval 18, 20
Scott, Cyril 33, 48, 53–68, 69, 71, 72, 83, 84, 92, 93, 99, 101, 102, 103, 109, 110, 116, 139, 140, 170, 172, 177, 180, 185, 220, 227–8
  Chinese Songs 61
  Handelian Rhapsody 54, 65, 220
  A Little Russian Suite 59
  Lotus Land 59, 61
  Nocturne 58
  Piano Quartet 65
  Piano Sonata Op. 17 (Unpublished) 54, 220, 227
  Piano Sonata No. 1 52, 53–66, 78, 108, 220, 227
  Piano Sonata No. 1 (revised version) 61–5, 220
  Piano Sonata No. 2 61, 66–7, 220. 227
  Piano Sonata No. 3 66, 67, 220, 225, 227
  Pierrot Piece No. 1 59
  Scherzo Op. 25 58
  Spring Song 58
  Vesperale 58
  Violin Sonata 65
Scriabin, Alexander 49, 54, 60–1, 67, 68, 69, 72, 73, 75, 77, 83, 84, 92, 93, 99–100, 101, 102, 105, 106, 107, 108, 109, 114, 116, 118, 119, 120, 123, 125, 158, 160, 171, 172
  Etude Op. 65/2 118
  Mystic chord 66, 103, 106, 117, 123
  Piano Concerto 69
  Prometheus 69
  Piano Sonata No. 1 72
  Piano Sonata No. 2 72
  Piano Sonata No. 4 61, 106
  Piano Sonata No. 5 61, 115
  Piano Sonata No. 6 61, 69, 117, 118
  Piano Sonata No. 7 69, 74
  Piano Sonata No. 9 115
  Piano Sonata No. 10 115
Searle, Humphrey 197
Seiber, Mátyás 200
Sellick, Phyllis 142, 145–6, 157, 165, 204, 212, 221, 228
Shelley, Howard 206, 226
Shepherd, Charles Henry 220
Sibelius, Jean 79, 82
  Finlandia 82
  Symphony No. 7 82
Simons, John 79
Sitwells 110, 129
Smalley, Roger 204
Smith, Bessie 141, 210
Smith, Cyril 159, 198, 204, 212
Smyth, Ethel 25–8, 33, 35, 53, 65, 220, 228
  Piano Sonatas 4
  Piano Sonata No. 1 in C 26–27, 28, 220, 226, 228
  Piano Sonata No. 2 in C sharp minor, *Geistinger* 27–28, 28, 220, 226, 228
  Piano Sonata No. 3 in D 28, 220, 228
  The Wreckers 28
Society of British Composers 47, 73
Society of British Musicians 1
Solomon, Yonty 112, 220
Sorabji, Kaikhosru Shapurji 49, 58, 66, 68, 69, 93, 100, 101–112, 114, 119, 121, 122–3, 125, 129, 132, 139, 140, 158, 171, 172, 220
  Opus Clavicembalisticum 101–2, 110, 111

Correspondances 106
Le jardin parfumé 106
Pantomime 106
Piano Sonata (unnumbered) 101, 220
Piano Sonata No. 1 101–12, 220, 228
Piano Sonata No. 2 101, 108, 109, 110, 112, 220, 228
Piano Sonata No. 3 101, 112, 220
Piano Sonata No. 4 101, 109, 110, 220, 228
Piano Sonata No. 5 101, 109, 220
Symphonic Variations 102
Speer, Charlton T. 221
Speer, William Henry 221
Spirituals (*see* Negro Spirituals)
Spohr, Louis 9
Stainer, John 35
Stanford, Charles Villiers 6, 7, 23, 23–5, 25, 33, 35, 39, 41, 65, 84, 85, 86, 113, 147, 160, 179–81, 187, 192, 206, 221
    Cello Sonata No. 1 Op. 9 25
    Irish Dances 65
    Piano Sonata in D flat Op. 20 4, 23–25, 184, 221
    Violin Sonata No. 1 in D Op. 11 24
Stevenson, Ronald 95, 217
Stockhausen, Julius 14
Strauss, Richard 39, 42, 43, 46, 49, 52, 56, 68, 69, 70, 94, 125, 171, 173
Stravinsky, Igor 82, 106, 113, 129, 132, 143, 158, 160, 167, 168, 170, 172, 180, 187, 196–7, 204, 208, 209, 210
    Concerto for two pianos 199
    Dumbarton Oaks 204
    Histoire du Soldat 208
    Les Noces 197
    Piano Rag Music 128
    Petrushka 87, 117, 208
    Ragtime 128
    Rite of Spring 138, 160, 180
    Sonata for two pianos 211
Suart, Evelyn 54, 220
Sullivan, Arthur 6, 30, 35, 185
    The Tempest 6
    Trial by Jury 6
    See also Gilbert and Sullivan
Symbolism 53, 106
Symphonic jazz 128–9, 141, 142, 158
    Symphonic poem 10, 57, 59, 71, 84
    Syncopation 127, 131, 132, 134, 135, 137, 138, 140, 142, 143, 151, 152, 154, 158, 164, 166

Szymanowski, Karol 109

Taylor, Franklin 3
Tchaikovsky, Peter Ilyich 15, 49, 53, 171, 180, 182
    Piano Trio in A minor Op. 50 44
    Symphony No. 4 57
    Symphony No. 6 36
Terroni, Raphael 170, 225, 228
Thomson, Bryden 83, 188, 230
Tippett, Michael 127, 129, 140–58, 159, 163, 165, 168, 171, 172, 188, 198, 199, 200, 201, 202, 206–13, 219, 221, 228–9
    The Blue Guitar 211
    A Child of our Time 153, 154, 157, 198
    Concerto for Double String Orchestra 146
    Concerto for Orchestra 211
    Fantasy Sonata 142, 206, 210, 221, 228
    King Priam 213
    The Mask of Time 213
    Piano Concerto 212
    Piano Sonata No. 1 94, 140–58, 162, 165, 166, 204, 206, 207, 210, 221, 228
    Piano Sonata No. 2 210–11, 213, 221, 228–9
    Piano Sonata No. 3 157, 212, 221, 229
    Piano Sonata No. 4 212, 221, 229
    Symphony No. 3 210–11
    Symphony No. 4 213
    Triple Concerto 213
Tobin, John 48, 111
Tone poem (*see* Symphonic poem)
Trinity College of Music 5–6
Tritone 12, 20, 44, 75, 86, 92, 103, 105, 119, 120, 121, 123, 124, 134
Truscott, Harold 34, 159, 221–2, 229

Uzielli, Lazzaro 53

Van Dieren, Bernard 110, 129, 196
Vaughan Williams, Ralph 68, 79, 83, 89, 95, 99, 139, 146, 147, 160, 171, 180, 181, 185, 187, 191, 193, 195, 196, 210
    Job 196
    London Symphony 83
    Pastoral Symphony 196
    Piano Concerto 185
    Symphony No. 4 149, 159, 161
    Symphony No. 5 159, 180
    Toward the Unknown Region 204
Virginal music 145

Index

Wagner, Richard 14, 15, 18, 20, 22, 23, 25, 28, 32, 35, 36, 37, 39, 43, 46, 49, 54, 61, 68, 69, 70, 94, 125, 171, 173, 175, 189, 196, 201, 204
   Piano Sonata 4
   Das Rheingold 15
   Ring cycle 15, 102
   Tristan und Isolde 15, 18
   Die Walküre 15
Walton, William 99, 128–9, 140, 158, 192, 193, 195, 209, 220
   Belshazzer's Feast 140
   Façade 129, 193
   Fantasia Concertante 128
   Portsmouth Point overture 129
   Symphony No. 1 159
   Troilus and Cressida 196
War 120, 123, 125, 167, 171
   World War I 23, 47, 49, 65, 68, 70, 74, 83, 88, 95, 101, 113, 114, 125, 127, 157, 161, 171, 173, 207, 209
   World War II 95, 125, 157, 159, 160, 161, 188, 197

Warlock, Peter (*see* Philip Heseltine)
Weber, Carl Maria von 2
Webern, Anton 123, 171, 183
Weill, Kurt 128
Wibaut, Frank 201
Wesley, Samuel 1
Wolstenholme, W. 222
Wood, Charles 166
Wood, Christopher 222
Wood, Henry 65, 167, 197
Wordsworth, William 222

Yeats, W. B. 70

Zimmermann, Agnes 12, 24, 219, 221

www.ingramcontent.com/pod-product-compliance
Lightning Source LLC
Chambersburg PA
CBHW071203240426
43668CB00032B/2004